Studies in Rhetorics and Feminisms

Series Editors, Cheryl Glenn and Shirley Wilson Logan

Other Books in the Studies in Rhetorics and Feminisms Series

Regendering Delivery
The Fifth Canon and Antebellum Women Rhetors
Lindal Buchanan

Feminism Beyond Modernism
Elizabeth A. Flynn

Liberating Voices
Writing at the Bryn Mawr Summer School for Women Workers
Karyn L. Hollis

Gender and Rhetorical Space in American Life, 1866–1910
Nan Johnson

Appropriate[ing] Dress
Women's Rhetorical Style in Nineteenth-Century America
Carol Mattingly

The Gendered Pulpit
Preaching in American Protestant Spaces
Roxanne Mountford

Vote and Voice
Women's Organizations and Political Literacy, 1915–1930
Wendy B. Sharer

Rhetorical Listening

Rhetorical Listening

Identification, Gender, Whiteness

Krista Ratcliffe

Southern Illinois University Press / Carbondale

This volume's epigraph, "The book of Ruth and Naomi," is from *Mars and Her Children* by Marge Piercy, copyright © 1992 by Marge Piercy and Middlemarsh, Inc. Used by permission of the Wallace Literary Agency and Alfred A. Knopf, a division of Random House, Inc.

Library of Congress Cataloging-in-Publication Data

Ratcliffe, Krista, 1958–
   Rhetorical listening : identification, gender, whiteness / Krista Ratcliffe.
      p. cm. — (Studies in rhetorics and feminisms)
   Includes bibliographical references and index.
   1. English language—Rhetoric—Study and teaching—United States. 2. Report writing—Study and teaching (Higher)—United States. 3. Listening—Study and teaching (Higher)—United States. 4. Minorities—Education (Higher)—United States. 5. Women—Education (Higher)—United States. 6. Multicultural education—United States. 7. Feminism and education—United States. I. Title. II. Series.
   PE1405.U6R384 2005
   808'.042'071173—dc22   2005012120
   ISBN 0-8093-2668-X (cloth : alk. paper)
   ISBN 0-8093-2669-8 (pbk. : alk. paper)

Printed on recycled paper. ♻

The paper used in this publication meets the minimum requirements of American National Standard for Information Sciences—Permanence of Paper for Printed Library Materials, ANSI Z39.48-1992. ∞

For Olivia Ratcliffe Brown
        (who is a wonderful listener)

When you pick up the Tanakh and read
the Book of Ruth, it is a shock
how little it resembles memory.
It's concerned with inheritance,
lands, men's names, how women
must wiggle and wobble to live.

Yet women have kept it dear
for the beloved elder who
cherished Ruth, more friend than
daughter. Daughters leave. Ruth
brought even the baby she made
with Boaz home as a gift.

Where you go, I will go too,
your people shall be my people,
I will be a Jew for you,
for what is yours I will love
as I love you, oh Naomi
my mother, my sister, my heart.

Show me a woman who does not dream
a double, heart's twin, a sister
of the mind in whose ear she can whisper,
whose hair she can braid as her life
twists its pleasure and pain and shame.
Show me a woman who does not hide

in the locket of bone that deep
eye beam of fiercely gentle love
she had once from mother, daughter
sister; once like a warm moon
that radiance aligned the tides
of her blood into potent order.

At the season of first fruits we recall
two travelers, co-conspirators, scavengers
making do with leftovers and mill ends,
whose friendship was stronger than fear,
stronger than hunger, who walked together
the road of shards, hands joined.

                    —Marge Piercy, "The book of Ruth and Naomi"

Contents

Acknowledgments   xiii

Introduction:
    Translating Listening into Language and Action   1

1. Defining Rhetorical Listening   17

2. Identifying Places of Rhetorical Listening:
    Identification, Disidentification, and Non-Identification   47

3. Listening Metonymically:
    A Tactic for Listening to Public Debates   78

4. Eavesdropping:
    A Tactic for Listening to Scholarly Discourses   101

5. Listening Pedagogically:
    A Tactic for Listening to Classroom Resistance   133

Appendix:
    Teaching Materials for Writing about Gender and Whiteness   175

Notes   187

Works Cited   205

Index   219

Acknowledgments

Rhetorical Listening invites a consideration of listening into rhetoric and composition studies. Defined as a stance of openness that a person may choose to assume in relation to any person, text, or culture, rhetorical listening may be employed in many different contexts for many different purposes. This project, however, explores how rhetorical listening may help listeners negotiate troubled identifications with gender and whiteness in public debates, scholarly research, and classroom pedagogy. And as with any project, many people helped this one come to fruition.

I want to thank Marquette University for the summer research fellowships and sabbatical, which gave me stretches of time to think, read, and write; I also want to thank Tim Machan, English department chair, for providing me with an administrative schedule conducive to completing this book.

I owe a debt of gratitude to colleagues in rhetoric and composition studies who, whether they know it or not, have helped me think and learn about listening: Michelle Ballif (especially for recommending Gemma Corradi Fiumara's work), Virginia Chappell, Cindy Cox, Diane Davis, Nancy DeJoy, Chris Farris, Alice Gillam, Paula Gillespie, Cheryl Glenn, Joe Harris, Shirley Wilson Logan, Andrea Lunsford, Joyce Irene Middleton, Beverly Moss, Roxanne Mountford, Jacqueline Jones Royster, Sarah Sloane, Kathleen Welch, and Lynn Worsham.

I am grateful to several people at Southern Illinois University Press: the Studies in Rhetorics and Feminisms Series editors, Cheryl Glenn and Shirley Wilson Logan, for listening to my manuscript, offering insightful editorial suggestions, and supporting this project; editor-in-chief Karl Kageff and the department heads for providing helpful revision comments; managing editor Carol Burns and copyeditor Mary Lou Kowaleski for carefully shepherding this book in its final stages; and Jackie Royster for taking time from her very busy schedule to write a very useful review that helped me to clarify connections among chapters as well as to reframe and rephrase this project for a broader audience.

Most importantly, I want to thank Kevin Brown and Olivia Ratcliffe Brown for supporting me with their patience, love, and laughter.

Parts of the introduction and chapter 1 were previously published in my article "Rhetorical Listening: A Trope for Interpretive Invention and A Code of Cross-Cultural Conduct," *CCC* 51.2 (Dec. 1999): 33–62. Copyright 1999 by the National Council of Teachers of English. Reprinted with permission. Parts of chapter 4 were previously published in another of my articles, "Eavesdropping as Rhetorical Tactic: History, Whiteness, and Rhetoric," *JAC* 20.1 (2000): 87–119. Reprinted with permission. I wish to thank these journals as well as Marquette University students—Paul Doro, Kamenka Robbins, Carol Sales, Sara Scheunemann, Ben Weiler, and Rachel. They and many other students greatly helped to make this book possible.

Rhetorical Listening

Introduction: Translating Listening into Language and Action

> How do we translate listening into language and action, into the creation of an appropriate response?
> —Jacqueline Jones Royster, "When the First Voice You Hear Is Not Your Own"

In 1994, Jacqueline Jones Royster posed the above question in the published version of her CCCC chair's address. In response to Royster's question, this book argues that listening should be revived within rhetoric and composition studies via a concept of rhetorical listening. This project defines *rhetorical listening* as a trope for interpretive invention and as a code of cross-cultural conduct. Defined generally as a trope for interpretive invention, *rhetorical listening* signifies a stance of openness that a person may choose to assume in relation to any person, text, or culture. Defined more particularly as a code of cross-cultural conduct, *rhetorical listening* signifies a stance of openness that a person may choose to assume in cross-cultural exchanges. To articulate this cross-cultural function of rhetorical listening, this book explores intersecting identifications of gender and whiteness in the public sphere, in rhetorical scholarship, and in composition pedagogy.

This concept of rhetorical listening is important to rhetoric and composition studies because it supplements Kenneth Burke's rhetorical theory. In *A Rhetoric of Motives*, Burke argues that *all* language use has a persuasive function: for example, when a person explains an idea, that person is trying simultaneously to explain the idea and to persuade an audience to accept the explanation. Burke further argues that if such persuasive functions are to succeed, identification must precede persuasion (55). But identifications, especially cross-cultural identifications, are sometimes difficult

1

to achieve. Such identifications may be troubled by history, uneven power dynamics, and ignorance. Curious about such troubled identifications, I use this project to investigate the following question: How may people employ rhetorical listening to foster *conscious* identifications with gender and whiteness in ways that may, in turn, facilitate cross-cultural communication about any topic?

To establish grounds for investigating this question, this introduction narrates the "origins" of this project and defines important terms.

Narrating "Origins"

My thinking about rhetorical listening has emerged during the past few years not just from an abstract, scholarly interest in the intersections of rhetorical theory and feminist theory but from several intertwining threads in my academic and personal lives. Some threads repeated here are taken from my 1999 *CCC* article "Rhetorical Listening"; still others reveal that there is (always) more to a story.

The first thread emerged when I presented a paper about Mary Daly at a Womanist Spirituality Conference in Columbia, Missouri. An African American woman in the audience told me afterwards that she refuses to read Daly because Daly's critique of women in patriarchy is really just a critique of white women in patriarchy, one that excluded this audience member by *erasing differences* among women, a charge much like the one leveled against Daly by Audre Lorde ("An Open Letter" 70). The second thread emerged when I taught a special topics course called "The Rhetorics of Women's Autobiographies" at Marquette University in Milwaukee, Wisconsin. A young white woman in class said that although she was extremely moved when reading excerpts from Lorde's cancer journals, she didn't want to read any more of Lorde's writings. When I asked her why, she cited Lorde's last line: "If one Black woman I do not know gains hope and strength from my story, then it has been worth the difficulty of telling" ("From a Burst" 295). The student felt that Lorde, by specifying "Black woman," was excluding her by *erasing commonalities* among women.

While I understand each woman's decision and recognize the power differentials of each situation, I find these threads troubling. Not only do they expose each woman's difficulty in imagining simultaneous differences and commonalities, these threads also resonate as metonymic echoes of larger cultural discourses repeated not just by other students but also by people all across the United States. What troubles me is that such reactions negate the possibility for cross-cultural dialogue not just about gender and race but about any subject, such as, feminist methodology in the first thread and cancer in the second. Although I certainly respect an individual's right to refrain from dialogue at a particular moment in her or his life, I do not accept U.S. culture's dearth of discursive possibilities either for articulating intersecting identifications of gender and race or for promoting cross-cultural dialogues.

Listening, it seems to me, might serve as one such possibility. But listening is hardly a simple solution; indeed, it raises many questions that pertain to all people: Why is it so hard to listen to one another? Why is it so hard to identify with one another when we feel excluded? Why is it so hard to focus simultaneously on commonalities and differences? Why is it so hard to resist a guilt/blame logic when listening? And how do power differentials of particular standpoints and cultural logics influence our ability to listen? Any definition of listening must account for these questions—and others.

A third thread complicates the first two by exposing an all-too-often missing component in discussions of gender and race as well as in cross-cultural discussions of any topic. That missing component is whiteness (as a racial category). While writing *Anglo-American Feminist Challenges to the Rhetorical Traditions: Virginia Woolf, Mary Daly, Adrienne Rich,* I was challenged by Susan Jarratt to consider how race informed gender in Woolf's, Daly's, and Rich's feminist theories of rhetoric. So I considered two issues: (1) the attitude that these women's texts expressed and represented about race and (2) the influence that whiteness played on their texts. Yet when I completed the project, I was left with more questions than conclusions. Theoretically, I wondered: What exactly is whiteness? For whom is whiteness (in)visible? And how does it function rhetorically, especially in relation with gender? Personally, I wondered: How does my life as a white woman affect my actions as a teacher at Marquette University, as a scholar in rhetoric and composition studies, as a mother who shops at Piggly Wiggly in Cedarburg, Wisconsin, after work? What lessons am I (un)consciously sending to my students, my readers, my neighbors, my daughter, myself?

A fourth thread provides language with which to contemplate one specific application of listening, that is, articulating intersecting identifications of gender and race to promote cross-cultural communication. When Royster gave her opening keynote address at the 1997 Feminisms and Rhetorics conference in Corvallis, Oregon, she challenged attendees to construct "codes of cross-cultural conduct," that is, rhetorical tactics for fostering cross-cultural communication.[1] Royster's challenge resonated with me.

Suddenly, I saw an opening for my interest in rhetorical theory (the absence of listening) to merge with my interest in feminist theory (the intersections of gender and whiteness) as a means of doing my own gender/race work, both professionally and personally. By weaving the above threads together, I have created a place from which to ponder listening, or rather what I have come to think of as rhetorical listening.

But . . .

There is more to the story, my story—a story whose narrative progresses from an "unawareness" of whiteness to the writing of this book. I tell my story not simply because it is my story, not because I am particularly proud of it (I'm not), but rather because it represents a much larger cultural narrative that still echoes in the U.S.—a narrative that renders whiteness invisible within the dominant white culture. This narrative needs to be interrupted if the U.S. is ever to encourage productive dialogues about gender and race and their intersections. My story simply demonstrates one attempt to interrupt this nonproductive narrative and move into a more productive one.

To illustrate the "more to the story," bear with me as I revisit thread #3. In the fall of 1992 while I was putting finishing touches on *Anglo-American Feminist Challenges,* someone suggested to me that Jarratt's challenge to foreground race might be implemented if I added a chapter on Alice Walker. I immediately rejected that suggestion. But then, wondering why I so quickly jumped to this conclusion, I reflected on the suggestion some more. After honest deliberation, I again rejected that suggestion, opting to keep my focus on three white women: Woolf, Daly, and Rich. I had many reasons to support my decision: (1) my scholarly research and, hence, my expertise centered around Anglo-American[2] feminist theories of rhetoric; (2) these women had important insights to offer rhetoric and composition studies; (3) adding Walker changed the focus of the manuscript; and (4) the manuscript was complete and, given the ticking of my tenure clock, I could not face a major rewriting. Armed with this logic, I justified my focus on Woolf, Daly, and Rich. And I still believe I made the correct decision.

Yet . . .

Perhaps more interesting than my logical reasoning was my emotional state. I was alternately satisfied and bothered—satisfied that I had addressed Jarratt's challenge and bothered by visceral doubts. If I have learned anything from my years as a writing teacher, it is to pay attention to dissonance (thank you, Nancy Sommers). So I did. And I finally realized the irony of my reasoning: by enthymemically arguing my case from existing common-sense assumptions about expertise, insights, focus, and tenure, I was retreating into an Aristotelian rhetoric of common sense (i.e., the sense we hold in common), which was the very rhetoric that my manuscript challenged. Now I grant you, Aristotelian rhetoric is a very powerful, very useful way to reason. But as I argued in *Anglo-American Feminist Challenges,* it can be gender blind, that is, naïvely blind to concerns of gender. What I was realizing in my own life was that it can also be race blind.

My first response was guilt—good old-fashioned liberal guilt. When asking myself whether my defense of Woolf, Daly, and Rich was as race blind as Aristotle's treatise of rhetoric was gender blind, I answered myself with a well-intentioned, "Of course it is." What did I do with this nonproductive guilt? I did what most white people trapped in a guilt/blame logic do: I focused defensively on myself, repeating to myself all the logical reasons why I had omitted Walker from my project. In other words, the subject of all of my sentences was *I.*

Unable to convince myself that I had made the right decision, I stumbled into a second response, which was a search for absolution, a search for someone else to validate my thinking, to tell me it was OK not to include Walker in my project. Suddenly, I didn't trust my own authority. I talked with former professors, colleagues, friends, students. Eventually, I sighed with relief. They assured me I had nothing to feel guilty for. Notice, though, that my subject—and the subject of all my sentences—was still *I.* One note: In my frenzied search for absolution, I did refuse an editorial suggestion that I call Shirley Wilson Logan, whom I did not know at the time, to ask her if she thought it would be "OK" for me to focus on three white women and not include Walker. I could only imagine the conversation: "Hello, Shirley. My name is Kris Ratcliffe. You don't know me, but I understand you're African American and, hence, the perfect person to give me permission *not* to include a chapter on an African American woman in my book." At that time, I may not have been able to articulate a theoretical definition of *whiteness.* But I felt it viscerally. Such a "white" move would have been insultingly essentializing, making Logan a spokesperson for an entire ethnic group; such a move would also have been reinforcing a pattern of behavior that Diana Fuss claims "historically underwrites cultural racism and . . . tenaciously upholds its academic institutionalizations" (*Essentially Speaking* 86). And echoing in my ears, I could also hear Maria Childers and bell hooks: "As long as white women within feminism still ask black women to teach them about race, [black women] are still being put in a servant/served relationship" (71).

And so I arrived at my third response: accountability. When questioning whether my Aristotelian defense of my first book on gender was race blind, I still responded with, "Of course." The difference was: I no longer wanted absolution; I wanted answers and was willing to do my own work to find them, which included (when necessary) asking for a little help from my friends, whether those friends be flesh-and-blood people or texts that have become the friends of my mind. In other words, I was, indeed I am, no longer saying, "Of course," from within a guilt/blame logic but rather from within an accountability logic. Convinced that wallowing in guilt and in the desire for absolution is not only nonproductive but narcissistic, I determined to bring my embodied racism to consciousness (well, as much as possible anyway) and use it to complicate my feminism, my scholarship, and my daily life.[3]

But how?

Growing up as the great-great-granddaughter of white Quaker abolitionists whose home was an Indiana link in the Underground Railroad has given me a historical sense of right and wrong "sides" in U.S. race relations. But growing up as a Midwestern, small-town, white American girl, I also learned the always present notion that the past was the past. My ancestors' activism was presented simply as a chapter in our family's history. At no time was I given a narrative in which their activism was linked to a script for my own life. Indeed, my town was so amazingly oblivious to the social insights of the 1960s (even as we watched boys . . . family . . . being shipped off to Vietnam) that by my middle school years (the early 1970s), I had learned via the gossip over the fences that it was "acceptable" for the sons in our community's only African American family to play basketball with the white boys but not "acceptable" for them to go to the prom with the white girls. Few people in my town found that odd. Our basketball team was named the Randolph Southern Rebels; painted on our gymnasium wall was a confederate general astride his white charger; the pep club regularly chanted, "From out of the South/With all his might/Came the Southern Reb/Ready to fight." Few people in my town found that odd either.

Obviously, growing up with such identifications, I had gender and race work to do. I realized that when I went to college. The problem was that I learned about race but I didn't learn *how* to critique whiteness as a racial category. Instead, I learned how to critique gender. I embraced feminism as a woman-centered project that helped me *to understand* history and literature as well as *to rewrite* a script for my own life. But for many years, my gender analyses acknowledged that gender intersected with race, age, etc., yet remained naïvely blind to the ways that gender and whiteness intersect.

Flash-forward a decade from my college years to the early 1990s. When I really started thinking theoretically about what it means to be a white woman in the U.S., I found myself echoing the claims of Rich ("Split" 122), Ruth Frankenberg ("'When We Are Capable'" 11), and Becky Thompson (95): Nothing in my education, academic or otherwise, had prepared me to recognize or articulate whiteness, and certainly nothing in my education had provided me with strategies for resisting certain versions of whiteness that may privilege me but oppress others. I state this lack and unearned privilege not to elicit sympathy, excuses, or pats on the back. I state them simply because I have now heard them and want to make them visible. For "only by visualizing this privilege and incorporating it into discourse can people of good faith combat discrimination" in ways that prevent their doing "more harm than good" (Wildman and Davis 660, 661).

To this end, I returned to the writers who had helped me before: Rich, Toni Morrison, hooks, and Judith Butler. They had greatly influenced my thinking about feminism, so I reread them, hoping they could help me articulate my thinking about feminism and race, particularly the history of whiteness as it intersects with gender. I read theorists in rhetoric and composition studies who discuss, among other things, how race inflects our field's scholarship and pedagogy: such as, Keith Gilyard, Amy Goodburn, Logan, Min-Zhan Lu, Joyce Middleton, Royster, Victor Villanueva Jr., Kathleen Welch, Lynn Worsham. I read other theorists in critical race studies and whiteness studies (both of which champion anti-racist agendas): such as, Kimberlé Williams Crenshaw's mapping of gender and race, Richard Delgado's challenging the black/white binary that haunts discussions of race in the U.S., Richard Dyer's critiquing visual manifestations of whiteness, Ruth Frankenberg's defining *white* as a racial category and exploring how it informs white women's lives, and Jayne Chong-Soon Lee's tracing multiple definitions of *race*.

And I started paying attention in my daily life.

I concluded that listening was necessary. I also concluded that identifications with gender and whiteness are inextricably intertwined—not only with each other but with a host of other cultural categories, such as class, age, religion, ethnicity, nationality, beauty, and political affiliation, In an effort to untangle this intertwining, I wrote this book. As I write this introduction, simultaneously situated in an accountability logic and in a predominantly white suburb of Milwaukee, I recognize my own responsibility to do my own race work so as to understand my feminism and my life; I also recognize the need to reflect beyond my own reading, observations, and experiences. For sight gets us only so far; we also have to listen to other people, not so that they will do the work for us but, as Morrison reminds us in *Beloved,* so that *we* and *they* may lay *our* stories alongside one another's. hooks reinforces this idea: "I have gone back to 'confession' not as a need to tell my story in public or to be narcissistic, but because I now realize that people really learn from the sharing of experience" (Childers and hooks 77). We can listen to other women's and men's stories—in books and, perhaps more importantly, in our daily lives—not so that these stories serve as the final word on gender and whiteness (or on any other topic for that matter) but so that they engage in dialogue with our own experiences and observations.

As hooks claims, such dialogues offer wonderful possibilities; however, they also offer potential problems. Alice Rayner points to two: (1) the "coercive force of dialectic" and (2) people's tendency to fall back on "already completed meaning" that makes us comfortable instead of "remain[ing] open to an 'impossible' answer" (19). To help us all resist the coercive forces within dialectic/dialogue while remaining open to impossible answers, I offer this book on rhetorical listening. I offer it not as a final stage of self-actualization about identifications with gender and whiteness. (I happen to think that self-actualization is one of our more insidious cultural myths although, to be fair, Abraham Maslow made it more palatable by redefining it as episodic, not as a final stage or point of stasis). Instead, I offer this book as a result of one white feminist's recursive struggle to "figure out" how listening to language (a language that is always figurative) may be used, first, to expose troubled identifications with gender and whiteness both in our culture and in our lives and, second, to conceptualize tactics for negotiating such troubled identifications.

But before I begin, I want to turn to language—to its figurative function and to defining terms of this study.

Defining *Gender* and *Race* and Their Cultural Logics

As Plato demonstrates via his method of dialectic, one of the first moves a rhetor should make when presenting an argument is to define his/her terms.

Given my focus on how rhetorical listening may help people hear intersecting identifications with gender and whiteness, it seems only apt that I define my use of the terms *gender* and *race*. Because *gender* and *race* are words, they function as do all words—not as transparent descriptors of thought that stipulate only dictionary definitions but rather as tropes (i.e., as rhetorical figures) that suggest multiple meanings. This tropological function of language is both representative and generative. It is representative in that language represents that which already exists; it is generative in that language generates that which does not yet exist or is not yet named. As such, this tropological function of language fuels both logic and imagination, much as Isocrates theorized long before the Western world split logic from imagination and the rational from the creative.

What grounds the tropological function of language is the symbolic systems within which words "play"; within such systems, words (such as *gender* and *race*) function as cultural categories through which people see, organize, analyze, and value the world. And because such symbolic systems are culturally and historically grounded, words-as-tropes emerge and function differently over time and place. In the U.S., *gender* and *race* have histories of use and effect. Unless we trace these histories, we may function under the misimpression that these categories are timeless and universal instead of historically situated, multiple and fluid. Therein lie both the problems . . . and the possibilities . . . for exploring intersecting identifications with gender and whiteness via rhetorical listening.

Gender is a trope that signifies socially constructed "common-sense" attitudes and actions associated with women and men. This definition is predicated on the existence of two sexes, men and women. For millennia, these two categories have reigned as a common-sense classification of humans (although recent science suggests that a more accurate classification might include more than two categories). Despite recent suggestions, the following commonplaces exemplify one way that bodies are sexed and gendered in the U.S.: Women are assumed to be nurturing; men, aggressive. While a particular woman or man may not perform these general cultural assumptions, she or he is still marked by them: If a woman is not nurturing, she may be labeled cold and somehow less than a woman; if a man is not aggressive, he may be labeled weak and somehow less than a man (and given the prevalence of terms such as *wuss* and *sissy*, "less than a man" often signifies "more like a woman"). These examples imply two important points. First, gender is an important area of study both for women and for men.[4]

And second, because the trope *gender* functions within culturally and historically grounded symbolic systems and attains its currency via a culture's ideologies and institutions, gender is always a question not only of commonality and difference but of unearned privilege and power—or lack thereof (Showalter 4).

Because the term *gender* is a trope within language and because language changes over time, the term *gender* has a history.[5] As a twentieth-century feminist category of analysis, *gender* arose in opposition to the category *sex*. The first principle of many early women studies programs in the 1970s was that *sex* referred to physical attributes of men and women and *gender* referred to cultural attributes (e.g., breasts were categorized under sex attributes while breast fetishes were categorized under cultural ones). By the early 1990s, however, feminists such as Judith Butler had called the sex/gender split into question, asking "how and why 'materiality' has become a sign of irreducibility" (28), that is, asking how and why *sex* had become a privileged category in feminist analyses, unmarked by cultural influence, even though the category *sex* is culturally troped onto bodies, too. Granted, men and women are born with particular, material bodies; however, they see, organize, analyze, and value their bodies as *men* and *women* because they are born into a culture with a symbolic system containing these terms and their associated meanings.

What complicates matters is that symbolic systems often house competing cultural logics. A cultural logic is a belief system or way of reasoning that is shared within a culture—for example, even though not all Green party members think exactly alike, certain tenets associated with the Green party form a recognizable Green cultural logic. In the U.S., competing cultural logics about gender inform the way the term *gender* signifies. For example, some common cultural logics associated with gender in the U.S. include: (1) the logic of patriarchy, (2) the logic of equal rights, (3) the logic of comparable worth, and (4) the logic of postmodern commonalities and differences.

First, the cultural logic of patriarchy imagines *sex/gender* as a biological difference between men and women; it uses this difference to claim physical, intellectual, and public-sphere superiority for men as well as to grant (on its own terms, of course) domestic "superiority" for women. Second, the logic of equal rights imagines *sex/gender* as biological and/or cultural differences but *human rights* as innate God-given commonalities; thus, this logic employs Enlightenment ideals to claim rights for women by arguing that human commonalities trump sex/gender differences. Third, countering the equal-rights' focus on human commonality, the logic of comparable worth imagines *gender* as cultural differences; this logic attempts to reassess the cultural value assigned to "women's work," the purpose being to comparably value the different work that has been culturally assigned to men and women. Fourth, interrupting the binary opposition of commonality versus difference, the logic of postmodern commonalities and differences imagines *gender* as a culturally constructed discursive category possessing socializing forces within cultural contexts; this logic posits gender as a factor in—but not the sole determinant of—a person's identity. Although cultural logics emerge at particular historical moments (e.g., equal-rights feminism emerged from eighteenth-century Enlightenment philosophy), their influence may resonate long past their moments of origin (e.g., equal-rights feminism still functions in 2005 U.S. culture as grounds for equal-pay arguments).

As a factor that marks identity, gender marks different things. For example, people are marked: A man who likes to cook every day for his family may be labeled feminine, unless he is a chef, which is a cultural position that has traditionally been marked for males, though both these markings are changing as more women become chefs and as more men cook regularly for their families. Objects are also marked: Dark leather office furniture may be labeled masculine and associated with CEO offices while pink walls are labeled feminine and associated with little girls' bedrooms. Cultural positions are marked, too: Listeners, whether men or women, may be labeled feminine because *feminine* has historically connoted passivity as a proper role for women.

What makes *gender* a slippery category, though, is that its associated meanings shift across time and place; for example, assumptions about women's roles differ when talking about women in India and in France, in 1805 and in 2005. What makes gender even more slippery is that its associated meanings always intersect with meanings ascribed to other cultural categories that classify people, such as age, class, race, ethnicity, nationality, and religion. For instance, a woman is not simply a woman; she may also be young, poor, white, of French ancestry, Canadian, and Catholic—all of which inform her identity. Thus, while gender marks her identity, her identity cannot be reduced solely to gender. Instead, gender functions as a cultural category that is embodied and performed differently by each person, depending upon his/her culture's socializing messages about gender, upon his/her particular identifications with gender, and upon his/her reactions to these messages and identifications.

Within this logic of intersecting categories, it is obviously logical to discuss how a culture's gender socialization affects women and men *in particular*. It is also logical to discuss how a culture's gender socialization affects women and men *in general* because socialization establishes general cultural patterns that emerge as norms; gender norms mark all women and men, but these norms function like statistics in that they may be performed by many—but not necessarily by all—women or men. Yet within this logic, it is not logical (not to mention not ethical) to stereotype women and men by rendering *all* women identical and *all* men identical—for instance, all U.S. women are nurturing, or all U.S. men are aggressive. Such stereotyping erases two important functions of identity formation: (1) how each person's identifications with gender intersect with her/his identifications with other cultural categories and (2) how intersecting identifications render each person a particular-yet-culturally-marked identity.

Like *gender, race* is a trope. It signifies socially constructed "common-sense" attitudes and actions associated with different races.[6] This definition is predicated on the double fallacy that multiple races exist and that race is grounded in biology. Historically, this double fallacy has been perpetuated in the U.S. via the twin pillars of religion (the Bible's mark of Cain) and science (biology textbooks' race theories).[7]

In terms of science, consider George William Hunter's 1914 *Civic Biology,* the textbook at the center of the 1925 Scopes "monkey" trial. Although advocating a revolutionary theory of evolution, the textbook reified classifying humans into five races:

> The Races of Man. — At the present time there exist upon the earth five races or varieties of man, each very different from the others in instincts, social customs, and, to an extent, in structure. These are the Ethiopian or negro type, originating in Africa; the Malay or brown race, from the islands of the Pacific; the American Indian; the Mongolian or yellow race, including the natives of China, Japan and the eskimos; and finally, the highest type of all, the Caucasians, represented by the civilized white inhabitants of Europe and America. (qtd. in Pennock)

This theory, which was taught in U.S. schools well into the twentieth century, is grounded in the observations of some white biologists who classify humans so as to put themselves on the highest rung of the racial chain of being. This theory reminds me of Plato's classification of souls in the *Phaedrus,* which places philosophers on the highest rung and relegates sophists pretty close to the bottom (479); it reminds me that people tend to create theories in their own images.

Through the years, this five-races-of-man theory has obviously been challenged by cultural critics and by scientists. Most recently, government scientists mapping human DNA in the Human Genome Project have concluded that humans are 99.9 percent similar and that, indeed, there is only one race, the human race. Commenting on information from the Human Genome Project, the Association of American Medical Colleges posted on their Web site that "all physicians need to be made aware that there are neither 'black' genes, nor 'white' genes" (Bonham) . . . or for that matter "brown" genes, "yellow" genes, or "red" genes. The Web site elaborates:

> Certainly, we must educate medical students about the concepts of genetic variation. It is scientific fact that, due to history and geography, certain alleles—a member of a pair or series of genes that occupy a specific position on a specific chromosome—are more common in some populations, but that does not mean they do not exist in other population groups. The doctors of tomorrow must understand that there are no genetic 'bright lines' [or racial lines] between population groups. (Bonham)

In sum, DNA variation occurs among groups of people, but DNA variation is not synonymous with racial difference.[8] Consequently, U.S. culture is left with the word or trope *race,* which is a fictional category possessed of all-too-realistic consequences. It has no scientific grounding but functions with tremendous ideological force (pun intended). This force can be positive when *race* signifies ethnicity and when cultural traditions are celebrated; however, this force can be deadly to the mind, spirit, and body when race and biology and character are falsely conflated into a five-races-of-man theory.

Despite being based in bad science, the races-of-man theory continues to permeate U.S. culture. Its continued resonance exposes that the distinguishing characteristics of race in the U.S. have often been a confused conflation of biology (pigmentation and phenotype) and culture (ethnicity), both of which have been further conflated with character traits and intelligence. This confused conflation engenders stereotypes—such as, whites as the intellectually superior majority, Asian Americans as the model minority, and African Americans as the athletically superior minority. To determine how such stereotypes emerge and to interrupt them, I turn now to a brief history of how the term *race* has been employed in the U.S.

Compared to the long history of classifying people as men and women, the tropes of *race* and *whiteness* have a much shorter but more convoluted history. Although initially used to refer to ethnic groups (as in the Irish race or the British race), by time the U.S. Constitution was signed in 1787 and ratified in 1788, *race* had shifted to signify color and blood as designators of biological differences among people. These "biological differences," in turn, designated social and economic hierarchies:[9] that is, "white people" were presumed to be the superior race, thus deserving of freedom (although white indentured servants did exist); "black people" were presumed to be at best childlike and at worst animalistic, thus deserving of slavery (although free blacks did exist); "red people" were presumed to be savages, thus in need of civilizing (although they had civilizations of their own). In all these scenarios, *white* functions overtly as a racial category that is privileged even if all white people did not share identical social and economic privileges. This unearned racial privilege was justified not only by the races-of-man theory but by a eugenics movement.[10] Their social implications resulted not just in separate restrooms and water fountains but in sterilization of American Indians and medical experimentation on African Americans.

During and after the civil-rights movement of the 1950s and 1960s, however, talking about *whiteness* became associated in the dominant white culture with racists and white-supremacist groups. As a result of these associations, polite white society deemed it bad manners to discuss whiteness in public. As a result of this "politeness," discussions of white privilege and its power went underground, ultimately becoming invisible to most whites even as it remained visible to most non-whites.

How may this history be interrupted? Because tropes, such as *race,* take their meaning from the symbolic systems in which they function, I find it useful to examine how the trope *race* signifies differently within different cultural logics. Some common ones are: (1) the logic of white supremacy; (2) the logic of color-blindness; (3) the logic of multiculturalism; and (4) the logic of critical race theory.

First, the logic of white supremacy imagines *race* as biological differences, positing a hierarchical racial chain of being via the five-races-of-man theory. This logic was used to justify the existence of slavery as well as the treatment of slaves, Chinese immigrants, American Indians, Jewish people, and others.[11] Although this logic has been publicly discounted, its legacy haunts the U.S. not just in fringe political groups like racist militias but in our everyday symbols and metaphors.

Second, as a counter to white supremacy, the logic of color-blindness denies the existence of *race* as a viable category, either biologically or culturally. This logic draws on assumptions from equal-rights philosophy to demand that all people be treated equally in the present moment. But this logic ignores history or cultural factors that may privilege or constrain people in the present moment; thus, it ignores how *equal treatment* sometimes resonates as *not just.*

Third, as a counter to the logics of white supremacy and color-blindness, the logic of multiculturalism argues that the category of *race* is an imaginary construct, based on bad science, and should be replaced with the category of *ethnicity,*[12] which is defined as cultural heritage. This logic demands that all ethnicities be valued for their differences and commonalities and, concurrently, that each person be seen as an individual whose identity is informed by ethnicity but not reduced *solely* to ethnicity. Despite its antiracist agenda, multiculturalism has recently come under attack for promoting feel-good ethnic differences while leaving racism intact (Villanueva, "Reading" 195).

Fourth, as a corrective to multiculturalism's intentional eliding of *race* and its unintentional eliding of racism, the logic of critical race studies posits *race* as a U.S. cultural trope that names a cultural location. While this trope is grounded in bad science, it remains steeped in very real material consequences for U.S. culture and for individual people's lives. This logic demands that *race* be studied, not to reify its existence but to expose its functions so as to interrupt injustices and promote social justice.[13] As such, this cultural logic posits an ethical imperative for people to study whiteness as a racial category along with all other racial categories, recognizing the power dynamics within and among the different categories in order to interrupt the negative resonances of the trope *race.*

What makes *race* such a slippery category in the U.S. is not simply that its use and associated meanings shift across time, place, and cultures (e.g., human race versus Irish race versus white race) nor simply that it always intersects with other cultural categories (e.g., ethnicity, age, nationality, and gender). What makes *race* so slippery is the confused conflation of definitions. Standard definitions of *race* usually fall within a binary opposition, somewhere between biological grounding (now discounted by science) and cultural grounding (now championed in the academy). But as Lee argues, this binary opposition is too reductive for analyzing race because it does not account for the multiple ways that the trope *race* is employed in the U.S. (442–43). Some of these ways include:[14]

- race as a biological essence: character, moral traits, and intellect are biologically determined
- race as biological ancestry: physical attributes are inherited
- race as ethnic ancestry: cultural heritage is passed on
- race as a cultural position: cultural categories are used to classify or locate people, ideas, and things
- race as political class: groups of people are brought together for political action

These definitions overlap, intertwine, complicate each other, and confuse discussions of race and of all other topics inflected by race. This confusion is especially evident in discussions wherein *race* is not defined and cultural logics are not stated, the result being that people may "talk past" one another (Duncan 44), often assuming that their own definitions of *race* are "the Truth" and that other people just "don't get it."

Couple these assumptions with the traumas associated with race in the U.S., and the result in public discourse is a dysfunctional silence and/or, at best, awkward conversations. This silence and awkwardness perpetuate the status quo wherein *race* functions as a highly contested term: that is, as a trope for that-which-does-not-exist-biologically-but-that-which-has-become-ideologically-"real" in U.S. culture, so real that for centuries people have died because of it. Such extreme consequences are explained by Michael Eric Dyson, who defines race as "a set of beliefs and behaviors shaped by culture, rooted in history, and fueled by passions that transcend reason" (42). Thus, like gender, race is always a question not only of difference but of unearned privilege and power—and the lack thereof.

Challenging such unearned privilege and power is one goal of this book. To that end, subsequent chapters explore how listeners may employ rhetorical listening to hear some of our troubled identifications with gender and whiteness. Specifically, subsequent chapters define *rhetorical listening,* demonstrate its necessary connection to conscious identifications, and offer three tactics[15] (eavesdropping, listening metonymically, and listening pedagogically).

1
Defining Rhetorical Listening

In the beginning was not the word. In the beginning is the hearing.
—Mary Daly, *Gyn/Ecology*

My hearing depends on detailed differences or similarities. . . . And sometimes and in varying degrees, I can choose the mode of my *conscious* listening.
—Alice Rayner, "The Audience"
(emphasis added)

And once we have a vocabulary for explaining what we do when we listen, it is easier to convince others to listen the way we do—and to change the way we listen ourselves.
—Peter Rabinowitz, "Fictional Music:
Toward a Theory of Listening"

In this project, *rhetorical listening* is defined generally as a trope for interpretive invention[1] and more particularly as a code of cross-cultural conduct. As a trope for interpretive invention, *rhetorical listening* signifies a stance of openness that a person may choose to assume in relation to *any* person, text, or culture.[2] Employed in this general way, it functions as one answer to Jacqueline Jones Royster's question: "How do we translate listening into language and action . . . ?" ("When the First Voice" 38). My particular interest, however, lies in how rhetorical listening may be employed to hear people's intersecting identifications with gender and race (including whiteness), the purpose being to negotiate troubled identifications in order to facilitate cross-cultural communication about any topic. Employed in this particular way, rhetorical listening functions as a response to Royster's call for "codes of cross-cultural conduct" ("Borderlands").

Royster's question and call are important because they pinpoint a lack of scholarly interest in listening within contemporary rhetoric and composition studies. What accounts for this lack? After all, for more than two thousand years, the four rhetorical arts of reading, writing, speaking, and listening were cornerstones of Western rhetorical studies (Murphy, "Rhetorical History" 5, 11). But in the early twentieth century, these arts were separated from one another during the divorce of English studies from communication studies. Custody of these arts was awarded to different disciplines, with reading and writing relegated to English studies and speaking and listening relegated to communication studies. This divorce still haunts English studies, even after the mid-twentieth-century recovery of rhetoric via the rise of rhetoric and composition studies within English departments. For within English studies and rhetoric and composition studies, reading and writing reign as the dominant tropes for interpretive invention; speaking places a respectable third; but listening runs a poor, poor fourth.

That is not to say listening has never been mentioned within recent scholarship. It has. For example, James Phelan and Andrea Lunsford employ listening to explore voices speaking or not speaking within written texts. Phelan posits listening as a means of constructing "some conceptual model for defining and investigating voice in written discourse," particularly narratives (132), and Lunsford offers it as a means for reclaiming "the voices of women in the history of rhetoric," voices of women long dead who need no longer be silent if only we know how to listen for them (6).[3] Yet, this scholarly focus on voice elides sustained theorizing about listening. As a counter to this focus on voice, Victor Vitanza and Michelle Ballif employ listening to (expose) language play with/in texts. Pondering Nietzschean, hermeneutic, and poststructuralist conversations about listening and the ear, Vitanza promotes listening as a means of questioning the *logos* and exposing its "duplicity"/"triplicity"/"complicity" with/in language (*Negation* 165–69). Pondering similar conversations, Ballif argues that traditional rhetorical theories subordinate listening as a way of knowing actual desires of actual audience members (51–58). Despite the aforementioned scholarly work, the dominant scholarly trend in rhetoric and composition studies has been to follow the lead of popular culture and naturalize listening, that is, assume it to be something that everyone does but no one needs study. The implication for rhetoric and composition studies is quite simple: Listening is rarely theorized or taught.

To counter this trend, this chapter offers an extended definition of *rhetorical listening* as a trope for interpretive invention and, more particularly, as a code of cross-cultural conduct. As mentioned in the introduction, this concept of rhetorical listening is important because it supplements Kenneth Burke's rhetorical theory. Just as Burke argues that identification must precede persuasion (*Rhetoric* 55), this chapter argues that rhetorical listening may precede *conscious* identifications. Such conscious identifications are important because they may provide grounds for revising identifications troubled by history, uneven power dynamics, and ignorance; as such, they may foster cross-cultural communication on any topic.

My purpose in offering this concept of rhetorical listening is not to construct a totalizing theory of listening; such an endeavor is impossible. Rather, my purpose is to invite further conversations on how listening may inform rhetoric and composition studies. To develop an extended definition of rhetorical listening, this chapter (1) explains disciplinary and cultural biases that displace listening, (2) justifies why listening is needed within rhetoric and composition studies and life; (3) defines rhetorical listening as a trope for interpretive invention; (4) explores one of its uses as a code of cross-cultural conduct; and (5) offers an example.

Explaining Biases Against Listening

One disciplinary bias that explains rhetoric and composition studies' neglect of listening may be found, most obviously, in the work we do: We have appropriated Western rhetorical theories to theorize writing and the teaching of writing. Because we focus primarily on written discourse and because listening is commonly associated with oral discourse, we have been slow to imagine how listening might inform our discipline. We have more readily paired writing with reading and, to a lesser extent, with speaking. We pair writing with reading because many teachers assume that improving students' reading skills improves their writing skills (Mailloux; Haas and Flower; Bartholomae and Petrosky). And although speaking is not our field's primary province, we also pair it with writing. It haunts our theories and praxes either as an invention strategy (students' talking with peers in review sessions and with teachers in conferences), as a proofreading strategy (students' reading papers aloud to check sentence flow), or as an influential metaphor (voice) (J. Harris; Yancey). As a result of these pairings, our field's dominant tropes for interpretive invention have been writing and reading and, to a lesser degree, speaking. To supplement these tropes, I offer rhetorical listening.

A second disciplinary bias that explains our neglect of listening is that Western rhetorical theories themselves have traditionally slighted listening. Classical theories foreground a rhetor's speaking and writing as means of persuading audiences; these theories are only secondarily concerned with how audiences should listen and hardly at all concerned with what Ballif calls the desires of particular audience members (51). Granted, Aristotle's *Rhetoric* assures students who study his rhetorical theory that they will learn not only how to *produce* enthymemes but also, by implication, how to *analyze* them (1.12); and in a culture whose texts were primarily oral, such analysis implies listening. But Aristotle's theory never delves into *how* to listen. Moreover, his production/reception linkage is more complicated than his assurance allows. Although most writing teachers and students link production (writing) with reception (reading), they also recognize differences, such as, most students are more comfortable with reading than with writing. And although writing teachers and students may link strategies of production (speaking with writing) and strategies of reception (reading with listening), they ascertain differences here, too: Speaking is second "nature" for most students, but writing is not; some students learn better by reading information, others by hearing it explained. Yet, classical and modern theories of rhetoric rarely delineate or question such production/reception differences.

Although poststructuralist theory calls such differences into question (Miller 41–42), it has inadvertently served as a third disciplinary bias in our field's neglect of listening. Jacques Derrida's project to deconstruct Western metaphysics reverses Plato's celebration of speaking and suspicion of writing. Consequently, deconstruction champions writing as a trope that more accurately describes textuality, or how we use language and how language uses us. Moreover, it collapses reading into this equation by arguing that writing is reading is writing. But because it denigrates speaking as the trope that fosters a metaphysics of presence, poststructuralist theory in the wake of Derrida finds itself suspicious of speaking and, by association, of listening, even though Derrida pays tribute to listening as a means of substituting the ethical for the ideal in his essay about Emmanuel Levinas ("Violence" 99). But even as Derrida flirts with listening, his focus is on reading: As Christie McDonald claims in her preface to Derrida's *Ear of the Other*, "what is at stake in [his] vast program is contemporary *reading* and how it becomes possible to assume political positions (viii; emphasis added).

One cultural bias that may partially account for our field's neglect of listening is exposed in the work of Deborah Tannen: gender bias. Citing personal observation, other researchers' case studies, and her own linguistic theory, Tannen claims that in U.S. culture, speaking is gendered as masculine and valued positively in a public forum while listening is gendered as feminine and valued negatively. Tannen further argues that U.S. culture socializes men and women to listen differently: Men often listen by challenging speakers to a verbal duel to determine who knows more and who is quicker on his feet; women often listen by smiling, nodding, asking questions, and providing encouraging verbal cues (*yes, uh huh, is that right?, hmmm*) (142). In other words, men are socialized to play the listening game via the questions "'Have I won?'" and "'Do you respect me?'" while women are socialized to play it via the questions "'Have I been helpful?'" and "'Do you like me?'" (129). Thus gendered, listening subordinates not only women to men but listening to speaking.

If true, Tannen's assertions have important implications for interactions among women and men in classrooms, in workplaces, and in general. When I asked undergraduate rhetorical-theory students to name these implications, they were quite adamant in their responses. They claimed that in an ideal world, men would learn how to listen just as women do, but given the reality of our world, that is probably not going to happen; therefore, they concluded that women must resist their socialization as nurturers and learn to duel verbally. I was not surprised by this conclusion; neither was I altogether accepting. I conceded that women may need to learn to speak up more. But why, I asked, cannot men also expand their repertoire of listening skills? And why, I continued, cannot listening itself be revalued, perhaps even reengendered?[4]

A second cultural bias that may inform our neglect of listening emerges in the writings of Nikki Giovanni: race bias. Giovanni argues that listening is not only gendered but also inflected by race. Specifically, she argues that listening is not as necessary in U.S. culture for white people as it is for non-whites; she also argues that this general trend can be complicated by class differences. To illustrate her point, Giovanni imagines a fictional scenario, a poet's internal dialogue with herself while composing a talk for the 372nd Annual Convention of Black and White Women in America:

> I suppose we shouldn't even talk about how the women's movement wouldn't listen to the Black women when we tried to say that the average white woman didn't understand her maid. I mean, [in the movie *An Imitation of Life*] when Lana Turner said to Annie, "I didn't know you belonged to a lodge," Juanita Moore replied, "Well, Miss

Laura [*sic*], you never asked." There was no *women's* movement; there was a white women's movement and Black women never were, nor felt, included. It's all been an *imitation of life* to us, and *the long walk home* won't change that." (85–86)

Giovanni points out that Lana Turner's Lora Meredith wears the blinders that privilege affords privileged people, in this case the blinders that white privilege affords white people. Despite that Annie is privy to the intimate details of Lora's life, Lora has not imagined her maid's life, Annie Johnson's life, beyond the services visibly rendered in their apartment. One question that may be asked of this scenario is: How may Lora change her complicity in the structural and personal racism that haunts all their lives if she cannot see it?[5]

This question exposes a third cultural bias that may have influenced our field's neglect of listening: U.S. culture privileges sight. This preference for interpretive tropes that proceed via the eye is what Martin Jay calls *ocularcentrism*.[6] The question that emerges is: What are the limits of ocularcentrism? As any camera operator will confirm, the limitation of sight is that when one object is foregrounded, other objects blur, fade into the background, fall outside the field of vision. To carry this metaphor further, I believe that the sight tropes of reading and writing may sometimes perpetuate our difficulty of bringing into focus two differences, such as gender and race. Adrienne Rich admits the difficulty of such a move, even as she exhorts us to "watch the edges that blur" ("Contradictions" 111, 29, lines 10–12):

> Sometimes I feel I have seen too long from too many disconnected angles: white, Jewish, anti-Semite, racist, anti-racist, once-married lesbian, middle-class, feminist, exmatriate southerner, split at the root—that I will never bring them whole. I would have liked, in this essay, to bring together the meanings of anti-Semitism and racism as I have experienced them and as I believe they intersect in the world beyond my life. But I'm not able to do this yet. ("Split" 122)

This difficulty is exemplified in Lora and Annie's situation: Lora does not understand Annie because the cultural "blinders" of white and class privilege impede Lora's ability to "visualize" Annie's life beyond how it "visibly" intersects with her own. And I believe this difficulty, in one way or another, haunts everyone's life. Despite this difficulty, Rich admonishes us to keep trying to understand our identifications by bringing blurred intersections together and then acting accordingly: "We can't wait to speak until we are perfectly clear and righteous. There is no purity and, in our lifetime, no end to this process" (123). So, for those times when we run into difficulty with blurred or invisible intersecting identifications, I suggest we switch from a sight trope to an auditory one and see, or rather listen to, where it may lead.

Making a Case for What the Ear Has to Offer

Having demonstrated how disciplinary and cultural biases displace listening, I now want to justify the need for rhetorical listening in rhetoric and composition studies and in life. For of all the questions that have haunted this project, two keep coming back to me from reviewers and audience members: How does listening differ from reading—and why do we need listening? When I presented an early version of this project at the University of Wisconsin–Milwaukee's rhetoric and composition lecture series, a graduate student responded, prefacing her remarks with, "Of course, what you're really talking about is a kind of reading." No, I tried to explain, I am not. I am talking about interpretive invention, a way of making meaning with/in language, with two different kinds being reading and listening. For if listening is to be revived and revalued within our field, it must occupy its own niche. Rather than be subsumed by reading, it should rank as an equal yet intertwining process of interpretive invention, for sometimes the ear can help us see just as the eye can help us hear.[7] I am not surprised at the graduate student's response. It is informed not only by the disciplinary and cultural biases previously mentioned but also by what I believe is the organizing principle of these biases: the divided *logos* that Martin Heidegger claims we have inherited in the West, the *logos* that speaks but does not listen.

One need not fully subscribe to Heidegger's philosophical project of *dasein*, or being in the world, to recognize the aptness of his divided *logos* theory. In general, the *logos* is a system of discourse within which a culture reasons and derives its truths. Although the Greeks had different concepts of *logos* (Jarratt, *Rereading* 42–61), Heidegger argues that these concepts imply both speaking and listening. He further argues that "this nature of language remains hidden from the Greeks. They have never expressedly stressed it, much less raised it to the level of a problem. But their statements operate in this realm" (*What Is Called Thinking?* 202). To explain his claim, Heidegger explores the relationship between the Greek noun *logos* and its verb form *legein,* which in its fullest sense means both "saying" and "laying" (198). The second meaning, "laying," entails laying others' ideas in front of us in order to let these ideas lie before us. This laying-to-let-lie-before-us functions as a preservation of others' ideas (194–215) and, hence, as a site for listening.

But because we have inherited a divided *logos*, we inhabit a culture where "saying" has assumed dominance and "laying" (and, thus, listening) has been displaced. Thus separated from a consideration of otherness, "saying" quickly becomes masterly expression; writing, a means of masterly expression; and reading, a means of mastering-the-masterly-expression. All three quickly subsume listening. But listening is not totally erased, just displaced . . . and almost always diminished from its potential as *legein*. Sometimes it is acknowledged because it cannot be physically ignored, as in the fields of psychology, theology, and communications. Sometimes it is assumed to be a natural process that we need not study, as in rhetoric and composition studies. Sometimes it is mistaken for silence, as in patriarchal histories of women and nondominant ethnic groups. And sometimes it goes by another name: reading,[8] as when we read for tone, rhythm, voice, silence, and a plethora of other elements associated with a h(ear)ring metaphor.

In *The Other Side of Language: A Philosophy of Listening,* Gemma Corradi Fiumara calls for both a reinterpretation of our *logos* to expose its divided nature and a restoration of a fuller *logos* based on the Greek action *legein* (11–17). Such reinterpretations and restorations would result in a philosophy of listening, which would offer us other codes for conducting ourselves in the world. For as Fiumara suggests, a philosophy of listening "is an attempt to retrieve the functions of listening which may allow for truer forms of dialogue" (13). That is, in a divided *logos* (one that speaks but does not listen), we commonly employ dialogue as Hegelian dialectic wherein the posited thesis subsumes the acceptable aspects of the antithesis with the unacceptable excess being exiled from the dominant logic. In an undivided *logos* (one that speaks and listens), we would employ dialogue as a dialectic-that-questions-dialectic, enabling a metonymic coexistence of ideas (Fiumara 15, 17).

I would like to echo Fiumara's call for listening by issuing a similar call in rhetoric and composition studies. For just as all texts can be read, so, too, can they be listened to. As a trope for interpretive invention, rhetorical listening differs from reading in that it proceeds via different body organs, different disciplinary and cultural assumptions, different figures of speech, and most importantly different stances. As Fiumara suggests, listening within a stance of openness maps out an entirely different space in which to relate to discourse: We may become "apprentices of listening rather than masters of discourse" (57). For when listening within an undivided *logos*, we do not read simply for what we can agree with or challenge, as is the habit of academic reading (in its multiple guises). Instead, we choose to listen also for the exiled excess and contemplate its relation to our culture and our selves. Such listening does not presume a naïve, relativistic empathy, such as "I'm OK, you're OK" but rather an ethical responsibility to argue for what we deem fair and just while questioning that which we deem fair and just. Such listening, I argue, may help people invent, interpret, and ultimately judge differently in that perhaps we can *hear* things we cannot *see*.

Within this more inclusive *logos* lies potential for personal and social justice. Perhaps through listening, people can engage more possibilities for inventing arguments that bring differences together, for hearing differences as harmony or even as discordant notes (in which case, at least, differences are discernible). Admittedly, we cannot hear everything at once (the din would no doubt madden us), yet we can listen to the harmony and/or discordant notes, knowing that more than meets the eye lies before us. Obviously, I am not arguing that we abandon reading, writing, and speaking. I am, however, suggesting that we recognize their limits and rethink them within an undivided *logos*, a *logos* that includes listening.

Defining a Trope for Interpretive Invention

Having established a need for listening within rhetoric and composition studies and in life, I now offer an extended definition of *rhetorical listening* as a trope for interpretive invention, that is, as a stance of openness that a person may choose to assume in relation to any person, text, or culture; its purpose is to cultivate conscious identifications in ways that promote productive communication, especially but not solely cross-culturally. This section unpacks this definition of rhetorical listening, first providing an example and then positing its moves.

An example of rhetorical listening emerges in Marge Piercy's poem, "The book of Ruth and Naomi." Even though the Biblical Ruth and Naomi are born into different ethnic groups (Ruth is Moabite; Naomi, Judean),[9] they forge a cross-cultural relationship that, for centuries, has represented an ideal friendship between women. Piercy attributes the success of the relationship, in part, to each woman's desire to connect with another woman via whispering:

Show me a woman who does not dream
a double, heart's twin, a sister
of the mind in whose ear she can whisper.

(277.19–21)

Yet this desire to whisper is predicated on the already existing possibility of another woman, one whose ear may hear the whisper, one who *listens* . . . and understands. Even though listening is a necessary component of these women's relationship, it is backgrounded in this poem, in its Biblical source, in much of our contemporary cultural consciousness, and in rhetoric and composition studies.

To foreground listening in rhetoric and composition studies, I offer a concept of rhetorical listening as a trope for interpretive invention. As the performance of a person's conscious choice to assume an open stance in relation to any person, text, or culture,, rhetorical listening challenges the divided *logos* of Western civilization. As such, it constructs a space wherein listeners may employ their agency (which Stanford drama theorist Alice Rayner defines as both "capacity" and "willingness" [7]) to foster conscious identifications that may, in turn, facilitate communication. Such rhetorical listening comprises the following moves:

1. Promoting an *understanding* of self and other
2. Proceeding within an *accountability* logic[10]
3. Locating identifications across *commonalities* and *differences*
4. Analyzing *claims* as well as the *cultural logics* within which these claims function

Though not necessarily linear, these moves foster in listeners the critical thinking skills that may lay grounds for productive communication.

Before unpacking these four moves, I want to address a question that haunts this study: Is rhetorical listening, as defined here, too idealistic to have a pragmatic effect? My response is: No, it is not. Dismissing rhetorical listening as too idealistic presumes a focus only on its obvious limitations: That is, rhetorical listening cannot solve all the world's problems, nor can it guarantee perfect communication or even productive communication in all instances. Then again, neither can Aristotle's enthymeme.

Championing rhetorical listening as potentially pragmatic presumes a simultaneous focus on its limitations *and* its possibilities. Rhetorical listening enables people to hear textual strategies associated with a h(ear)ing metaphor, such as voice and silence; relatedly but more encompassingly, it enables people to hear what Toni Morrison calls "the sound that [breaks] the back of words" (*Beloved* 261), thus enabling people to question the *logos* as we know it. Such questioning *may* serve as grounds for communicating across troubled identifications. In this way, rhetorical listening does not simply assume that identifications will precede persuasion; rather, it offers one tactic for attempting to negotiate troubled identifications that haunt many rhetorical exchanges. Sometimes rhetorical listening will fail. But sometimes it will work—just like Aristotle's enthymeme.[11]

For rhetorical listening to have a pragmatic effect, its practitioners must identify and understand its four moves. The following definition of these four moves is indebted to Phelan and Lunsford, to Vitanza and Ballif, to Heidegger, Royster, Rayner, and Morrison.

1. *Promoting an understanding of self and other.* By stipulating *understanding* as an end of rhetorical listening, I recognize that I am invoking a troubled term. *Understanding* has a complicated history in narrative studies and in philosophical studies[12] in that it is often coupled with authorial intent. And as many scholars caution, this coupling often gives birth to a naïve idealism. For example, Julia Kristeva claims that because Westerners "are entitled only to the ear of the virginal body [of Mary] . . . , there arises a possible tendency to eroticize [and, hence, idealize] hearing, voice or even understanding" (173). Steven Mailloux claims that coupling understanding and intent often circles "back to all the problems of textual realism and readerly idealism and ignores the specific rhetorical contexts of power-knowledge" (148). By posing understanding as an end of rhetorical listening, I am not proposing that we idealize understanding or authorial intent: My purpose is neither to promote a "textual realism" wherein a text is perceived as a repository of *the* truth nor to celebrate a naïve "readerly idealism" wherein the contexts of speaker/writers are simplified and the contexts of reader/listeners erased. Rather, my purpose is to wed Giovanni's real to Piercy's ideal, to collapse the real/ideal dichotomy into a strategic third ground where rhetorical negotiation is exposed as always already existing and where rhetorical listening is posited as one means of that negotiation.

Granted, such a purpose resonates with remnants of idealism. But, as mentioned earlier, I like to consider these remnants strategic. Just as Gayatri Spivak justifies subalterns' employing a "*strategic* essentialism" in their critique of postcolonial oppression (205) and just as Amy Schuman justifies ethnographers' employing a "strategic Romanticism" when constructing and analyzing the subjects of their studies, I am advocating a strategic idealism when listening with the intent to understand. Strategic idealism implies a conscious identification among people that is based on a desire for an inter-subjective receptivity, not mastery, and on a simultaneous recognition of similarities and differences, not merely one or the other. The idealism is strategic in that people should recognize the difficulty and dangers inherent in such a project . . . and proceed knowingly.

As employed in this study, *understanding* means more than simply listening *for* a speaker/writer's intent. It also means more than simply listening *for* our own self-interested readerly intent, which may range from appropriation (employing a text for one's own ends), to Burkean identification (smoothing over differences to achieve common ground), to agreement (affirming only one's own view of reality). Instead, *understanding* means listening to discourses not *for* intent but *with* intent—with the intent to understand not just the claims but the rhetorical negotiations of understanding as well. To clarify this process of understanding, rhetorical listeners might best invert the term *understanding* and define it as *standing under*,[13] that is, consciously standing under discourses that surround us and others[14] while consciously acknowledging all our particular—and very fluid—standpoints. Standing under discourses means letting discourses wash over, through, and around us and then letting them lie there to inform our politics and ethics.[15]

Standing under our own discourses means identifying the various discourses embodied within each of us and then listening to hear and imagine how these discourses might affect not only ourselves but others. The question that arises, of course, is the same dilemma that haunts Lora Meredith: How can we know what is so naturalized for us that it is no longer visible to us? One answer to that question, according to Rayner, is listening. Her claim echoes Hans-Georg Gadamer's belief that "the primacy of hearing is the basis of the hermeneutical phenomenon" (420): That is, we speak because someone is listening. If we pull Rayner's theory into rhetoric and composition studies, we may argue that those of us listening to our own discourses return our discourses to ourselves somehow unchanged but changed. To exemplify this process, Rayner points to Virginia Woolf, who writes of a longing to hear the echo of her own words. Rayner deems Woolf's desire as

> the need for a return (echo) of speech and gesture, a return that occurs in time as openness, not in a static image or closed meaning. The echo is life-giving because while it is rooted in the past, it is not fixed

by the past. It returns the voice to the speaker, the same but different. (21)

Because our returning discourses may look the same but resonate differently, we need to cultivate both our eyes and our ears.

Standing under the discourses of others means first, acknowledging the existence of these discourses; second, listening for (un)conscious presences, absences, unknowns; and third, consciously integrating this information into our world views and decision making. The question that arises here is: How may we listen for that which we do not intellectually, viscerally, or experientially know? Or as Pocahontas sings to John Smith in that travesty of a Disney movie, how will you "learn things you never knew you never knew?" Again Rayner provides a way of thinking about this issue that may be borrowed for rhetoric and composition studies, a way of thinking that echoes Heidegger's reminder that in addition to silence, hearing is also a possibility of discursive speech ("Phenomenology" 234). Rayner argues that a theater audience (not as a collective whole but as a collection of individuals) should listen to a performance, perceiving it "not as a referential intention but as a desire to be heard as meaningful or as meaningfully breaking the conventional frames. The emphasis . . . is on the attempt and effort, not success or failure" (18), at least not as *success* and *failure* are defined by dominant social conventions.

This "desire to be heard" echoes not simply as a speaker's conscious use of a discourse but also as a speaker's unconscious desires and as the socializing functions of discourse. If this "desire to be heard" is met with opposing desires—for example, pretending the "desire to be heard" does not exist, hoping it will disappear, or waiting for someone else to handle it—then potential dialogue is stymied. But standing under the discourses of others and rhetorically listening to them have the potential to transpose a desire for mastery into a self-conscious desire for receptivity. As such, this process both invites the desires of others into our consciousness and accords these desires a place in which to be heard (Rayner 18).

Standing under discourses (whether our own or others') does not guarantee agreement; it should not foster idealism; it does, however, present a possibility for hearing what we cannot see. In this process, the unknown becomes not a perpetually purloined letter, that is, "an irretrievable absence or gap which symbols replace and displace, as in the Lacanian formula"; rather, the unknown becomes "more simply and more radically a limit to understanding" (Rayner 14). Limits may be moved and re-moved. According to Rayner, the agency for moving and re-moving such limits involves a "capacity" and "willingness" (7): We all possess that capacity; what must be supplied is the willingness. This focus on willingness, on conscious action, does not deny the socializing power of discourse on our unconscious. Rather, this focus simply articulates the space within which we may interject our own agencies, albeit partial and complicated, into our socializing identifications.

The result of such understanding is a broader cultural literacy, which affords us opportunities for negotiating our daily attitudes and actions, our politics and ethics. Rayner provides theatergoers with a definition of one such literacy, a definition that might be applied more generally to rhetoric and composition studies via rhetorical listening:

> It is perhaps a borderland more than a boundary between the capacity to hear and the obligation to listen to what one cannot immediately understand or comprehend. And it leads to the *learning* of community . . . in the exchange of signs. . . . At the very least, such choice involves a decision to recognize and become self-conscious toward the limitations of [one's] own 'imaginary' version of self and other—a limitation that does not acquiesce to . . . an unknowable, but takes that unknowable as a pre-condition within which action is still necessary and a confrontation with another inevitable. (18–19)

Because confrontation is inevitable, this literacy has the potential to effect more productive discourses about, and across, commonalities and differences. Given this potential, acquiring such literacy becomes both an ethical issue and a political issue for people with power and for people without it.

Linking the ethical to understanding is a necessary element of rhetorical listening. Granted, we may not always choose or control the discourses that socialize us; neither may we choose or control our unconscious responses to these discourses. But we can, to a limited degree, articulate our conscious identifications and choose to respond to them (or not); in this way, we become responsible for our words, our attitudes, and our actions. Because attitudes and actions are the means through which we negotiate conventional truths as well as our behaviors based upon these truths, Diane Davis argues:

> What is needed now is an *ethics* of decision; to the extent that we may no longer simply be guided by ontological Truth, by light or *logos,*

decisions have to be made. And any ethics of decision necessitates first a "hearing"—double entendre intended: it necessitates both a listening and a judging. ("Just Listening" 6; emphasis added)

Rayner agrees, claiming that listening as presence and as judgment presumes "an ethics of relation not simply power over" (21).

Once the question of power relations among people enters the conversation about understanding, the political also emerges as a necessary element of rhetorical listening. Because the political assumes not just one person but a collection of people, rhetorical listening recognizes the other as a *necessary* consideration in the making of meaning for the listener.[16] In terms of the political, rhetorical listening opens up not only possibilities of but responsibilities for interpretive invention, that is, for making meanings via language via others. Although rhetorical listening does not guarantee that everyone will concur about intersecting identifications and their functions, it does guarantee that considerations of the ethical and the political will haunt discussions of *understanding*.

2. *Proceeding from within an accountability logic.* Rhetorical listening invites listeners to position our stances of openness within a logic of accountability, which is quite simply a way of reasoning whose grounding principle is accountability. But what is *accountability*? As suggested by bell hooks in "Race and Feminism: The Issue of Accountability," *accountability* does not mean continually beating oneself up for one's history, culture, or Freudian slips; such a move is, at best, narcissistic. Nor does *accountability* mean believing that apologizing for unintended slights is enough; such a thought is, at best, self-indulgent. Nor does *accountability* mean claiming that the past is the past and, thus, has no effect on the present; such a claim is, at best, myopic. Nor does *accountability* mean arguing that things have always been this way and that acting for change will do no good; such an argument is, at best, cowardly, self-interested, and/or self-defeating. Instead, *accountability* signifies recognizing that none of us lives autonomous lives, despite the grand narrative of U.S. individualism. *Accountability* means that we are indeed all members of the same village, and if for no other reason than that (and there *are* other reasons), all people necessarily have a stake in each other's quality of life.

Because a logic of accountability focuses us on the present, with attention paid to the resonances of the past, a logic of accountability suggests an ethical imperative that, regardless of who is responsible for a current situation, asks us to recognize our privileges and nonprivileges and then act accordingly. A logic of accountability tries to interrupt our excuses of not being personally accountable *at present* for existing cultural situations that originated *in the past* (e.g., personal excuses such as "I never denied a woman a promotion" or "My family never owned slaves"). A logic of accountability invites us to consider how all of us are, at present, culturally implicated in effects of the past (via our resulting privileges and/or their lack) and, thus, accountable for what we do about situations now, even if we are not responsible for their origins.

As discussed further in chapter 3, such an accountability logic offers rhetorical listeners an alternative to a guilt/blame logic. As such, an accountability logic offers listeners a place to hear (some of) our conscious identifications, articulate these identifications, and even talk back to them.

3. *Locating identifications across commonalities and differences.* When attempting to identify identifications, we frequently gravitate, almost by default, toward places of common ground, that is, places of commonalities with other people, texts, and cultures. But when practicing rhetorical listening, we are invited to consciously locate our identifications in places of commonalities *and* differences. With this double focus, rhetorical listening juxtaposes traditional and postmodern rhetorical concepts of identification. Traditional theories of rhetoric theorize identification as commonality, that is, as a metaphoric common ground, a Burkean sharing of substance, a place that leads to persuasion (Burke, *Rhetoric* 55). Postmodern theories of discourse theorize identification differently. These theories question the possibility of substance and common ground and, instead, champion a metonymic juxtaposition of differences as the place of identification or disidentification (Fuss, *Identification* 3; Butler 93–121). The problem with traditional identification is that differences are often glossed over or erased, left outside the circle of consubstantiality; the problem with postmodern identification and disidentification is that commonalities are often perceived as impossible or as impossibly naïve.

As detailed in chapter 2, rhetorical listening interrupts this modern/postmodern binary opposition by theorizing identification as metonymic places of commonalities and differences. In such identifications, discourses (not substances) converge and diverge. In such identifications, dialogue emerges as a dialectical conversation that questions the process of dialectic, a conversation that "seeks not the clarification and rigidification of difference [or commonalities] but rather the murky margins between, those margins of overlap which inaugurate and which limit the very functioning of dialectic" (D. Williams 218). Within such borderlands, rhetorical listening helps listeners analyze discursive convergences and divergences. This analysis, in turn, helps listeners articulate our identifications and communicate about—and across—both differences and commonalities.

As exemplified in chapters 3, 4, and 5, rhetorical listening simultaneously focuses on commonalities and differences within textual claims and their cultural logics. In this way, rhetorical listening ties the personal (a person's claim) to the political (a cultural logic) without totally collapsing differences between the two.

4. *Analyzing claims as well as the cultural logics within which claims function.* If a claim is an assertion of a person's thinking, then a cultural logic is a belief system or shared way of reasoning within which a claim may function. Although claims and cultural logics are both rhetorical constructs, our arguments and analyses of arguments too often focus only on claims, such as, "I'm right that John Kerry should have been elected" versus "No, I'm right that George Bush should have been elected." Rarely do arguments and analyses of arguments focus on the cultural logics that ground such claims. But rhetorical listening invites listeners to acknowledge both claims and cultural logics. For example, the above political claim about President Bush might be functioning within a conservative religious logic, a Republican logic, a neoconservative logic, a military-hawk logic, or some combination of these and other logics. What is important to understand is that the claim would signify differently within each cultural logic.

By focusing on claims and cultural logics, listeners may still disagree with each other's claims, but they may better appreciate that the other person is not simply wrong but rather functioning from within a different logic. For example, instead of seeing a Bush supporter as just wrong, a Kerry supporter may recognize that a Bush supporter is functioning from a different set of principles and/or from different ways of interpreting common principles; a Bush supporter may have similar recognitions about a Kerry supporter. Such recognitions enable listeners, when appropriate, to appreciate the reasoning powers of others, even when disagreeing with their assertions. Thus, such recognitions function as grounds for negotiation and communication.

While there are obvious benefits of rhetorical listening, there are also caveats. The first caveat is: Rhetorical listening with the intent to understand, not master, discourses is not a quick fix nor a happy-ever-after solution; rather, it is an ongoing process. Rhetorical listening will not result in an ideal world in which rhetorical negotiation is no longer necessary. Such hopes are not only naïve but dangerous. Instead, rhetorical listening is another way of helping us continually negotiate our always evolving standpoints, our identities, with the always evolving standpoints of others. It is also another way of helping us recognize that our standpoints are not autonomous points of static stases but rather complex webs of dynamically intermingled cultural structures and subjective agency.

A second caveat is: Although listening with the intent to receive, not master, discourses can motivate a particular listener to take political and ethical action, this listener's desire cannot control how other readers, writers, speakers, or listeners will, in turn, receive the listener's desire, discourse, or actions. A listener should certainly not expect a pat on the back either for rhetorical listening or for speaking, reading, or writing based on rhetorical listening. After all, rhetorical listening is the responsibility of everyone. Expectations to the contrary are not only condescending but reduce rhetorical listening to simple intent.

And, finally, a third caveat is: As Marquette University undergraduate Sara Scheunemann wrote in a student essay, "Listening with the intent to understand opens [people] up . . . to being challenged, convicted, and hurt by the truth." It may be more another's truth than *the* truth that hurts us; however, this challenge, this conviction, this hurt exposes a space of dissonance. When responding to this dissonance, we should not accuse the person foregrounding it, deny its existence, or bristle defensively. Such reactions only shut down dialogue and reinforce the status quo. Rather, we should question ourselves—our attitudes and our actions—to determine whether we need to affirm, revise, or reject them. If such questioning makes us more uncomfortable, so be it. In fact, good. Such discomfort simply signifies already existing troubled identifications, and it underscores the need for standing under the discourses of ourselves and others—and listening.

Defining a Code of Cross-Cultural Conduct

Because rhetorical listening functions generally as a trope for interpretive invention, it has innumerable uses. One particular use that this project investigates is rhetorical listening's function as a code of cross-cultural conduct. This use assumes that listening is predicated upon respect for self and others; it also assumes that listeners possess the agency for acknowledging, cultivating, and negotiating conventions of different discourse communities. Used as a code of cross-cultural conduct, rhetorical listening may foster understanding of intersecting gender and race identifications in ways that may promote cross-cultural communication on any number of topics.

Although many troubled identifications haunt cross-cultural communications, I focus on intersecting identifications of gender and whiteness. Why? To explain, I want to revisit a thread in my thinking about rhetorical listening. As mentioned in the introduction, when Susan Jarratt challenged me to consider how race complicated my first book project on Anglo-American feminist theories of rhetoric, I found it fairly easy to write about the overt race claims that Woolf, Daly, and Rich make or do not make; however, I found it more difficult to write about how whiteness haunts these writers' discussions of women, language, and culture. What complicated my musing at that moment was my own standpoint as a white feminist who had an abhorrence of racism and who had considered how racism works in the lives of non-white people but who had never really been taught nor had taken it upon herself to learn how racism functions in relation to whiteness and/or white people beyond the narrative that begins, "Once upon a time, white people were racists." Jarratt's challenge to investigate race in my book project afforded me an opportunity to question and complicate this narrative.

Given this opportunity, I decided to start a new project in order to find tactics for conceptualizing and articulating intersections of gender and whiteness. I reasoned that if I could not see the way whiteness worked, perhaps I could hear it. Thus, I came to link rhetorical listening with articulating gender and race identifications, particularly gendered constructions of whiteness. The question that emerged next, of course, was: What should I listen to in order to hear intersections of gender and whiteness? Given my thinking about rhetorical listening, the obvious answer was: to the discourses of myself and others. For my purposes, I settled on three types: (1) autoethnography, (2) academic research, and (3) the stories of others.

Listening to Autoethnography

My interest in listening to autoethnography[17] initially emerged from a fascinating discussion that erupted a few years ago in an undergraduate rhetorical-theory class. In response to Cornel West's *Race Matters,* an exasperated white student told the class, "I don't see what the big deal is. I don't wake up every morning, look in the mirror, and say, 'Hey, I'm a white man.'" I paused for a moment, letting the tension in the room build, and then I asked him, "Do you think that is West's point? That *you* don't have to think about race but *he* does?" What followed was the longest silence and then the most lively debate I have ever encountered in an undergraduate classroom, a debate about gender and race that still echoes in my ears.

Listening rhetorically to the textual strategies associated with a h(ear)ing metaphor in this exchange, I hear echoes of multiple voices: I hear the young man's tone of authority and frustration along with an underlying defensiveness (he seemed to think he was expected to keep quiet about such ideas); I hear the cultural voice of a white America that imagines itself racially unmarked; I hear the silence of the classroom, of students not knowing whether and/or how to speak; and I also hear my teacherly tone, questioning yet subsuming the young man's thinking back into West's.

Such listening creates a space in which it becomes possible to question the *logos* as it plays out in myself, in the students, and in our culture. For example, would I have modeled a better listening technique if I had asked the class a less slanted question, such as "What happens when we lay this response alongside West's text?" And, how implicated am I in the fact that students felt they had few tactics for talking about gender and race, particularly whiteness? And, how often do I actually create pedagogical spaces that encourage such discussions? And, how frequently am I just as dismissive of how my own racial markings complicate my behavior, gendered or otherwise? And, why is white America so vested in being racially unmarked? Without this opportunity for listening, the young man and those who agreed with his ideas would never have been challenged nor would have those students who wholeheartedly agreed with West nor would have I.

This young man reminded me of an important lesson: We learn by listening to those who do not agree with us, provided the listening occurs in the context of "genuine conversation" (Copeland), where there is a desire in all parties to move our understanding forward. If the context is not one of genuine conversation, then refusing to listen may be appropriate. The trick is recognizing the differences as well as the possibilities for transforming the latter into the former. As a result of this young man's comments, I now try to see beyond my own reflection by listening to the discourses surrounding me in order to ask myself how my being a white woman affects my being and becoming in the world. In this way, I try to bring bits of my own embodied sexism and racism to consciousness and to deal with them one question at a time.

Though valuable, autoethnography is admittedly limited in its perspective. So to explore intersections of gender and whiteness further, I decided to listen to academic research about whiteness. Instead of reading to master the knowledge or to find a point of agreement and/or attack, I listened to studies of whiteness, laying them alongside my own (lack of) knowledge about intersections of gender and whiteness. I wanted to understand how these intersections function within contemporary U.S. culture and how they are inscribed differently within each person. The following ideas about whiteness are just a few that I uncovered.

As discussed in the introduction, *whiteness* is a trope that functions in the U.S. as a racial category often signifying biological differences among people. The problem with this racial category is that it is a myth, a social construct predicated on bad science. As biologists now tell us (and as cultural critics have been telling us for centuries), race is a false category: Its presumed biological grounds simply do not exist. Thus, the U.S. is left with a racial term such as *whiteness* that is scientifically invalid yet culturally powerful in that it informs everyone's daily life.

Because *whiteness* is a trope, a "conditional" relationship exists between people coded as white and practices coded as white in that not everyone can be classified as a white person but everyone can perform white practices, albeit with varying degrees of success (Keating 907). Although whiteness (like all cultural categories) is historically grounded (changing over time and space) and multiple (including lots of ethnic subcategories), in the U.S., it has consistently signified "privilege"; as such, it has resisted and denied difference (Frankenberg, *White* 236–37). While this privilege of whiteness has been translated into great achievements for some, it has also been translated into domination, even violence, for others, especially non-whites.

Functioning as a cultural norm (Hill 1; Dyer 2; Keating 904), whiteness and its privileges are often invisible to white people yet very visible to non-whites. Although impossible to understand apart from its intersections with gender, class, sexual orientation, age, and so forth.(Thompson 94), whiteness is often a missing ground in cultural conversations even as it appears in census reports and on college application forms. Perhaps AnnLouise Keating says it best: Whiteness "—whatever it is, and I would argue that at this point no one really knows—" is slippery (916).

Listening rhetorically to this research, I hear competing cultural logics: the *status quo* (which ignores whiteness) and the above theorists (who promote whiteness studies). Further, I hear differences among the latter. I hear an adamant tone in Ruth Frankenberg's argument that feminists should legitimize within academic discourses the study of whiteness, especially as it pertains to white women, by articulating this often invisible ground of our cultural discussions.[18] I also hear a more tentative tone in Keating's text, a care taken with words such as "conditional" and "whatever it is" in recognition of both the values and dangers of studying whiteness.

Despite the current prominence of whiteness studies within literary studies, sociology, history, art, film studies, anthropology, etc., critics do exist. Even proponents of antiracist agendas voice concerns. For example, some feminist scholars question the study of whiteness, fearing it may be a politically conservative move that returns discussions once again to white people, especially white men (Hill 4–8). Some ethnicity scholars question such study, fearing as Michael Eric Dyson cautions, that it may be "a sneaky form of narcissism . . . [that shifts] the focus and maybe even the resources back to white people and their perspectives (qtd. in Talbot 118). Still other scholars fear that studying whiteness risks reifying and perpetuating false categories of race (Keating 913).

Listening rhetorically to this research invites me to consider the (im)possibilities of studying intersections of gender and whiteness: Such study will not solve all discord; indeed, it may incite more. Even given these caveats, listening rhetorically to this research invites me to conclude that whiteness studies may actually help conceptualize better ways of articulating the intersecting identifications with gender and race—as well as the ways these identifications are rhetorically constructed and negotiated. At the same time, listening to this research makes me aware of the strategic idealism underlying such a claim.

Listening to the Stories of Others

By listening to autoethnography and academic research, I can test one against the other, but this juxtaposition also has its limits. Although both are useful means for understanding how identifications with gender and whiteness function in U.S. culture, these means should not be used or taught unreflectively, nor should they be the only modes of critical thinking passed on to students. For although autoethnography has become popular, it risks lapsing into a narcissistic confessional solipsism—and a privileged one at that[19]—unless we tie the personal to the cultural in ways that expose how our experiences speak metonymically for larger cultural issues and unless we make such storytelling a viable option for all academicians, not simply a select few. Moreover, for those of us trained in the academy, scholarly research too often resembles Tannen's definition of men's listening, that is, let's duel verbally or in writing so that I can prove how much I know, and, hence, you'll respect me.[20]

Consequently, scholars and teachers need to listen and to offer students opportunities for listening to the stories of others—all others. This idea echoes hooks' realization that telling her stories to others is a politically effective tactic because "people really learn from the sharing of experience" (Childers and hooks 77). Such learning occurs when we listen not only to the claims in other people's stories but also to their cultural logics, or rather to the competing cultural logics that such stories expose.

To understand how intersecting identifications with gender and whiteness are inscribed within white bodies,[21] we need only listen to the stories of others, such as Lillian Smith's reflections on her early-twentieth-century childhood as a white Southern girl in *Killers of the Dream:*

> The mother who taught me what I know of tenderness and love and compassion taught me also the bleak rituals of keeping Negroes in their "place." The father who rebuked me for an air of superiority toward schoolmates from the mill and rounded out his rebuke by gravely reminding me that "all men are brothers," trained me in the steel-rigid decorums I must demand of every colored male. They who so gravely taught me to split my body from my mind and both from my "soul," taught me also to split my conscience from my acts and Christianity from southern tradition. (27)

Listening rhetorically to the textual strategies, I hear contradictory sounds and rhythms in the first sentence: the mellifluous vowels in "tenderness and love and compassion" juxtaposed with the harsh consonants of "bleak rituals of keeping Negroes in their 'place.'" I also discern voices of competing cultural logics: the status quo versus social activism. By teaching Smith to "split" the inscripted identifications with gender, class, sex, religion, race, and regional tradition that are interwoven within her young body, Smith's parents un/consciously perpetuate what Rich calls "white discourse" ("Distance" 182), wherein whiteness is a privileged norm split from other cultural categories in ways that render it invisible, hiding its violence behind parlor manners and polite language. Listening rhetorically to question the *logos*, I have to ask myself if and how this version of white discourse is still being played out in my own life and culture, masked by middle-class, gendered manners.

To understand how intersecting identifications with gender and whiteness are inscribed within non-white bodies but in ways that preclude these bodies from fully participating in the privileges of whiteness, we need to listen to stories like Jeanne Wakatsuki Houston's *Farewell to Manzanar*. In her reflections on her family's life at Manzanar, a World War II, Japanese-American internment camp, she remembers a story about her brother:

> My oldest brother, Bill, led a dance band called The Jive Bombers. . . . He didn't sing *Don't Fence Me In* out of protest, as if trying quietly to mock the authorities. It just happened to be a hit song one year, and they all wanted to be an up-to-date American swing band. (73–74)

Listening rhetorically to the textual strategies, I hear Wakatsuki Houston's disclaiming sisterly tone, denying any political intent on her brother's part; I also hear her more savvy writerly tone, using this "nonpolitical" incident to expose the political intent of white America as well as its taken-for-granted gendered privileges, like roaming. Though Bill desires to be nonpolitical, his body is undeniably politicized, marked simultaneously by his Japanese ancestry and by his desire to be an all-American male.

In the textual moment of Wakatsuki Houston's reflections, I hear competing cultural logics of the Manzanar camp culture and the dominant white culture. From her perspective as a once wrongfully interned American citizen, she hears "Don't Fence Me In" very differently from how most white America heard it at the time of its release or from how most Americans heard it in the late 1990s Embassy Suite commercials. For Wakatsuki Houston, the role of the masculinized roamer rings falsely from the mouth of Bill, a young American imprisoned solely because his ancestry differed from the cultural norm.[22] While his desire to be an all-American male functions as a metonym for the gendered, white discourse of his time, the ancestry classifications within that white discourse preclude his full participation in the privileges of whiteness and, hence, the fulfillment of his desire. Indeed, within 1940s white culture, Bill's ethnicity trumps his gender even as his gender privileges him within the Manzanar camp.

Listening rhetorically to question the *logos*, I not only question the fairness and legality of Jeanne's and Bill's situations, but I also have to ask myself, once again, if and how I ever participate in white discourses in ways that might unknowingly erase the desires and material existence of others?

As a result of this project, listening to autoethnography, academic research, and stories of others now informs my life, my research, and my teaching.

Listening to a Student's Listening

I am not the only player in my thinking about rhetorical listening. In addition to listening to my own life, to academic research, and to the stories of others, I have developed my ideas about rhetorical listening by listening to students. For example, consider an experience I had with a student named Rachel in an undergraduate, women's literature course. While Rachel was writing her second paper for our course, she put rhetorical listening into action as a trope for interpretive invention and as a code of cross-cultural conduct. By listening to her untheorized and unconscious praxis of rhetorical listening, I was able to conceptualize and articulate the concept of rhetorical listening; as a result, both my teaching and my scholarly research have benefited. To this day, I am grateful to Rachel for helping me theorize rhetorical listening.

During one class session, we read aloud from Toni Morrison's *Beloved*, specifically the shed scene where the escaped slave Sethe attempts to kill her children and herself before her former owner Schoolteacher can recapture them all. The first telling of this scene, which is narrated from four white men's points of view, perfectly captures the logic of white slaveholders. This slavery logic dehumanizes slaves by likening them to animals; it justifies slavery on the grounds of slaves' "animalistic" essence; and it evaluates treatments of slaves (e.g., beatings) on the grounds of productivity, not humaneness. After our class discussion, Rachel e-mailed me about a possible paper topic, one that would relate our class discussion to a guest lecture in her political-science class, which she had attended earlier in the day.

> Hi! Something "strange" just occurred, and I was wondering if I could bounce it off you because the oddity of the situation just intrigues me, and I can't quite see how to put it into perspective, so I'm hoping you can help. (Quite a sentence!) First off, we just finished with class, and for you to understand the story, you have to know that I have Dr. [X's] Corrections class right before yours. (I'm a Poli Sci and Crim major.)
>
> Okay, well today in that class, we had a guest speaker. . . . Now the man was entertaining and informative, and I enjoyed the class and his lecture immensely (one of those people who appear so energized

you can't help but wonder how much coffee they drink in a single day—but still, they are fun to listen to as energy is infectious). Now to the point . . . He started his lecture by asking how many people believed in parole and whether it was a good thing or not. The class was overwhelmingly against it (typical), and the overall opinion was that it was kind of a necessary evil (due to overcrowding, etc.). Well, to give us an example of one main reason parole and institutions like it were a necessity, he told a metaphor. The metaphor was one about a mean dog in the neighborhood who gets into trouble. If you chain the dog up and keep it on a short leash and punish it for it's [*sic*] wrongs, you are only causing the dog to become more angry. He compared this to prisoners who are kept in high security/maximum prisons. He then went on further to say that chaining someone/thing up for a long time and punishing it is only going to allow its hate and anger to grow, and that once the "dog" is let off the leash, it would be a mess to see what the reaction to society and the community would be. Therefore, parole and institutions like it are necessary to reward those who attempt change and reformation, because if you just resort to a strict punishment approach, the "dogs" that are returned to the community will be beyond human reason and will only seek vengeance.

Now if you haven't figured it out already, the reason I'm bringing this up is because it shares a striking similarity with the words that the schoolteacher says to his nephew about breaking Sethe, as well as having a connection to the idea of people as animals. I'm sure this man that was speaking is a very nice guy, and maybe I'm just jumping onto this because the two classes were juxtaposed right next to each other, allowing for the realization of the similar aspects to occur, but this just seems amazing to me. I was planning to write my paper #2 on something entirely different, but now this just seems to be completely interesting. I suppose it would work into how slaves were treated as prisoners and how prisoners are in turn treated like animals (as slaves were also), but I just find this similarity too shocking to let it go. I'm wondering if you think there is a connection I could make and I guess how you think I could go about this. (The quote was on page 149 in *Beloved* is what I'm referring to.) If there is a weak connection in his metaphor, please just say so. I just am wondering if there is rather a distinctly definite one which ties into the fact that [the guest speaker] is white and that this chapter [in *Beloved*] was the only one written in the white perspective. I see why he used his metaphor, yet at the same time, I find it striking that he compared criminals to dogs and that schoolteacher compares slaves to animals and both are referencing to treatment. Hmmmmmm. . . . Well, I just really felt the need to get another person's perspective on this, and you definitely are the person with the most knowledge into what Beloved is "saying."

So if you could help, I'd appreciate it. Sorry that this explanation was so long—I didn't intend it to be! (I hope it all is clear too!) Anyways, thank you for thinking it over. (Personal correspondence)

Rachel sent this e-mail, she later told me, because she had shared her idea with a good friend, and he thought she was crazy, reading more into the situation than was really there. Was she? she wanted to know. Her friend thought she was accusing the speaker of being a hypocrite. She was not, she assured me. She simply wanted to understand the discourses surrounding her, especially those relating to the prison system she hopes to work within after graduation. That way, she could become more responsible for the discourses she internalizes as her own.

Coincidentally, Rachel e-mailed me a few days before I spoke about rhetorical listening at the University of Wisconsin–Milwaukee. By listening to her listening, I not only heard but began to see the moves of, and the possibilities for, rhetorical listening. For Rachel, by laying the criminology and literature class sessions in front of her and letting them lie there, was attempting to invent topics and arguments for her second essay; hence, she was employing rhetorical listening as a *trope for interpretive invention*. Rachel was proceeding with her project for a number of reasons. First, she wanted to *understand* the discourses surrounding her so that she could act ethically as an employee within the criminal justice system. Second, she wanted to embrace an *accountability logic* and avoid a guilt/blame logic. Her intent was not to nail the guest lecturer for hypocrisy; she went to great lengths in paragraph two to describe the guest speaker positively, calling him a "nice guy" in paragraph three. Her intent was to work within an accountability logic wherein she could question his discourse and, albeit limitedly, participate in her own socialization. Third, she was intrigued by the *commonalities and differences* in the two discourses in that they both likened people to animals and justified behaviors on the basis of productivity even though Schoolteacher perpetuates a belief that some people are animals while the guest lecturer resists this notion. Fourth, Rachel heard commonalities and differences not just in *claims* of the two texts but also in their *cultural logics*. Both texts' claims and cultural logics seem haunted by privileges of gender and whiteness even as Schoolteacher reinscribes a cultural logic of an inhumane slave economy and the guest lecturer inscribes a cultural logic of reform for the prison economy in Wisconsin.

Was Rachel's listening process as neat and orderly as the previous paragraph makes it appear? Of course not. You can tell that from listening to her e-mail. She notes that something "'strange'" is haunting her, which she cannot pinpoint for herself. She is hesitant about her ideas so she waits until paragraph two to announce "Now to the point" although she follows that assertion with an ellipsis, which signifies a gap, an absence (of clarity? connection? confidence?). And although Rachel is quite articulate, summarizing the guest lecture and noting its possible connections to *Beloved,* she feels the need for someone else to put it into perspective; she has heard the commonalities and differences, but she cannot see the connections clearly. The two discourses are lying before her, but she cannot connect them for herself in ways that make sense within her concept of *logos*. Because part of my job as a teacher is to help students conceptualize their thinking processes, I analyzed her e-mail for method and experienced the serendipitous pleasure of having my thinking about rhetorical listening clarified, which, in turn, enabled me to offer her a perspective on her topic.

So what perspective did I offer Rachel? Did I think she was crazy? Obviously not. I think she has a definite talent, not for "reading more into the situation" as her friend had suggested but for listening to the exiled excess in our daily dialectical dialogues. And I think this talent was spurred, in part, by Rachel's literally hearing the two discourses side by side and then listening to them as they echoed in her ears. I encouraged her to write the paper.

Was Rachel's second essay a success? That depends on how one reads/listens to it. Briefly, here is an outline of her paper. To establish the issues and to signal the importance of context, she begins by juxtaposing narratives of the two class sessions in an opening section, which is separated from the rest of the essay not only by a white space but also by being set in italics. Then she asserts her main claim: The dehumanization that occurred in the slavery logic is occurring today in the criminal-justice–reform logic because (she cites an authority here to drive home her point) "'a practice often lasts for a long time after the theory which inspired it has lost its hold on the belief of mankind'" (2). To illustrate this claim, she makes three moves: (1) She turns to her guest lecturer, arguing that his dog metaphor continues a practice of dehumanization even though he does not believe in dehumanization; (2) She turns to slavery, arguing that the practice of owning other people directly contradicted the principles and ideals upon which our nation was founded; and (3) She turns to the residuals of slavery that still exist in our culture, exploring how one white woman's discourse about whiteness in Frankenberg's study exactly parallels Stamp Paid's analysis of whiteness in *Beloved,* thus implying but never quite circling back and connecting how gender and whiteness informed the guest lecturer's talk. She concludes by asserting, "The dehumanization of any person . . . and . . . large groups of people over long periods of time is wrong."

But for me, her most interesting writing occurs in her final paragraph:

> It seems that white "rule-abiding" society could be suffering from fear. They could be worried that both criminals and blacks are inherently no different than themselves, and with that as fact, how do they make themselves feel superior? If everyone is equal, they are the same, and if whites are the same as blacks and "rule-abiding" citizens are the same as criminals, how can we compare ourselves to an Other? How can we bolster the feeling of superiority over the inferior groups of people who are just a bit behind us evolutionarily, if they are really not inferior or evolutionarily behind? The question is: why do we need to feel superior? What does this say about us? What have we become?

Rachel's conclusion intrigues me on many levels. One is its pronoun usage. In thinking through this cultural concern, she has trouble with pronoun shifts, not in terms of grammatical agreement but in terms of who-is-what. Her category of "white rule-abiding society" is a *they* to her; yet because she is a white rule-abiding citizen herself, the category is also a *we*. But that implication is not yet articulated in her writing, perhaps because she does not see herself as being someone who needs to make others feel inferior. While she can listen to her guest lecturer and Toni Morrison, she seems not yet able to listen to herself, at least not here, hence the importance of teaching rhetorical listening as a trope for interpretive invention that applies not just to the discourses of others but also to the discourses of one's self. A second level that intrigues me is her use of questions. She concludes with questions that teachers might traditionally suggest should occur in her introduction as a frame for her paper, around which her paper would be developed. Although Rachel had initially desired to answer these questions in her paper, she could not, she told me when she handed in the paper, because the questions—especially as they related to whiteness—were too new to her world view, hence the importance of teaching rhetorical listening as a code for cross-cultural conduct.

Should I, as a teacher, read Rachel's paper as weak or reward her for helping me think through a critical question? I certainly have a responsibility to read her paper for structural weaknesses and suggest different strategies for remedying them, but I also have a responsibility to listen rhetorically with an intent to understand what she is doing in her paper. And I have a responsibility to listen rhetorically in order to question my concept of the *logos*. Sometimes, I am richly rewarded, as when Rachel helped me to define rhetorical listening. And sometimes, I am challenged to be a better pedagogue.

So Where Does That Leave Us?

Defining rhetorical listening as a trope of interpretive invention not only emphasizes the discursive nature of rhetorical listening but also plays with the etymology of the term *trope* as "a turning." For rhetorical listening turns hearing (a reception process) into invention (a production process), thus complicating the reception/production opposition and inviting rhetorical listening into the time-honored tradition of rhetorical invention.[23] Second, rhetorical listening turns the realm of hearing into a larger space, one encompassing all discursive forms, not just oral ones. Third, rhetorical listening turns *intent* back on the listener, focusing on listening *with intent* to hear troubled identifications, instead of listening *for intent* of an author. Fourth, rhetorical listening turns the meaning of the text into something larger than itself, certainly larger than the intent of the speaker/writer, in that rhetorical listening locates a text as part of larger cultural logics. And fifth, rhetorical listening turns rhetoric's traditional focus on the desires of the speaker/writer into a harmonics and/or dissonance of the desires of both the speaker/writer and the listener.

In sum, rhetorical listening maps new possibilities for interpretive invention. When specifically employed as a "code of cross-cultural conduct," rhetorical listening has the potential to identify troubled identifications and to negotiate them, with the goal being to generate more productive discourses, whether these discourses be narratives or arguments, whether they be in academic journals or over the dinner table. As such, rhetorical listening responds to the need exemplified by Annie and Lora and promotes the possibility exemplified by Ruth and Naomi.

2

Identifying Places of Rhetorical Listening: Identification, Disidentification, and Non-Identification

> Identification is . . . an assumption of place.
> —Judith Butler, *Bodies That Matter*

> But put identification and division ambiguously together, so that you cannot know for certain just where one ends and the other begins, and you have the characteristic invitation to rhetoric.
> —Kenneth Burke, *A Rhetoric of Motives*

> Identification names the entry of history and culture into the subject, a subject that must bear the traces of each and every encounter with the external world. Identification is, from the beginning, a question of *relation,* of self to other, subject to object, inside to outside.
> —Diana Fuss, *Identification Papers*

> "Identification with" is . . . a political choice.
> —Barbara Harlow, "Sites of Struggle"

If rhetorical listening is to facilitate cross-cultural communication, then rhetoric and composition studies needs to extend its discussions of identification to include troubled identifications, that is, those identifications troubled by history, uneven power dynamics, and ignorance. When rhetoric and composition scholarship invokes identification, it most commonly cites Kenneth Burke's modern theory of consubstantial common ground. As a place for rhetorical listening, however, Burke's concept of identification is limited. It does not adequately address the coercive force of common ground that often haunts cross-cultural communication, nor does it adequately address how to identify and negotiate troubled identifications; moreover, it does not address how to identify and negotiate *conscious* identifications functioning as ethical and political choices.

To counter this scholarly gap, this chapter critiques the limitations and possibilities of Burke's modern theory of identification for the project of rhetorical listening. In addition, this chapter complicates Burke's theory by engaging and critiquing Diana Fuss's postmodern theory of identification as well as T. Minh-ha Trinh's postcolonial one. By juxtaposing the aforementioned theories of identification, this chapter identifies a modern/postmodern divide:[1] Modern theories of identification often foreground personal agency and commonalities while backgrounding differences; postmodern theories of identification and disidentification[2] often foreground differences while backgrounding personal agency and/or commonalities.

Given this modern/postmodern divide, this chapter asks: How may scholar/teachers in rhetoric and composition studies navigate this divide so as to theorize identification as a place for rhetorical listening? As one response to this question, this chapter argues that just as identification necessarily precedes persuasion (Burke, *Rhetoric* 55), rhetorical listening may precede our *conscious* identifications (and, yes, I do acknowledge the plethora of unconscious identifications over which we have little, if any, control). To demonstrate my argument, this chapter (1) examines competing definitions and functions of identification; (2) analyzes the (im)possibilities of Burke's modern concept of identification as a place for rhetorical listening; (3) analyzes the (im)possibilities of Fuss's postmodern concepts of identification and disidentification as places for rhetorical listening; and (4) puts Burke's and Fuss's theories into play with Trinh's in order to offer a concept of non-identification to supplement identification and disidentification as places for rhetorical listening.

Identification: Competing Definitions and Functions

When employed as a code of cross-cultural conduct, rhetorical listening assumes the possibility of conscious identifications. But to construct conscious identifications, rhetorical listeners need to understand definitions and functions of identification. To that end, this section traces multiple definitions of identification, explores connections between identification and identity, explains the modern/postmodern divide in theories of identification, and argues for a reformist concept of identification that enables it to serve a place of rhetorical listening.

Thanks to Sigmund Freud,[3] *identification* is inescapably associated with the tradition of psychoanalytic theory.[4] Within this tradition, identification emerges as doubled and interrelated sites: (1) the place of ego/id interactions and (2) the place of self/other interactions. The ego/id site of identification directs attention to *inner* forces that inform subjectivity, specifically the relations between a person's conscious and unconscious processes. Within this site, according to Fuss, *identification* signifies "change [that] happens whenever the ego, under pressure from an instinctual [id's] demand for an unattainable object, transforms itself into the object 'for the sake of the id'" (*Identification* 48). The self/other site of identification directs attention to *outer* forces that inform a person's subjectivity. Within this site, according to Fuss, *identification* signifies "psychical change [that] occurs whenever we are confronted with a new object in the external world" (48).

These doubled sites of identification—that is, ego/id and self/other—blur commonsense distinctions between inside and outside, demonstrating a mobius-strip relationship between the two. As such, these doubled sites of identification hold particular importance for the project of rhetorical listening. The ego/id site conceptualizes identification as a psychical place that affects one's agency, specifically one's capacity and one's willingness to listen rhetorically. The self/other site conceptualizes identification as a historical/cultural place that affects one's interactions with other people and cultures.

Though grounded in psychoanalytic studies, the concept of identification is not limited solely to that tradition. For example, in rhetorical theory, Burke assumes identification to be a place where conscious and unconscious rhetorical exchanges transpire (*Rhetoric* 25). In feminist theory, Fuss assumes identification to be a place where the boundaries between the personal and the political become inextricably and inexplicably intertwined (10), where the "detour through the other that defines a self" occurs (*Identification* 2). Whatever their academic discipline, theorists of identification tend to agree with Judith Butler that identification always invokes "an assumption of place" (99), with *place* signifying both bodily and historical/cultural locations. In sum, theorists agree that because people are always historically and culturally situated, so, too, are their embodied identifications—hence the linkage of identification with *place*.

But despite this agreement, theorists offer radically different interpretations of the functions of identification:

> Are identifications conscious or unconscious? active or passive? immediate or belated? creative or lethal? Some theorists view every identifi-

cation as a cross-identification, while others read cross-identification as less a psychological given than a social mandate; some see identification as already in play and therefore relatively effortless, while other see identification as dangerous and difficult; some understand identification as a form of regressive nostalgia, while others view identification as a means of achieving real psychological change; and some highlight identification's tendency to align and to shore up identity, while still others emphasize identification's capability for dislocation and destabilization. (Fuss, *Identification* 10)

So although the project of rhetorical listening focuses on conscious identifications, it recognizes that other types of identification exist and that identification is an inescapable element of academic theories and daily life.

Identification directly informs or indirectly haunts academic theories in many different fields, such as, psychoanalysis, philosophy, communications, drama and performance studies, queer studies, feminist studies, and, of course, rhetoric and composition studies. How? Every theory from rhetoric to philosophy to astronomy assumes a concept of human identity and, hence, identification. For example, Aristotelian philosophy posits people as ineluctable essences, either superior masculine or inferior feminine ones (*Politics* 35–36); poststructuralist theory posits people as lexical constructs (Barthes, "Death" 54); and extragalactic astrophysics posits people as carbon-based proteins existing for only a few seconds of galactic time (Preston). Because every theory assumes a concept of human identity, it also assumes a means for human subjects to interact with themselves and the world in ways that inform their identities; such interactions presume the inescapable presence of identification. For example, neo-Aristotelians, such as Burke, imagine consubstantial identifications; poststructuralists imagine discursive (dis)identifications; and astrophysicists imagine chemical ones.

Identification also directly informs or indirectly haunts everyone's life . . . from reading newspapers in the morning to putting children to bed in the evening, from ordering cheese at the deli to negotiating trade with China, from analyzing presidential debates to teaching first-year composition. For example, throughout her lifetime, a U.S. woman experiences innumerable identifications with gender. As a preteen, she may view a clothing commercial on TV and be encouraged to dress older than her years; as a forty-year-old, she may read a magazine article and be encouraged to look younger than her years. Moreover, this woman also experiences innumerable identifications with other cultural categories that intersect with gender: race, class, nationality, family role, etc. So just as a person's identity encompasses more than a single identification (e.g., watching one commercial or reading one ad), her or his identity also encompasses more than identification with a single cultural category (e.g., gender). For a person is always more than just his gender or just her race or just his class.

As these academic-theory and daily-life examples demonstrate, identification is inextricably linked with identity but does not directly correspond to it. In other words, although an identification may inform a person's identity, a person's identity cannot be reduced to a single identification. No single identification solely defines a person's identity; he or she is a compilation of many identifications.

This distinction between identification and identity is incredibly important. It demonstrates how people are influenced by their identifications with cultural categories but also how people are not rendered identical by these identifications. When people's identities are interpreted as identical in terms of a single identification (e.g., defined in terms of one TV ad) or in terms of a single cultural category (e.g., defined in terms of gender), then opportunities for stereotyping abound.

This linkage of identification with identity has implications for academic researchers and for our objects of study. According to Vincent Leitch, researchers' assumptions about identification inform researchers' assumptions about their own identities:

> How a critical theory construes the issue of identification is . . . significant because it ultimately involves how the [researcher's] own author-function is situated in relation to regimes of reason. The regimes may be forgotten, repressed, "purged," celebrated, analyzed, or criticized—all such operations go into constituting the subject-position of the [researchers]. (37)

Likewise, assumptions about identification also inform researchers' assumptions about the identities of people, histories, cultures, or artifacts being studied. Indeed, our (un)conscious assumptions about identification inform not just who we are but what we expect from ourselves, from others, and from language. And all of these assumptions affect the data and conclusions of a scholarly study, whether it be in sociology, nursing, or rhetoric and composition studies.

How is rhetoric and composition studies informed and/or haunted by theories of identification? As stated earlier, modern and postmodern theories of rhetoric construct a theoretical divide about identification. On one side, modern rhetorical theories recover language from its "effacement" in the Enlightenment (Berlin, *Rhetorics* xvii) and champion the idea of a human agent trying to control language for his own ends, for example, the theories of I. A. Richards, Stephen Toulmin, James Kinneavy, and Burke. Such theories imagine identification as a metaphoric space wherein the substance of one person is synthesized with substances of other people in order to bridge differences and create common ground for persuasion and political action (Burke, *Rhetoric* 55). Visually, this process is often represented as interlocking circles with a shared middle space of common ground signifying a place of identification.

On the other side of the divide, postmodern rhetorical theories may acknowledge some space for personal agency; however, they foreground the agencies of discourse and cultural structures in the construction of subjects and their identities, for example, the theories of Michel Foucault, Jacques Derrida, Jean-François Lyotard, and Butler. Though distinct in their differences, these theories question the possibility of substance as well as the possibility of shared substance or common ground. Instead, they posit identification as a discursive process (both psychical and historical/cultural) whereby subjects, because they have lost the object of their desire, metaphorically construct mental images of those objects and then act upon those images. This metaphoric replacement of object with image occurs via internal interactions of conscious and unconscious processes; it also occurs via confrontations with external sources (e.g., people, history, culture, artifacts). Hence, for postmodernists, the figurative function of discourse, not substance, figures prominently in identification. For figuration is what enables the construction of mental images and also conceptualization of the cultural structures into which we are born and socialized at particular historical moments.

In an attempt to interrupt this modern/postmodern divide,[5] rhetoric and composition scholars informed by feminist studies, ethnic studies, cultural studies, and postcolonial studies (or some combination thereof) have mapped spaces for a rhetorical agent who possesses personal agency (albeit limited) even as that agent is socialized by enveloping cultural discourses (Royster, "When the First Voice" 36–38; Gilyard, "African American" 642; Berlin, *Rhetorics* 68–76; Lu 349–54). As cultural discourses become embodied in people (differently, of course, depending upon each person's particular experiences and identifications), the gaps and/or conflicts between the embodied discourses construct spaces from which a person's agency may emerge. Moreover, as cultural discourses become embodied, boundaries between inside and outside blur and beg discussions of one's accountability to self and other. These blurring boundaries, in turn, beg questions of identification. Yet just as feminist studies has mostly ignored the "reformist potential" of identification, talking around it while celebrating the reformist potential of everything else (Fuss, *Identification* 6), so, too, has rhetoric and composition studies.[6]

To interrupt this trend, this chapter explores how a reformist potential of identification may be theorized and practiced via rhetorical listening. To that end, this chapter revisits and challenges the modern/postmodern divide in rhetoric and composition studies. This chapter revisits the modern/postmodern divide by establishing how it is often interpreted as a binary opposition; this chapter challenges this divide by exposing it as a *false* binary opposition. To focus this challenge, this chapter returns to the question posed in its introduction or, rather, to a slightly revised version of that question: How may scholar/teachers in rhetoric and composition studies navigate the modern/postmodern divide so as to theorize reformist concepts of identification, disidentification, and non-identification as places for rhetorical listening?

To begin identifying and defining these psychical and historical/cultural places for rhetorical listening, let us turn now to Burke's modern concept of identification.

Modern (Im)Possibilities: Kenneth Burke

As the most widely circulated modern concept of identification in rhetoric and composition studies, Burke's identification deserves consideration as a place for rhetorical listening. Although I greatly admire his theory, his concept of identification provides a limited site for rhetorical listening. Granted, Burke's identification does provide a place of personal agency and a place of commonality, yet it often does so at the expense of differences. As a place of common ground, Burke's identification demands that differences be bridged. The danger of such a move is that differences and their possibilities, when bridged, may be displaced and mystified. In this section, I demonstrate this claim first by explaining how Burke defines and interconnects the terms *identification, consubstantiality, substance,* and *identity* and then by exploring how these interconnections inform questions of (1) personal agency and (2) coexisting commonalities and difference in ways that promote and limit rhetorical listening.

Burke's definitions of *identification* are scattered throughout his texts, which is a common pattern in Burke's writings. In *The Philosophy of Literary Form*, Burke offers this extended discussion:

> By "identification" I have in mind this sort of thing: one's material and mental ways of placing oneself as a person in the groups and movements; one's way of sharing vicariously in the role of leader or spokesman; formation and change of allegiance; the rituals of suicide, parricide, and prolicide, the vesting and divesting of insignia, the modes of initiation and purification, that are involved in the response to allegiance and change of allegiance; the part necessarily played by groups in the expectancies of the individual . . . ; clothes, uniforms, and their psychological equivalents; one's ways of seeing one's reflection in the social mirror. (227)

Although many modern theories interpret identification within a psychoanalytical tradition, Burke's definition, though grateful to Freudian psychoanalysis, also foregrounds cultural aspects of identification. By foregrounding how Freud's "intrapsychic" process of identification functions in a social realm, Burke explains the implications of identification for communication, community, and, hence, rhetoric (Wright 308).[7] As such, Burke's identification contains a personal, a cultural, and a discursive dimension. Christine Oravec explains it this way: Burke's identification "never strays very far from earlier versions of the three ruling analytically schema of the twentieth century: Freudianism, Marxism, and structural linguistics"; as such, it "tracks the interpenetration of subject, environment, and discourse" (175).[8]

To identify connections between rhetoric and identification, Burke links identification with the persuasive and socializing functions of discourse in *Language as Symbolic Action*. Initially, he posits a speaker's persuasive use of discourse as both conscious and unconscious: "Aristotle's Rhetoric centers in the speaker's explicit designs with regard to the confronting of an audience. But there are also ways in which we *spontaneously, intuitively,* even *unconsciously* persuade ourselves" (301). Interestingly, this unconscious persuasive function of discourse invites a consideration of socialization into the realm of rhetoric, for people may be unconsciously persuaded, or socialized, into performing certain attitudes or acts via the discourses of other people, texts, and cultures. But whether identification is conscious or unconscious, Burke argues in *A Rhetoric of Motives* that identification is inextricably connected to rhetoric because identification necessarily precedes persuasion: "You persuade a man only insofar as you can talk his language by speech, gesture, tonality, order, image, attitude, idea, *identifying* your ways with his" (55). As such, Burke's identification extends the realm of rhetoric to all human interaction and becomes "the key rhetorical process through which poets and ordinary people attempt to persuade others" (Gusfield 39).

In Burke's rhetorical theory, identification functions via consubstantiality (*Rhetoric* 62), with consubstantiality functioning via the merging of substances (21). *Consubstantiality* signifies a place of bridged differences and common ground, a place from which to act for common cause. As noted earlier, such consubstantiality may be visualized as the shared space of two distinct but interlocking circles. For Burke, consubstantiality is not simply a matter of choice but an inescapable part of living a life: "A doctrine of *consubstantiality*, either explicit or implicit, may be necessary to any way of life. For substance, in the old philosophies, was an *act*; and a way of life is an *acting-together*; and in acting together, men have common sensations, concepts, images, ideas, attitudes that make them *consubstantial*" (21).[9] This consubstantial "*acting-together*" assumes a place where a person "is both joined and separate, at once a distinct substance and consubstantial with another" (21).

What exactly is Burke's substance that can be both consubstantial and distinct in itself? In his *Grammar of Motives,* Burke offers an extended discussion of *substance* in which he makes three moves: (1) he historicizes the term, (2) he offers it as a paradox, and (3) he claims it to be indefinably ambiguous (21–58). To define *substance,* Burke culls both a common usage and an etymology: "The word is often used to designate what some thing or agent intrinsically *is* [i.e., its essence]. . . . Yet etymologically 'substance' . . . would be something that stands beneath or supports the person or thing (21–22).[10] Thus, we arrive at what Burke calls "the paradox of substance" because "though used to designate something *within* the thing, *intrinsic* to it, the word etymologically refers to something *outside* the thing, *extrinsic* to it" (23); the implication is that "the given subject both is and is not the same as the character with which and by which it is identified" (32). According to Burke, this indefinable ambiguity of the paradox of substance serves the rhetorician well: "What handier resource could a rhetorician want than an ambiguity whereby he can say 'The state of affairs is substantially such-and-such,' instead of having to say 'The state of affairs *is* and/or *is not* such and such'?" (52).

Yet, within our contemporary theoretical milieu, the mere mention of the term *substance* immediately raises specters of the term *essence* (dreaded for its potential slippery slide into a naïve biological essentialism).[11] In 1957, Roland Barthes charged that the "disease of thinking in essences is at the bottom of every bourgeois mythology of man" (*Mythologies* 75). Burke readily concedes this point, noting that the terms *essence* and *substance* have been in disrepute since, at least, the writings of John Locke. But Burke argues for a reconsideration of *substance* because "in banishing the *term*, far from banishing its *functions* one merely conceals them" (*Grammar* 21):

> At the very best, we admit, each time you scrutinize a concept of substance, it dissolves into thin air. But conversely, the moment you relax your gaze a bit, it re-forms again. For things *do* have intrinsic natures, whatever may be the quandaries that crowd upon us as soon as we attempt to decide definitively what these intrinsic natures are. And only by systematically dwelling upon the paradoxes of substance could we possibly equip ourselves to guard against the concealment of "substantialist" thought in schemes overtly designed to avoid it. Yet these schemes are usually constructed by men who contemn dialectical operations so thoroughly that, in their aversion, they cannot adequately observe them, and are accordingly prompt to persuade themselves that *their* terminology is not dialectical, whereas every terminology is dialectical by sheer reason of the fact that it is terminology. If you will, call the category of substance sheer error. Yet it is so fertile a source of error, that only by learning to recognize its nature *from within* could we hope to detect its many disguises from without. (56–57)

Thus, for Burke, the play of "substance" is inescapable. What is negotiable is its definition.

Consequently, substance emerges as central to Burke's theory of rhetoric. *Substance* signifies a site where material reality and rhetoric merge but do not directly correspond:

> [M]en are not only *in nature*. The cultural accretions made possible by the language motive become a "second nature" with them. Here again we confront the ambiguities of substance, since symbolic com-

munication is not a merely external instrument but also intrinsic to men as agents. (*Grammar* 33)

For Burke, first-nature substance (the material body and its natural environment in which we live) is inextricably intertwined with second-nature substance (rhetorically constructed discursive and cultural categories, both extrinsic and embodied, within which we think and feel). For example, a woman in U.S. culture has a material body (i.e., first-nature substance), yet she has difficulty thinking of her material body without the terms *woman's body;* and given the value terms that our dominant culture associates with *woman's body* (e.g., *young, thin, beautiful, sexy,* often *white*), a woman may have difficulty feeling good about her body (or coming to terms with it) when it does not conform to the norms established by these cultural terms (i.e, second-nature substance).

Burke's interrelated first-nature and second-nature substances construct identity (*Language* 41–42) in that it enables a person to declare "me" and/or "not me." Yet this declaration of identity is never quite complete, just as identifications are never quite complete, for names (such as "me" or "not me" or "Kris" or "Mama") are always synecdoches of identity (Burke, *Philosophy* 27). Moreover, for Burke, identity is never merely individual: "The individual's identity is formed by reference to his membership in a group" (306); indeed, "*one is never a member of merely* one '*corporation*'"(307). Because a person's substance is constantly encountering other substances via the consubstantiality of identification, a person's identity is not fixed in time, in place, or in a particular group. Instead, identity is malleable. But for myriad reasons, this malleability fosters fear and resistance of itself. The irony, then, is that, despite the malleability of identity, the fear and resistance of this malleability render identity not easily changed: For as Burke says somewhat ironically, "a change of identity . . . would require a change of substance" (41).

In sum, Burke defines *identification* as a consubstantial merging of substances that helps constitute a person's identity. In a place of identification, a person is consubstantially this *and* that, simultaneously "me" and "not me." Each identification offers new opportunities for consubstantiality, which, in turn, influences a person's substance and, hence, a person's identity; thus, identity is continually informed by, but not totally determined by, each new identification.

Given this definition, I find myself asking: Does Burke's identification work for rhetorical listening? And my answer is a conflicted "yes" . . . and "no." For as I will demonstrate in the following discussion, Burke's identification makes space for personal agency and commonalities but not for differences.

On the question of personal agency, Burke's identification provides a space for rhetorical listening in that it theorizes a personal agency coexisting within first-nature substances (material bodies and environments) and second-nature substances (cultural and discursive constructs). Thus, Burke's first- and second-nature substances construct a concept of identity that neither reverts to an Aristotelian essentialism nor anticipates a Barthesian lexical subject but instead provides a third option. Frank Lentricchia explains:

> Burkean rhetoric would occupy the space between the old rhetoric of pure will and the . . . postmodernist aesthetic of antiwill: between a subject apparently in full possession of itself, and in full intentional control of its expression, and a subject whose relation to "its" expression is very problematic. . . . Burke is giving rhetoric an unconscious, something unheard of in the ancient traditions, but in the process of doing so he is not going to lose sight of the conscious and the willful. (159–60)

Burke's third option has implications for personal agency. According to Lentricchia, "the rhetorician is the not-always-knowing carrier of historical and ideological forces, while at the same time he acts within and upon the present and thereby becomes an agent of change" (160). This agent of change both shapes and is shaped by identification, which is a site where the agent of change may transform him- or herself and/or others and/or cultural practices even as he or she is transformed by them. Such a concept of personal agency provides a place conducive to rhetorical listening.

On the question of coexisting commonalities and differences, however, Burke's identification does not so easily make a place for rhetorical listening. That is, Burke's identification (in its search for common ground) does not easily escape charges that it mystifies unfair ideological power plays (in its erasure of differences). Because Burke's place of identification posits conjoined substance (i.e., the metaphoric place of common ground), it demands commonalities. Yet problems haunt such metaphoric places of common ground.

One problem is the coercive function of common ground. As Cornel West claims, common ground often assumes "an unmediated identification and resemblance (between subject and object, ideas and world) in which correspondence is attained and unity achieved" (10). In other words, Burke's identification-as-common-ground may occur at the expense of differences. Or in Burke's own words, identification should "confine differences solely to those areas where differences are necessary" (*Philosophy* 313). Granted, Burke's discussion of rhetoric posits identification and division equally: "put identification and division ambiguously together, so that you cannot know for certain just where one ends and the other begins, and you have the characteristic invitation to rhetoric" (*Rhetoric* 25). Although I greatly admire Burke's thinking about rhetoric, the equality he posits between identification and division is short lived. Because "divisions" are posited as differences that must be bridged in order to construct a place of identification, Burke's place of identification emerges as a site of commonalities, ranging from consubstantial beliefs to necessarily bridged differences.

A question that Burke's concept of identification begs is: What happens to the *unnecessary* differences? A corollary question is: Who defines and who decides what is *necessary* and *unnecessary*—or in other words, who defines the terms of commonality, and who decides which differences must be bridged and which differences must be deemed excess and relegated outside the consubstantial place of identification? In most cases, the answer is: the "I" with the power. For the "I" without power, Burke's metaphoric common ground of identification may feel more like "not me" than "me." Or worse, as Frantz Fanon points out, it may feel (as it does for the colonized) neither like the subject "me" or the subject "not me" but rather "like an object in the midst of other objects" (109; qtd. in Fuss, *Identification* 143). Given these considerations, the politics of identification emerge as incredibly complex.

What further complicates the politics of identification is that each party involved may experience an identification differently, depending upon one's subject position, which depends (in part) on how one is positioned culturally. Moreover, these different identifications offer different risks. For the "not me" and the "object among objects," the risk of identification in "me" terms is violence—psychical, cultural, and physical. In such cases, "the 'risk of identification' may not always be worth the taking; in fact, identification, and the symbolic violence it can wield, poses the very trap to be avoided in the already perilous process of forging political alliances across identities" (Fuss, *Identification* 9). Conversely, for the "me," identification in one's own terms risks a blindness to ways of life other than one's own, a blindness to naturalized cultural violence against others (and inevitably against oneself), indeed a blindness to one's own blindness. For all of the above parties, identification risks a personal and cultural displacement that is too often imagined only as loss, not as gain. The resulting blindness and aversion to risk do not offer opportunities for identifying and negotiating troubled identifications, especially those that haunt cross-cultural communications.

So how may rhetoric and composition studies interrupt this trend? Given the aforementioned blindness and risks, our field would do well to remember that "identification is not only how we accede to power, it also how we learn submission" (Fuss, *Identification* 14). To help us enact such remembering via rhetorical listening, Burke's identification does provide a personal agency that escapes the trap of essentialism. In valorizing commonalities, though, it does not provide a sufficient recognition of differences as a place for rhetorical exchanges and subsequent actions. In Burke's theory, differences do not "accede to power," they learn to submit. Consequently, Burke's identification constructs a limited space for rhetorical listening. As such, it exposes a need for postmodern concepts of identification and disidentification that engage differences.

Postmodern (Im)Possibilities: Diana Fuss

Because rhetorical listening insists that identification function as a place not just of personal agency but also of coexisting commonalities and differences and because a modern Burkean concept of identification only partially fulfills this need, I turn to Fuss's postmodern concept of identification as outlined in her 1995 *Identification Papers*. Her study explores the psychoanalytic and cultural functions of identification, particularly its workings in sexual orientation and colonization.[12] Fuss's concepts of identification and disidentification foreground differences, such as gender and whiteness, in ways that invite these differences to accede to power; thus, differences may emerge as places of rhetorical listening. To demonstrate this claim, this section explains Fuss's definitions of *identification, disidentification, identity,* and *nonidentity* and explores how these interconnections inform questions of personal agency and questions of coexisting commonalities and difference in ways that promote and limit rhetorical listening.

In *Identification Papers,* Fuss introduces *identification* as "the play of difference and similitude in self-other relations" (2). In her introduction, she expands this definition, demonstrating how identification is grounded in daily life and psychoanalytic theory:

> Identification is an embarrassingly ordinary process, a routine, habitual compensation for the everyday loss of our love-object. Compensating

for loss may be one of our most familiar psychological experiences, coloring every aspect of our relation to the world outside us, but it is also a profoundly defamiliarizing affair, installing surrogate others to fill the void where we imagine the love-object to have been. . . . Identification, in other words, invokes phantoms. By incorporating the spectral remains of the dearly departed love-object, the subject vampirisitically comes to life. . . .

Identifications startle us by the apparent suddenness of their emergence, the violence of their impact, the incalculability of their efforts. Identifications are the origins of some of our most powerful, enduring, and deeply felt pleasures. They are also the source of considerable emotional turmoil, capable of unsettling or unmooring the precarious groundings of our everyday identities. (1–2)

Thus, like Aristotle's concept of rhetoric, Fuss's concept of identification has tremendous power for good or ill.

This power of identification is made possible via its metaphoric function. To prove this point, Fuss explores three metaphors most associated with Freud's concept of identification: "gravity, ingestion, and infection" (*Identification* 13).[13] As these three metaphors imply, identifications invite external forces (i.e., discourses, images, other people) inside a person's body; hence, the outside becomes the inside. And because a person's internal forces (i.e., the conscious and the unconscious) manifest themselves externally via a person's relations with other people and discourse, the inside becomes the outside. This endless process, resembling a stroll on a mobius strip, drives our lives. As such, identifications inform a person's identity, but a person's identity cannot be reduced to a single identification.

Because identifications emerge from encounters with forces both internal (ego-id) and external (self-other), Fuss defines identification as a place both psychical and cultural. With more than a passing nod to Freud and Jacques Lacan, Fuss posits identification as the process that "names the entry of history and culture into the subject, a subject that must bear the traces of each and every encounter with the external world. Identification is, from the beginning, a question of *relation*, of self to other, subject to object, inside to outside" (*Identification* 3). For Fuss, such identification is incredibly complex, being "both voluntary and involuntary, necessary and difficult, dangerous and effectual, naturalizing and denaturalizing . . . , the point where psychical/social distinction becomes impossibly confused and finally untenable" (10). As such, identifications emerge as both conscious and unconscious.

In addition to a concept of identification, Fuss posits a concept of disidentification. Invoking Butler's theory from *Gender Trouble* and *Bodies That Matter,* Fuss claims that *disidentification* signifies an identification that is not so much "refused" as "disavowed" (*Identification* 6); in other words, a disidentification is "an identification that has already been made and denied in the unconscious" (7). For example, xenophobia (one kind of disidentification) results when, say, an American disavows an identification with a Syrian, which the American is only able to do because she has first identified with the Syrian or, more precisely, *with what she imagines a Syrian to be.* (Remember, identifications are replacements of actual objects with mental images.) Within this logic, disidentifications are dependent upon previous identifications however faulty or stereotypical.

The effects of disidentification are consequential, even monumental. According to Diane Davis, they pose "some serious trouble" (*Breaking* 40). According to Butler, disidentification renders the object of a person's disidentification "abject" (*Bodies* 112). This phenomenon plays out in rhetorical history. For example, Plato disidentifies with the sophists and renders them abject when he denounces them as lower-level souls (479), but he is able to do so only after first identifying with his mental image of sophists. The questions that haunt such identification and disidentification are: How accurate are mental images that drive our identifications and disidentifications? Who decides and defines what is accurate? What actions do this deciding and defining make (im)possible? When such mental images are fairly accurate, the disidentifications may be productive, as when a society refuses to embrace serial killers and decides to incarcerate them. On the other hand, when such mental images are mostly inaccurate, disidentifications may be nonproductive (even dangerous), as when a society refuses to embrace the intellectual and managerial talents of women and decides to disenfranchise them.

A disidentification based on faulty identifications demonstrates why imagination alone is not enough when attempting to understand a person from a different tradition. Imagination must be grounded in material reality via a kind of cultural/historical archaeological/ethnographic work that the subject doing the conscious identifying must be willing to perform. In Jacqueline Jones Royster's terms, people need to learn about one another's "home place" because such learning helps construct places of identification

("When the First Voice" 32).[14] This work, however, is not an equal opportunity employer. People from nondominant cultures must learn about dominant cultures' home places if they are to work and survive within them, but people from dominant cultures need not necessarily learn about nondominant cultures' home places. People from dominant cultures often possess the unearned *privilege to choose* to learn about nondominant home places; moreover, people from dominant cultures possess the unearned *privilege to choose* to recognize that *dominant* and *nondominant* are cultural constructs and that the identities of each group are always interdependent and often multiethnic.

The idea that a culture's identity is dependent upon both dominant and nondominant influences is best explained by Ralph Ellison who argues that although mainstream America may be coded white (by which he means that mainstream America's power has historically flowed through whites), the dominant culture is not solely white:

> Without the presence of blacks, [*Huckleberry Finn*] could not have been written. No Huck and Jim, no American novel as we know it. For not only is the black man a co-creator of the language that Mark Twain raised to the level of literary eloquence, but Jim's condition as American and Huck's commitment to freedom are at the moral center of the novel. (164)

Given Ellison's point, rhetoric and composition studies needs to become more cognizant of how identifications and disidentifications function.

Fuss's linkage of identification and disidentification proves invaluable to the project of rhetorical listening. For the interplay of identification and disidentification constructs a place of differences where rhetorical exchanges, such as cross-cultural communication, may occur, that is, a place where these exchanges may result in genuine understanding, not patronizing acceptance or silent resistance. If such disidentifications can be brought to consciousness (and obviously not all of them can), then places for negotiating coexisting commonalities and differences may emerge. Such a project is far from simple. For identifications and disidentifications are always evolving, always slippery. And according to Butler, so, too, are the times and places of their occurrences:

> But where or how does identification occur? When can we say with confidence that an identification has happened? Significantly, it never can be said to have taken place; identification does not belong to the world of events. Identification is constantly figured as a desired event

or accomplishment, but one which finally is never achieved; identification is the phantasmatic staging of the event. (*Bodies* 105)

As a "phantasmatic staging," an identification that occurs today may surface today, or it may reappear years later, or both, or, conceivably, not at all. To the extent that such "phantasmatic stagings" may be brought to consciousness, rhetorical listening provides a means for negotiating them.

Regardless of when an identification originates, it informs a person's identity by its conscious and/or unconscious presence. Yet Fuss's identification and disidentification claim a troubled link to identity, a link too often unnamed and unspoken in rhetorical theories. According to Fuss, identity "is actually an identification come to light" (*Identification* 2); simultaneously and conversely, identification is also "a process that keeps identity at a distance" (2). Fuss credits Eve Sedgwick's books (*Between Men, Epistemology of the Closet,* and *Tendencies*) with helping her conceptualize connections between identity and identification in ways that provide a "challenge to the silent presumption that identities wholly correspond to identifications" (6). Just as words cannot directly correspond to material objects (e.g., the word *chair* is not the exact same thing as the four-legged wooden, steel, or plastic object it references), identities cannot directly correspond to identifications. Instead, Fuss claims "identity is 'the Self that identifies itself.' Identification is the psychical mechanism that produces self-recognition. Identification inhabits, organizes, instantiates identity" (2). Given this concept of identity, Fuss's identification functions as a place where "the play of difference and similitude in self-other relations, does not, strictly speaking, stand against identity but structurally aids and abets it" (2). Note that she emphasizes a loose cause-effect distinction between identity and identification, not wanting them to be seen as synonyms nor as different grammatical versions of an identical process.

Furthermore, according to Fuss, just as identification includes the possibility of disidentification, identity incorporates "nonidentity within it": that is, "To be 'like' the other is to be different from the other, to be precisely *not* the same" (*Identification* 19.n 27). With this claim, which echoes Butler's theory, Fuss asks her readers to consider the implications of this question:

> How might it change our understanding of identity if we were finally to take seriously the poststructuralist notion that our most impassioned identifications may incorporate nonidentity within them and

that our most fervent disidentifications may already harbor the identity they seek to destroy? (10)

Responses to this question differ, of course, depending upon the cultural
position of a particular subject and upon his or her particular identifications.

But this question possesses powerful resonances for rhetorical listening.
Indeed, Fuss's concepts of identification, disidentification, identity, and
nonidentity foreground differences as well as commonalities. In the process, differences emerge as mapped places of rhetorical exchanges where
personal agency may be exerted.

On the question of personal agency, Fuss's concept of identification (like
Burke's) does provide a space for rhetorical listening. Because discourse is
not totalizing but, rather, contains contradictions and gaps, personal agency
may arise from the contradictions and gaps within the embodied discourses
that socialize a person via identifications and disidentifications. In other
words, socializing discourses both shape a person and afford a person opportunities to reinforce, revise, and/or interrupt identifications with such
discourses. Although discursive contradictions and gaps provide the potential for agency, the consequences for reinforcing, revising, and/or interrupting a person's identifications are different for different people, depending
upon their particular experiences within culture and upon their particular
un/conscious processing of these experiences via (dis)identifications at specific historical moments.

Within the above logic, the space for personal agency as conscious choice
is limited by the unconscious. Moreover, because it is difficult to delineate
between the conscious and the unconscious (in terms of motivations for
action) and between the inside and the outside (in terms of identifications
with other people, ideas, and so forth), Fuss's concept of personal agency
is difficult to pinpoint as autonomously belonging to any one individual's
identity. And so we arrive back at Fuss's introduction: "[I]t is precisely identity that becomes problematic in and through the work of identification"
(*Identification* 2). Yet, even if personal agency is limited and slippery in Fuss's
theory, it does exist.

On the question of coexisting commonalities and differences, Fuss's
concept of identification offers more possibilities for rhetorical listening than
does Burke's theory. Indeed Fuss's identification and disidentification give
commonalities and differences equal play. This rhetorical reconsideration of
difference is important not just for personal well-being but also for societal

survival: The "reconstitution of opposition as difference is . . . an imperative at the society level, for humanity can no longer afford the interpretive
errors of hypostatization which heighten difference into conflict into war."
This reconsideration of difference emerges as a

> dialogue, a conversation which is engaged in dialectically but which
> concerns the very processes of dialectic, one which seeks not the clari-
> fication and rigidification of difference but rather the murky margins
> between, those margins of overlap which inaugurate and which limit
> the very functioning of dialectic. (D. Williams 218)

Rhetorical listening, I argue, may foster such a dialogue, such a "dialectic," wherein awareness of the disidentifications lurking in such "margins
of overlap" makes us attentive to power plays that are ideologically (un)fair
and to the resulting troubled identifications. In rhetorical listening, power
plays and troubled identifications do not simply vanish. With increased
attentiveness, they may perhaps become more audible . . . and then perhaps more visible . . . and then perhaps more possible to negotiate—with
perhaps, of course, being the operative term.

This possibility of negotiation raises the question of politics in relation
to identification. Indeed, a controlling question throughout Fuss's study is:
"What, then, is political about identification?" (*Identification* 8). To answer
that question, Fuss explores identifications associated with sexual orientation and racial colonization. She argues that Butler's concept of disidentification helps differences accede to power; indeed, that

> Butler's comments on disidentification . . . encourag[e] a reconceptu-
> alization of the political, laying the theoretical groundwork for a poli-
> tics of affiliation fully cognizant of the sacrifices, reversals, and repa-
> rations involved in every imaginary identity formation. (6–7)

She also invokes the culturally inflected psychoanalytic claims of Fanon to
remind us that identification is "neither a historically universal concept nor
a politically innocent one" (141).

Indeed, Fuss argues that identification runs the risk of "annihilating the
other *as other*" (4), as in Burke's theory of identification, which begins by
associating identification with killing (*Rhetoric* 19–20) and ends by frequently mystifying differences. But for Fuss, identification also offers a place
for resisting this risk.[15] To navigate such political currents and foster resistance, Fuss invokes the doubled sites of identification (i.e., the psychical

site of ego/id and the historical/cultural site of self/other) and argues that both sites are political constructs: "*the psychical operates precisely as a political formation*" (*Identification* 165; emphasis original), and there are "historical and social conditions of identification" that are inevitably political (165). To argue that these two sites are inextricably interwoven, Fuss again invokes Fanon's theory:

> It reminds us that identification is never outside or prior to politics, that identification is always inscribed within a certain history: identification names not only the history of the subject but the subject in history. What Fanon gives us, in the end, is a politics that does not oppose the psychical but fundamentally presupposes it. (165)

With this claim, Fuss provides concepts of identification and disidentification that may function as places for rhetorical listening. Employing Fanon's theory to complicate the feminist anthem "The personal is the political," Fuss blurs but does not collapse lines between the personal and the political. In this way, Fuss via Fanon posits identification and disidentification as places wherein people may access agency to listen rhetorically not just for commonalities but also for differences.

The only limitation haunting Fuss's concepts of identification and disidentification is their figuration only as metaphor.

Refiguring Identification as Metonymy

Traditionally, identification has been configured via metaphor. As discussed earlier, Freudian theorists most often represent identification via the metaphors of "gravity, ingestion, and infection" (Fuss, *Identification* 13). Rhetoric and composition theorists most often represent identification via the metaphor of overlapping circles. Fuss explains this impulse to metaphor:

> Metaphor is not simply one approach among many to the problem of identification. To the extent that identification is a desire to be *like* or *as* the other, to the extent, in other words, that identification is fundamentally a question of *resemblance* and *replacement,* metaphor provides the most direct point of entry into the internal workings of a complex cultural and psychical process. (51)

I agree. But . . . although metaphor may function as the dominant trope for identification, metaphor succeeds because it privileges commonalities more than differences. To counter this privileging of commonality, other productive "point[s] of entry" may be theorized for identification, such as, the figuration of metonymy.

The differences between these two figures are important. Metaphor foregrounds resemblances based on commonalities, thus backgrounding differences; metonym foregrounds resemblances based on juxtaposed associations, thus foregrounding both commonalities *and* differences. This subtle but important distinction exposes the limits of metaphor and hints at the supplemental possibilities of metonym for figuring identification. This consideration of refiguring identification prompts several questions. What would happen, in terms of rhetorical listening, if identification's metaphoric places of conjoined circles (a la Burke) and ingested food (a la Fuss via Freud) were supplemented by metonymic places of juxtaposed commonalities and differences? Within such a place, could new opportunities for identifications emerge? Could disidentifications be more readily called into question? Could the limitations of metaphoric identification be turned, at least sometimes, into possibilities? My answer to all these questions is: possibly.

To see where *possibly* may lead in terms of articulating productive places for rhetorical listening, this section offers three proposals for rhetoric and composition studies.

Proposal #1: Put Burke's theory into play with Fuss's theory so as to expand rhetoric and composition studies' understanding of metaphoric identification and disidentification as places for rhetorical listening. This first proposal may seem odd, given that Burke and Fuss represent opposite sides of the modern/postmodern divide. But as the previous sections have demonstrated, resonances exist between modern and postmodern theories of identification. Thus, putting Burke and Fuss into play results not in a theoretical incompatibility but rather in an interesting theoretical dance.[16] Their dance resembles the one David Williams choreographs for Burke and Derrida:

> In a sense, Derrida's ontodeconstruction and Burke's ontological construction revolve around each other, arguing with each other in ways that at times, under the dialectical pressure of the conversation, seem to place them in opposition. But since each problematizes the rigidity of structures of opposition, the margin between—the margin of overlap—reasserts itself. In the end there is no end to the conversation: the revelation of the end . . . is to begin again, to engage in the endless process of interpretation, and to find what joy, what affirmation we may in it. (218)

This "margin between" may function as overlap. And as Adrienne Rich reminds us in poem 29 in "Contradictions," such metaphoric overlap functions heuristically:

> you can learn
> from the edges that blur   O you who love clear edges
> more than anything   watch the edges that blur.
>
> (111.9–12)

When rhetoric and composition studies watches the blurring of Burke's and Fuss's theories of identification, what becomes visible is multiple places for rhetorical listening. Multiple places are important because if in a particular situation, one place of identification does not work, then having other places available increases the chances that rhetorical listening may succeed.

Proposal #2: Represent this play of Burke's and Fuss's theories of metaphoric identifications visually via an energy-field image. To represent the play of Burke's and Fuss's theories visually, rhetoric and composition studies needs to supplement the metaphoric images of conjoined circles and ingestion with another metaphoric image of identification: shared energy fields.[17] Energy-field imagery posits identifications as places where discourses, acting as energy fields, pass by and through a person's body as well as by and through the bodies of others.

Like rays of sunlight, discourses are invisible to the human eye and yet may simultaneously permeate multiple bodies as when millions of people view a movie, read the same book, or listen to a president's speech. Depending on a person's psychical and historical/cultural locations, he or she may internalize the discourses differently. In this way, a person is continually socialized into general cultural discourses while particularized as a subject. Such identification draws from Burke's consubstantiality via second-nature substances as well as from Fuss's discursive identifications and disidentifications.

Energy-field imagery clearly represents how such discursive identifications and disidentifications provide people lenses for seeing the world. Consider how the competing discourses of "the good mother" may permeate all our bodies and socialize us. Such discourses abound in the U.S. whether in books, movies, or families' oral traditions. Though all these discourses are external to people's bodies, they also permeate bodies and become embodied. Whether I identify or disidentify with these discourses, they affect my attitudes and daily interactions with my daughter, my husband, my friends, and even students in my classes. And because my daughter, husband, friends, and students are exposed to similar if not identical discourses, my encounters with these people are also informed by their encounters with "the good mother" discourses. These discourses are multiple with definitions differing depending upon the people and/or institutions promoting each discourse. Moreover, these discourses compete with other socializing discourses, such as those of individualism and self-affirmation.

As becomes obvious with the-good-mother example, socialization proceeds via identification and disidentification. This process does not proceed via simple cause and effect but, rather, via complicated causes and effects that are inextricably knotted, intertwined, and recursive. As such, socializing discourses continuously provide grounds for identifications and disidentifications that construct the evolving lenses through which people and nations see the world (or not) and act (or not). The idea of seeing the world via evolving lenses draws from Burke's concept of terministic screens (*Language* 44–62); the idea of not seeing draws from Fuss's concept of disidentification.

Socialization via identification and disidentification is not a one-way burst of energy running from discourse to people. Once discursive energy fields become embodied in people, the discourses are channeled and changed— sometimes greatly, sometimes minutely—by the bodies they occupy. In other words, people may reinforce, revise, and/or resist the discursive energy fields in which they find themselves. What affords people such agency? Gaps and contradictions in embodied discourses. Ideally, gaps and contradictions become places from which people may assert their own voices. Pragmatically, a person's personal agency is limited in varying degrees by psychical and cultural locations at particular historical moments, especially as they are informed by power differentials.

Consider, for example, James Baldwin's explanation of how individuals and societies may talk back to the socializing discourses of history:

> [T]he great force of history comes from the fact that we carry it within us, are unconsciously controlled by it in many ways, and history is literally *present* in all we do. It could be scarcely otherwise since it is to history that we owe our frames of references, our identities, and our aspirations. . . . [O]ne enters into battle with that historical creation, Oneself, and attempts to recreate oneself according to a principle more humane and more liberating; one begins the attempt to achieve a level of personal maturity and freedom which robs history of its tyrannical power, and also changes history. (321)

For Baldwin, as for bell hooks, talking back becomes not merely an option but sometimes a necessity for personal and social survival. When talking back becomes necessary, then understanding how the socializing functions of discourse construct identifications and/or disidentifications makes talking back more productive. Energy-field imagery enhances this understanding.

Energy-field imagery makes visible the functions of metaphoric identifications and disidentifications that are sometimes mystified by images of interlocking circles or ingestion. First, energy-field imagery makes visible the doubled function of discourse: That is, discourse both socializes us and enables us to talk back to our socialization. Within the play of this energy-field imagery, discourses permeate us, and we permeate them, each being changed by the other. Second, energy-field imagery shifts the place of identification from common ground to shared atmosphere, making visible the facts that multiple places of identification coexist and that we may stand in different cultural locations even as we share identifications. Third, energy-field imagery posits discursive socialization as a metaphoric process of continual identifications and disidentifications. For whether discourses are socializing us or we responding to them in ways that blur inside and outside, grounds for identifications and disidentifications are continually being constructed. Fourth, energy-field imagery suggests how discursive fields may be strengthened or dissipated. Our encounters with discourses depend upon our particular circumstances at particular historical moments; moreover, our encounters add energy to or help dissipate always already evolving discursive categories, such as, race, class, gender, nationality, age (Linn 25–26). Fifth, energy-field imagery makes visible how discourse abets the construction of our identities and how our identities may reinforce, revise, and/or resist these cultural discourses.

Proposal #3: Supplement metaphoric concepts of identification and disidentification with a metonymic concept of non-identification as places for rhetorical listening. Metaphoric identifications—whether represented as common ground, ingestion, or shared energy fields—possess certain limits. At times, identifications (via common ground) are arrogant and coercive—as when the U.S. defines *freedom* in terms of U.S. democracy and imposes this definition on other countries without consulting those countries' traditions. At times, disidentifications (via disavowed identifications) are faulty and discriminatory—as when gender stereotypes are invoked to argue that women are too emotional to be president of the U.S. And at times, identifications and disidentification are unconsciously dehumanizing because the "object" falls under the radar of the "subject" doing the identifying—as when white characters in 1930s Hollywood movies talk in front of African American workers as if the latter were invisible men or women. At best, these limitations result in misunderstandings among people at home, at school, at work, at play. At worst, these limitations result in violation, murder, or war.

To address these problems, rhetoric and composition studies needs to map more theoretical terrain and provide more pragmatic tactics for peaceful, cross-cultural negotiation and coalition building. One such tactic is to supplement metaphoric identifications and disidentifications with metonymic non-identification.

To map a space for *non-identification* in rhetoric and composition studies, I return briefly to David Williams's claim about the dance of Burke and Derrida, specifically to Williams's term *margin between* (218). Although Williams reads the term as metaphoric "overlap" (or shared space), the term may also be read as a metonymic "gap" (or space between juxtaposed subjects). Both figurations are useful to rhetoric and composition studies because, together, they map expanded rhetorical terrain for identification, which, in turn, increases opportunities for rhetorical listening.

When Williams interprets *margin between* as a space of metaphoric "overlap," the resulting identifications and/or disidentifications may mystify as much as they reveal. For example, although listening rhetorically in places of identification appears fairly easy, what people sometimes forget is that easy identifications may mask power differentials and coerced differences. Although listening rhetorically in places of disidentification may be difficult, what people enmeshed in disidentifications sometimes forget is that choices still exist—such as, to stay enmeshed or to try to move on. One tactic for moving on entails consciously shifting ground from metaphoric places of identification and disidentification to metonymic places of non-identification.

When Williams's term *margin between* is interpreted as a "gap" or as a space between juxtaposed subjects, it may signify metonymic non-identification. To define non-identification, I look first to its visual representation. The hyphen in *non-identification* signifies a place where two concepts are metonymically juxtaposed—that is, where concepts of the negative and of identification are associated but not overlapping. As such, the hyphen represents the "margin between," a place wherein people may *consciously choose* to position themselves to listen rhetorically. This "margin between" does not transcend ideology; it does, however, provide a place of pause, a place of reflection, a place that invites people to admit that gaps exist. Admissions of gaps may take the form of "I don't know you," "I don't know what I don't know about you," or even "I don't know that I don't know that you exist"—whether that *you* is a person, place, thing, or idea. In some cases, rhetorical listening in the place of non-identification may precede new identifications; in other cases, it enables us to revisit former identifications and disidentifications. As such, this perpetual process resembles a chicken-and-egg phenomenon.

What's important in the process of non-identification, however, is that people recognize the partiality of our visions and listen for that-which-cannot-be-seen, even if it cannot yet be heard. Although the tactic of listening rhetorically in metonymic places of non-identification cannot guarantee successful results in every situation, the concept of non-identification is important to rhetoric and composition studies because it maps a place, a possibility, for consciously asserting our agency to engage cross-cultural rhetorical exchanges across both commonalities *and* differences. Such a performance of rhetorical listening makes hearing a possibility; in turn, hearing provides a ground for action motivated by accountability.

This performance of rhetorical listening fosters a rhetorical stance of humility (not weakness), a stance that recognizes interdependency among subjects. Within an interdependent place of non-identification, X and Y are imagined not as subject and object but as two very different subjects—that is, as subjects who are juxtaposed but not necessarily on common ground, as subjects who are encountering the same socializing discourses but processing them very differently, as subjects whose juxtaposition presupposes an interdependency upon one another that is integral to the identity formation of each. Within such an interdependent place of non-identification, metaphor and metonymy coexist.

This interdependency has been theorized by Trinh as one that "consists in creating a ground that belongs to no one, not even to the creator. Otherness becomes empowerment. . . . Furthermore, where should the dividing line between outsider and insider stop?" (932). Linking Trinh's interdependency to non-identification engages Burke's recovery of substance as an "acting together" (*Rhetoric* 21), but non-identificatory acting together is a conscious choice. That is, non-identification stipulates that when acting together, people must *choose* to recognize their interdependency as well as their movements among different insider and outsider cultural positions. Such recognitions of cultural positions do not deny interlocutors their subjectivity or their identities as historical *Is*. Instead, such recognitions expose simply (and, of course, it is never simple) that identities are complex and multiple (Desser 318) and that they "can hardly be submitted to the old subjectivity/objectivity paradigm" (Trinh 932).

The logic of Trinh's subject-to-subject interdependency has an important effect. Because rhetorical listening recognizes that people may move in and out of multiple cultural locations, it also recognizes that these movements affect how people see the world:

> [The] moment the insider steps out from the inside she's no longer a mere insider. She necessarily looks in from the outside while also looking out from the inside. Not quite the same, not quite the other, she stands in that undetermined threshold place where she constantly drifts in and out. (Trinh 932)

Desmond Tutu defines such interdependency via the South African term *umbuntu*: "Our humanity is caught up in that of all others. We are humans because we belong. We are made for community, for togetherness, for family, to exist in a delicate network of independence." *Umbuntu* served as the grounds for the Truth and Reconciliation Commission, which Tutu chaired; the commission invited all who lived under apartheid to come forward and publicly name abuses and consequences of apartheid without fear of legal or vigilante penalties. In this way, stories were juxtaposed with one another without having to be synthesized to construct grounds for legal action. These stories were "simply" allowed to lie alongside one another as a cultural quilt whose purpose was to provide an understanding of the past in hopes of reinventing the future. Did the commission heal all wounds? No. Did it map a more inclusive public history? Yes. Perhaps the most important question is: How is this more inclusive public history affecting South African society today?

What Trinh implies and what Tutu demonstrates is this point: Just as identification precedes persuasion (Burke, *Rhetoric* 55), rhetorical listening in a place of non-identification *may* precede conscious identifications; as such, rhetorical listening may help people consciously navigate troubled identifications and disidentifications. The operative term, of course, is *may*.

The possibility of consciously navigating our own identifications and disidentifications circles back to the question of personal agency. If non-identification is a place that assumes the existence of gaps and if gaps in discourse provide spaces that a person may choose to fill and, thus, assert personal agency, then non-identification offers people a place to assert personal agency. In a place of non-identification, people may *act* in a variety of ways. They may pause and reflect on people, places, and things that are similar, different, and unknown. They may exercise their capacity and willingness to listen to themselves and to others. They may reconsider previous identifications and disidentifications and decide whether to say "yes" and/or "no" and/or "maybe" to them. They may contemplate the existence of that-which-they-cannot-see and even of that-which-they-cannot-yet-hear. They may question how conscious personal agency competes with the unconscious and recognize that any answers to this question will always be partial. Finally, they may consider how personal agency competes with discursive agency and cultural agency—that is, how cultural discourses and structures delimit personal agency just as personal agency *may* interrupt cultural discourses and structures.

One caveat about personal agency and non-identification is worth mentioning. Even as a person invokes personal agency to interrupt unethical discourses or unethical cultural structures and practices, that person cannot control the effects of her or his interruption. Sometimes, the interruption is successful; sometimes, partial; sometimes, unsuccessful. Whether successful or not, interruptions have consequences.

The possibility of consciously navigating (some of) our own identifications and disidentifications also circles back to the question of coexisting commonalities and differences. Because non-identification is a place that assumes the existence of both commonalities and differences, it provides a place for listening rhetorically across both. Within Western logic, however, this simultaneous focus is hard to maintain. What often occurs is a reductive comparison and contrast within the terms of a person doing the identifying; what should occur, according to Royster, is a consideration within all the terms of the people involved in an identification ("When the First Voice" 29–30). This simultaneous focus on commonalities and differences challenges a rhetorical listener to be accountable for diverse points of views and to factor these views into her or his thinking—or to choose not to. The attempt to maintain this simultaneous focus is important in that it may offer ways to productively complicate cross-cultural discussions. For example, in U.S. culture (in all its multiplicity), non-white America has had to know the discursive fields of white America as a means of economic and physical survival. White America, on the other hand, has had the unearned privilege to remain "blind" to non-white America's discursive fields even as non-white discourses permeate all of American life from architecture to music to the economy to literature to history.

In a place of non-identification, it is incumbent upon anyone finding herself or himself in a dominant cultural position to *choose* to engage discursive fields other than her or his own, and it is incumbent upon those in less-dominant cultural positions to foster an involvement in, along with a healthy suspicion of, the dominant group's choosing (Royster, "When the First Voice" 32–33). It is incumbent upon anyone in a place of non-identification to remember that all people circle in and out of dominant and nondominant positions on a daily basis, depending on whether they are at home, at work, with friends. And finally, it is incumbent upon anyone in a place of non-identification to recognize that listening to multiple discourses produces not only harmony but disharmony; hence, a person must *choose* to stick with the work that needs to be done in such a place, realizing that such work may take patience, may require multiple hearings (pun intended), may not succeed, may even be misinterpreted. Yet, such choosing potentially provides a means of physical, psychical, cultural, and spiritual survival—personally, locally, nationally, and globally.

Some Concluding Thoughts on Ethics

Why are rhetorical listening and its places of identification, disidentification, and non-identification necessarily linked to ethics? Perhaps because, as Nietzsche claims, "'It is the ear of the other that signs'" (qtd. in McDonald ix) or perhaps because as Derrida claims, echoing Nietzsche, "everything comes down to the ear you are able to hear me with" ("Otobiographies" 4). Given this function of the ear, rhetorical listening begs the question: "what do we do at the boundaries of comprehension?" (Rayner 6). General questions of "What do we do?" always land us within the realm of ethics; likewise, more particular questions such as how do we use "the power of identification . . . in the service of a nonviolent, progressive-thinking politics"? (Fuss, *Identification* 9) also land us within the realm of ethics.

For an ethics of rhetorical listening to exist, two conditions must be met. First, a listener must be imagined with an agency that enables him or her to *choose* to act ethically, either by listening and/or by acting upon that listening. As demonstrated earlier, rhetorical listening in places of identification, disidentification, and non-identification affords people just such agency, albeit limited. Second, given this agency, listeners must be provided with a lexicon and tactics for listening and for acting upon their listening. In rhetoric and composition studies, many people, such as Royster, Davis, Michelle Ballif, and Joyce Middleton, are theorizing such a lexicon and tactics. In this chapter, my contribution to the scholarly lexicon is to theorize non-identification as a place for rhetorical listening, a place that supplements metaphoric identification and disidentification. In subsequent chapters, my contribution is to model tactics for rhetorical listening as a code of cross-cultural conduct.

A final question about ethics that haunts this study is: What are the ethical possibilities and risks of theorizing and practicing identification, disidentification, and non-identification as places of rhetorical listening? The ethical possibilities include: coalition building across cultural boundaries; denaturalizing and, when appropriate, delegitimizing dysfunctional cultural categories and their boundaries; and acknowledging mutual disidentifications in hopes of constructing Fanon's "world of reciprocal recognitions" (218; qtd. in Fuss, *Identification* 144) or Trinh's world where "difference replace[s] conflict" (930). Yet, ethical risks also exist: appropriation, misunderstanding, and the possibility of grounding "a social movement on the precarious ground of psychical fantasy" (Fuss 8).

Given these possibilities and given these risks, perhaps the most ethical action is to acknowledge the risks and to act anyway, for as Rich claims, "[W]e can't wait to [act] until we are perfectly clear and righteous" ("Split" 123). As I listen to Rich, what resonates in my ear is that one such action, one such choice, may be to listen rhetorically to our troubled identifications and disidentifications . . . and to attempt to listen from the place of non-identification. And as I listen to the previous sentence, what echoes hauntingly in my ear is the voice of my teacher Ed Corbett, whom I imagine saying, "Krista, those places of non-identification foster rhetorics of open hands."

3

Listening Metonymically: A Tactic for Listening to Public Debates

> [W]hat I must engage/ . . . is meant to break my heart and reduce me to silence.
>
> —Adrienne Rich, "North American Time"

> I had decided never again to speak to white women about racism.
>
> —Audre Lorde, "An Open Letter to Mary Daly"

> It continues to be my judgment that public response in kind would not be a fruitful direction.
>
> —Mary Daly, "New Intergalactic Introduction," *Gyn/Ecology*

> Responsibility is the "ability to respond," which means being accountable for and proactive in terms of options.
>
> —Sonja Foss, Karen Foss, and Cindy Griffin, *Feminist Rhetorical Theories*

If one function of rhetorical listening is to foster cross-cultural communication in places of identification, disidentification, and non-identification, then particular tactics of rhetorical listening must be conceptualized and defined for listeners. This chapter is meant to do just that. To identify and negotiate troubled identifications that haunt public debates, this chapter posits one tactic: listening metonymically. *Listening metonymically* signifies the rhetorical-listening moves that listeners may make in public discussions when identifying a text or a person with a cultural group; specifically, this tactic invites listeners to assume that a text or a person is associated with—but not necessarily representative of—an entire cultural group.

As employed in this chapter, listening metonymically provides listeners a means of resisting a gendered and racialized silence that haunts U.S. public discourses. Although this gendered and racialized silence is only one kind of public silence,[1] it is important to identify and negotiate because it is a marker of troubled identifications and, as such, is dysfunctional. This dysfunctional silence results from and perpetuates a differend,[2] or discursive disconnect, between interlocutors (whether people or institutions) who occupy competing cultural logics about how gender and race intersect. To exemplify how a gendered and racialized silence may be interrupted by listening metonymically, I circle back to the late 1970s and early 1980s to the public "debate" between Audre Lorde and Mary Daly.

The debate arose in 1978 over a disagreement between the two women about feminist research methods. Daly sent Lorde a copy of *Gyn/Ecology: The Metaethics of Radical Feminism;* in return, Lorde sent Daly a private letter outlining her thanks and her concerns; after some time, Daly replied in kind with a private letter.[3] Although the two women agreed on feminist issues, they disagreed about Daly's scholarly method. Daly emphasized commonalities among all women; Lorde encouraged her to emphasize differences. When their disagreement was not resolved privately, Lorde (because she believed Daly's method represents a larger cultural pattern) publicly published "An Open Letter to Mary Daly" in Cherríe Moraga's and Gloria Anzaldúa's collection *This Bridge Called My Back: Writings by Radical Women of Color* (1983) and later in Lorde's own collection *Sister Outsider* (1984). Although Daly publicly acknowledged Lorde's letter in a revised 1990 introduction to *Gyn/Ecology,* she refused to engage in a public debate. Consequently, this "debate" just sits there in Lorde's essay and Daly's introduction, enshrouded mostly in silence. And it is this particular kind of dysfunctional silence that intrigues me.[4]

If the debate were only an historical anomaly, I would let it sit there. But it is not. It represents a current mode of exchange in the U.S. about gender and race: namely, an uncomfortable and unproductive silence. Such dysfunctional silence is not happenstance; it functions via a rhetorical structure that plays out again and again, reinscribing a powerful cultural desire in the U.S. *not* to talk publicly and cross-culturally about how gender and race intersect. This chapter's opening quotation from Adrienne Rich identifies the reason for this desire: Such talk may break our hearts. Still, Rich, Lorde, and Daly risk their hearts in their public writings. The lesson we may learn from rereading this debate is twofold: first, how to identify the structure and function of a rhetoric of dysfunctional silence and, second, how to posit the structure and function of a more productive rhetoric of listening.

Before I analyze this dysfunctional silence, however, let me clarify my reasons for selecting this "debate" to illustrate the movement from a rhetoric of dysfunctional silence to a rhetoric of listening. First, I do *not* intend to assume the mantle of "the one who knows best" in order to settle this particular debate; the right of settlement belongs, or rather belonged, to Lorde and Daly at particular historical moments. Indeed, I respect both women too much to make such a presumption. Second, I do not intend to script a hero/villain scenario in which one woman gets the *white* hat and the other gets the *black* one (note how perfidious our cultural commonplaces are). Third, I do not intend to imply that race in the U.S. functions only in terms of a black/white binary. And fourth, I am not privy to *nor* do I intend to delve into the private musings of Lorde and Daly. Rather, my interest lies in the public performance of this debate. Specifically, as a concerned citizen, teacher, and mother, I am interested in how the "debate" offers us (as a culture and as individuals) tactics for recognizing a dysfunctional gendered and racialized silence as well as tactics for resisting it.

My purpose in this chapter is to revisit the Lorde-Daly debate in hopes of illustrating how we—and by *we* I mean *all* women and men—may learn to move from a rhetoric of dysfunctional silence to a rhetoric of listening, a rhetoric within which we may communicate with one another about and across our commonalities and differences. To that end, this chapter (1) briefly defines the Lorde-Daly debate; (2) articulates a structure of a rhetoric of dysfunctional silence; (3) posits an alternative structure of a rhetoric of listening; and (4) discusses implications for rhetoric and composition studies.

The Debate

In *Gyn/Ecology,* Daly argues that women's oppression is transcultural and transhistorical, that is, that all women have been similarly exploited within patriarchy. To prove her claim, Daly identifies five rituals from different cultures and different historical moments and analyzes how they similarly victimize women. These five rituals are Indian widow burning, Chinese foot-binding, African genital mutilation,[5] European witch burning, and nineteenth-century American gynecology. Though different in particulars, these rituals represent to Daly a common cross-cultural impulse—indeed, a general method—for victimizing women within patriarchy.

Daly names this method the Sado-Ritual Syndrome (130–33) and articulates its seven steps:

Step 1: Perpetrators obsess about purity (131). In both European witch burning and Indian widow burning, fire purifies the women. In African genital mutilation and Chinese foot-binding, the procedures are performed to keep young girls pure, which ironically simultaneously eroticizes them.

Step 2: Perpetrators erase their own accountability for these atrocities by grounding their actions in a transcendent truth (132). Foot-binding is done in the name of beauty, widow burning in the name of honor, witch burning in the name of God, and gynecology in the name of science.

Step 3: Perpetrators ensure that the rituals catch on and spread quickly (132). Chinese foot-binding plays on class biases by encouraging lower-class Chinese women and men to imitate upper-class rituals. Indian widow burning plays on gender biases by encouraging the Indian widow to prove herself a "good wife" by leaping onto her husband's funeral pyre.

Step 4: Perpetrators use women as "scapegoats and token torturers" (132). In both African genital mutilation and Chinese foot-binding, mothers and other older women are the ones who perform the rituals on young girls.

Step 5: Perpetrators obsess on order, repetition, and detail (132). In Chinese foot-binding, European witch burning, and American gynecology, elaborate how-to manuals were developed.

Step 6: Perpetrators accept behavior that in other contexts would appear appalling (132). For a thousand years in China, foot-binding was seen as normal; it was outlawed only when Mao Tse-tung came to power in the twentieth century. Sadly, women whose feet had been bound before Mao's takeover were caught in a double bind. Before the revolution, the women were rendered lame; after the revolution, they were ridiculed by the communists and denied positions of power in the new regime.

Step 7: Perpetrators validate a ritual's existence through academic scholarship (133). For instance, African genital mutilation gets classified in scholarly texts as female circumcision, as if infibulation were somehow comparable in process and effect to male circumcision and as if infibulation were the only genital ritual practiced.

According to Daly, this seven-step Syndrome has been so naturalized—that is, so ideologically inscribed within cultures and bodies—that it keeps women and men from questioning their plights and imagining other possibilities. For example, within particular cultural contexts, foot-binding and infibulation have been viewed as normal acts of beautifying or celebrating a woman's body; hence, these practices have often not been questioned by perpetrators or survivors. Daly's purpose in *Gyn/Ecology* is to demystify such practices, demonstrating how they adversely affect women—all women, all over the world, at all points in human history.

After reading Daly's gift of *Gyn/Ecology*, Lorde wrote Daly a letter originally dated 6 May 1979 that expressed both her admiration for the book and her concerns. Lorde's concerns were twofold: (1) Under the term *woman*, Daly masks some very important differences among women from different cultures and (2) Black women are portrayed only as perpetrators and victims of patriarchal rituals. For readers unfamiliar with Lorde's letter, here is an excerpt:

> Thank you for having *Gyn/Ecology* sent to me. So much of it is full of import, useful, generative, and provoking. As in *Beyond God the Father*, many of your analyses are strengthening and helpful to me. Therefore, it is because of what you have given to me in the past work that I write this letter to you now, hoping to share with you the benefits of my insights as you have shared the benefits of yours with me.
>
> This letter has been delayed because of my grave reluctance to reach out to you, for what I want us to chew upon here is neither easy nor simple. The history of white women who are unable to hear Black women's words, or to maintain dialogue with us, is long and discouraging. But for me to assume that you will not hear me represents not only history, perhaps, but an old pattern of relating, sometimes protective and sometimes dysfunctional, which we, as women shaping our future, are in the process of shattering and passing beyond, I hope. ("Open Letter" 67)

Lorde continues, commending Daly for her "good faith toward all women" (67) and agreeing with her that the oppression of women crosses all ethnic, racial, and cultural boundaries.

But Lorde shifts from compliment to critique, arguing that by focusing on transhistorical and transcultural *commonalities* among women, Daly's Sado-Ritual Syndrome erases important *differences* within the oppression of women: "To imply . . . that all women suffer the same oppression simply because we are women is to lose sight of the many varied tools of patriarchy" ("Open Letter" 60). For example, while Lorde concurs that too little has been written about African genital rituals, she also asks Daly to consider their *differences* from European witch burning and Indian widow burning. Moreover, Lorde argues that Daly might want to consider the possibility that African women function as powerful foremothers and role models, not just as perpetrators and victims of patriarchy.

In closing, Lorde makes an offering of her letter:

> This letter attempts to break a silence which I had imposed upon myself. . . . I had decided never again to speak to white women about racism. I felt it was wasted energy because of destructive guilt and defensiveness, and because whatever I had to say might better be said by white women to one another at far less emotional cost to the speaker, and probably a better hearing. But I would like not to destroy you in my consciousness, not to have to. So as a sister Hag, I ask you to speak to my perceptions. Whether or not you do, Mary, again I thank you for what I have learned from you.
>
> This letter is in repayment.
>
> In the hands of Afrekete,
Audre Lorde
("Open Letter" 71)

Although Lorde and Daly exchanged private letters and met to discuss these concerns, their private communications resulted in no public debate or dialogue. Instead, each woman later published her own thoughts on the issue. In 1984, Lorde published a slightly revised version of the letter she had sent Daly under the title "An Open Letter to Mary Daly." In 1990, Daly acknowledged Lorde's letter in the introduction to a new edition of *Gyn/Ecology:*

> Explosions of Diversity do not happen without conflict, however. One of the responses to *Gyn/Ecology* was a personal letter from Audre Lorde, which was sent to me in May 1979. For deep and complex reasons, I was unable to respond to this lengthy letter immediately. However when Lorde came to Boston to give a poetry reading that summer, I made a point of attending it and spoke with her briefly. I told her that I would like to discuss her letter in person so that we would have an adequate opportunity to understand each other in

dialogue, and I suggested places where we might meet for such a discussion. Our meeting did in fact take place at the Simone de Beauvoir Conference in New York on September 29, 1979. In the course of that hour-or-so-long meeting we discussed my book and her response. I explained my positions clearly, or so I thought. I pointed out, for example, in answer to Audre Lorde's objection that I failed to name Black goddesses, that *Gyn/Ecology* is not a compendium of goddesses. Rather, it focuses primarily on myths and symbols which were direct sources of christian myth. Apparently Lorde was not satisfied, although she did not indicate this at the time. She later published and republished slightly altered versions of her originally personal letter to me in *This Bridge Called My Back* and *Sister Outsider* as an "Open Letter."

It continues to be my judgment that public response in kind would not be a fruitful direction. In my view, *Gyn/Ecology* is itself an "Open Book." I regret any pain that unintended omissions may have caused others, particularly women of color, as well as myself. The writing of *Gyn/Ecology* was for me an act of Biophilic bonding with women of all races and classes, under all the varying oppressions of patriarchy. Clearly, women who have a sincere interest in understanding and discussing this book have an obligation to read not only the statement of critics but also the book itself, and to *think* about it. (xxx–xxxi)

In sum, Daly claims that Lorde misunderstood her intent in *Gyn/Ecology* and contends that a public debate about this issue will serve no purpose.

Respectfully, I disagree. Without downplaying how personally painful this debate undoubtedly was for both women (as Rich says, such debates *are* meant to break our hearts), perhaps the rest of us can now benefit from the debate if we revision[6] it, using it to imagine not who was right and who was wrong but rather how one moves from a rhetoric of dysfunctional silence to a rhetoric of listening. To define these rhetorics and articulate their attendant practices, I turn next to an examination of their terms, their cultural logics, their rhetorical stances, and their dominant interpretive tropes.

A Rhetoric of Dysfunctional Silence

Only recently has feminist scholarship, such as Cheryl Glenn's *Unspoken,* examined silence in terms of its negative and positive functions. In the last half of the twentieth-century, silence is often defined negatively. White feminists document the absence of white women's voices in a variety of cultural contexts and challenged these silences with the possibility of white women's speaking. In psychology, Carol Gilligan gives us *In a Different Voice;* in literary studies, Elaine Showalter offers us *Speaking of Gender.* White feminists have also factored racial differences into their critiques of silence. In communication studies, Karlyn Kohrs Campbell gives us *Man Cannot Speak for Her;* in philosophy, Diana Fuss offers us *Essentially Speaking.*

Many non-white feminists have complicated the idea of silence as the absence of speaking voices, shifting the focus from voice to ear. Gloria Anzaldúa argues in *Borderlands/La Frontera* that silence may occur when a *mestiza* speaks but the dominant culture refuses to hear her (xx).[7] Echoing Anzaldúa, Ana Castillo argues in *Massacre of the Dreamers* that Chicanas have not necessarily lacked a voice but, rather, have lacked a hearing; indeed, she claims that Chicanas have not entered the rhetorical realm of "public discussion" because the dominant white culture has chosen not to hear their voices (5). Likewise, bell hooks argues in "Talking Back" that while white women may have needed to escape silence by coming to voice, African American women have always already had powerful voices; they just have needed cultural spaces in which their voices were valued enough to be heard (6–7). Anzaldúa's, Castillo's, and hooks's critiques expose a more complex concept of gendered and racialized silence. No longer is it merely the absence of speaking voice(s); it is also the absence of hearing ears. This definition both constructs a space for and demonstrates a need for rhetorical listening, with listening metonymically serving as a tactic for moving from a rhetoric of dysfunctional silence to a rhetoric of listening.

The rhetoric of dysfunctional silence that haunts discussions of gender and race in the U.S. often emerges via the following four functions: (1) It is driven by negatively resonating terms; (2) It proceeds via a cultural logic that masks coexisting commonalities and differences; (3) It offers interlocutors dysfunctional rhetorical stances of denial, defensiveness, and guilt/blame; and (4) It proceeds via the interpretive trope of reading metaphorically. This rhetoric fosters a guilt/blame logic, which fosters dysfunctional silence, which fosters guilt/blame, which fosters dysfunctional silence . . . and the discordant music of this dysfunctional dance plays on for centuries. If this rhetoric is to be interrupted, its presence must be made audible and then visible.

Function 1: A rhetoric of dysfunctional silence obsesses on negative terms in order to dismiss those terms. As Plato wisely demonstrates in any number of Socratic dialogues, the first move in analyzing a debate is to define its terms.

But as we all know, terms are more than simple dictionary definitions, more than even contextual definitions. Figuratively speaking (pun intended), terms both construct and represent our understanding of reality, and as such, they resonate with history, with culture, and with a community's stipulated definitions of *logos*, *ethos*, and *pathos*. A rhetoric of dysfunctional silence fostered via U.S. history and culture encourages readers to obsess on only negative interpretations of Lorde's terms (emphasis added):

- Lorde feels a *grave reluctance to reach out* to Daly.
- She believes white women are *unable to hear* black women or maintain dialogue with them.
- She knows black women often *decide never again to speak* to white women.
- She knows black women's speaking to white women is often perceived by black women as *wasted energy.*
- She believes white women too often retreat *into destructive guilt and defensiveness.*
- She believes white women can speak to white women at less *emotional cost.*
- She does reach out to Daly, though, because she desires not to have to *destroy [Daly] in [her] consciousness.*

A rhetoric of dysfunctional silence encourages readers to dismiss these "negative" terms—either by accepting them without critique or, worse, by rejecting them without critique. Such acceptances and dismissals reaffirm the status quo, preventing public debate on what Lorde's terms may tell us about the rhetorical situations of many African American women functioning within this rhetoric. What issues do Lorde's terms offer for public debate? Well, what I hear are these: For African American women, there is a sense of danger in speaking back to the dominant white culture; there is the pain of not being heard; there is the impulse to shut down dialogue and make whites do their own race work; there is a common expectation about how white women will respond to challenges; and there are two "successful" ways of coping—being silent and erasing painful knowledge from consciousness.

A rhetoric of dysfunctional silence also encourages readers to obsess on only negative interpretations of Daly's terms (emphasis added):

- Daly *regrets any pain* she may have caused herself or her readers.
- She *regrets unintended* oversights.

- She says that, *for me, Gyn/Ecology* was the means of bonding with all women.
- She uses the word *women* to refer *to women of all races and classes.*
- She claims that a public response to Lorde would *not be a fruitful direction* for feminism.

Again, a rhetoric of dysfunctional silence encourages readers to dismiss these "negative" terms—-either by accepting them without critique or, worse, by rejecting them without critique. Such acceptances and dismissals reaffirm the status quo, preventing public debate on what Daly's terms may tell us about the rhetorical situations of many white women functioning within a U.S. rhetoric of dysfunctional silence. What issue do Daly's terms offer for public debate? Well, what I hear are these: White women may assume (or be perceived as assuming) that to say "I'm sorry" is sufficient; they may assume that unintentionality is a valid excuse for not considering other peoples' possible reactions; they may assume that one's own pain is a sufficient lens through which to view others' pain; they may assume that commonalities among women should take precedence over differences, and, finally, they may assume that silence (even a dysfunctional silence) is the more polite and perhaps more politically expedient response.

But within a rhetoric of dysfunctional silence, the aforementioned issues proffered by Lorde and Daly are rarely debated publicly.

Function 2: A rhetoric of dysfunctional silence proceeds via a cultural logic that masks coexisting commonalities and differences. Implicit in this logic is one of our more popular rhetorical tactics, either/or reasoning. In the Lorde-Daly debate, two manifestations of this binary reasoning occur: (1) either commonalities among women are foregrounded or their differences are foregrounded and (2) either women speak or they remain silent.

In terms of the first manifestation of this either/or reasoning, implicit in Lorde's and Daly's terms are different logics about feminist analyses: that is, whether to foreground *commonalities* among women or whether to foreground *differences*. Daly uses the term *woman* to refer to all women who, she claims, have been transhistorically and transculturally subjected to patriarchal disciplining. But despite Daly's good intentions, she cannot escape history, particularly the ways white feminists have employed the word *woman*. As hooks and Barbara Christian remind us,[8] white women's use of *woman* has too often resonated as a code word for "white woman," a resonance that obviously diminishes differences. And this cultural history haunts Daly's use of the word *woman*, regardless of her private intent. Likewise, Lorde uses the term *Black woman* to recognize differences, a recognition that (however well-intentioned and historically understandable) diminishes commonalities. By perpetuating such binary oppositions, a rhetoric of dysfunctional silence discourages simultaneous imaginings of commonalities and differences.

In terms of the second manifestation of the either/or reasoning, implicit in Lorde's and Daly's terms is the idea that speaking and silence occupy opposite ends of a binary continuum. Lorde sees her options as speaking to white women or remaining silent; Daly sees her options as speaking back to Lorde in private or remaining silent. Within each woman's logic, both speaking and silence are marked as dangerous—albeit dangerous in different ways. Although Rich has shown that both speaking and silence may be marked positively, especially when silence is employed to listen to others (Ratcliffe, *Anglo-American* 122–25), a rhetoric of dysfunctional silence discourages both speaking and listening. Within such a rhetoric, the silence is deafening.

Function 3: A rhetoric of dysfunctional silence offers interlocutors three dysfunctional rhetorical stances—denial, defensiveness, and guilt/blame. The Lorde-Daly "debate" is no exception. Denial is a person's "[f]ailure to recognize obvious implications or consequences of a thought, act, or situation" ("Defense"). In terms of the Lorde-Daly debate, denial emerges when Lorde admits that she had decided never again to talk to white women about race (although her private and published letters to Daly function as her attempt to interrupt this denial). Denial also emerges when Daly sidesteps Lorde's question about negative representations of African women by arguing that *Gyn/Ecology* was not intended to focus on African goddesses.

In terms of white feminists, the denial of racism is not really the issue I want to discuss, for I have run into none who claim that racism does not exist in our culture. But I have run into a few who seemingly deny that race inadvertently informs our actions and attitudes. For instance, I was once part of a women's studies program that exploded over a race question (as many women's studies programs did in the 1980s). A decision of certain white feminists was called into question during a committee meeting, but these feminists refused to debate the question of whether race may have been a factor in the deliberations, claiming that the charge was politically motivated and that their participation in civil rights activities evidenced their antiracist ideologies. I do not doubt the sincerity of these women; their points might even have been valid. But my point is that the lack of public debate fostered by immediate denial prevented the group from coming to terms with the issue of *how* race intersects with gender in institutional politics; it also prevented the committee from banding together to produce effective institutional change on this or other feminist issues.

In terms of non-white feminists, denial may take a different form. I understand Lorde and many other non-white feminists' personal decisions not to talk to white women (with nonhearing ears) about race during the 1980s (or any other time for that matter) in an effort to make such white women "see" that they must do their own race work. For example, a few years ago, a white graduate student came to my office quite upset. She felt that her offer of friendship had just been rejected by another student in one of her classes, and she couldn't understand why.

"What happened?" I asked.

"Well," she explained, "the woman is black, and she was insulted when I asked her what it feels like to be black."

The graduate student is a highly ethical woman, and she honestly felt her classmate could give her insight into racism in our culture. Her classmate probably could have, but that is not the issue. I suggested to the graduate student that perhaps she should do her own race work—that is, not put the burden on her classmate to explain, not seemingly objectify her classmate as representative of all blacks, and not make curiosity about race the basis for a friendship.

"That's not what I intended," she said.

"But," I suggested, "perhaps that was the effect."

And there are important implications of this effect: It allows whites to become voyeurs of race, it targets non-white people as the only ones for whom race is an issue, and, consequently, it enables whiteness to remains invisible and unarticulated as a "color" or, more precisely, as a racial coding that intersects gender and other cultural categories.

A second rhetorical stance encouraged by a rhetoric of dysfunctional silence is defensiveness, which is a person's resisting a competing point of view in order to (1) minimize anxiety, (2) protect the ego, and (3) maintain repression ("Defense"). In terms of the Lorde-Daly debate, defensiveness emerges when Lorde claims white women have not heard black women's voices (although her imagining that Daly might hear her is clearly an attempt to interrupt this defensiveness); defensiveness also emerges when Daly claims that "for her" *Gyn/Ecology* was a project for bonding with all women (although I believe the sincerity of her claim).

As indicated by the aforementioned graduate student, in a rhetoric of dysfunctional silence, defensiveness is closely linked to denial. For example, if white feminists such as myself explain away every criticism of our actions by asserting our good intentions, then we leave no room for negotiating the (in)advertent effects of our actions or perhaps even worse assure that negotiation occurs only within our own terms. In "Race and Feminism," hooks illustrates this point:

> Whenever black women tried to express to white women their ideas about white female racism or their sense that the women who were at the forefront of the movement were not oppressed women they were told that "oppression cannot be measured." White female emphasis on "common oppression" in their appeals to black women to join the movement further alienated many black women. Because so many of the white women in the movement were employers of non-white and white domestics, their rhetoric of common oppression was experienced by black women as an assault, an expression of the bourgeois woman's insensitivity and lack of concern for the lower class woman's position in society.
>
> Underlying the assertion of common oppression was a patronizing attitude toward black women. White women were assuming that all they had to do was express a desire for sisterhood, or a desire to have black women join their groups, and black women would be overjoyed. They saw themselves as acting in a generous, open, non-racist manner and were shocked that black women responded to their overtures with anger and outrage. (144)

A defensive stance taken by white women affects everyone in that white women's defensiveness breeds non-white women's defensiveness. Pretty soon, each is seeing the other as the offender (for defensiveness presumes the existence of offensiveness). To protect ourselves from offenses (real or imagined), we all construct barriers as defenses, barriers that manifest themselves physically (who lives where), emotionally (who is friends with whom), and intellectually (whose knowledge is considered more valid). Such barriers may reinforce a rhetoric of dysfunctional silence. Yet even (especially) with U.S. history in mind, both white and non-white feminists must remain as open as possible to coalition building; otherwise, the dysfunctional silence—and the status quo—endures.

The third rhetorical stance encouraged by a rhetoric of dysfunctional silence is guilt/blame. Guilt means feeling that one has done wrong and, further, that one should feel shame and regret about having done wrong. Blame means holding someone accountable for a wrong or an unfortunate situation. In terms of the Lorde-Daly debate, the rhetorical stance of guilt/blame haunts their exchanges. Lorde may be read as blaming Daly for *Gyn/Ecology*'s methodology; Daly may be read as feeling cornered into a guilt stance. Or Daly may be read as not personally responsible for establishing the social realm in which we all dwell and, thus, as not warranting guilt or blame. The result? Guilt and blame hog the discussion and are eventually dismissed via denial and defensiveness. As a result, Lorde's concerns as well as Daly's are never given a full public hearing.

The guilt/blame stance, however, is more than an just an individual's internal or self-other dynamic. It is structurally embedded in U.S. public discourses.[9] As Lorde implies in her letter to Daly, white women often feel racial guilt or often feel as if they should feel racial guilt. While narrating her southern U.S. childhood during the first half of the twentieth-century, Lillian Smith describes this cultural pattern, explaining how awareness of racial guilt emerged early in white children and was just as quickly repressed:

> The mother who taught me what I know of tenderness and love and compassion taught me also the bleak rituals of keeping Negroes in their "place." The father who rebuked me for an air of superiority toward schoolmates from the mill and rounded out his rebuke by gravely reminding me that "all men are brothers," trained me in the steel-rigid decorums I must demand of every colored male. They who so gravely taught me to split my body from my mind and both from my "soul," taught me also to split my conscience from my acts and Christianity from southern tradition. (27)

Repressed guilt—whether southern, northern, eastern or western—is an identification that must be dealt with. But within a rhetoric of dysfunctional silence, a white woman's (or man's) dealing with repressed guilt means continually finding alternative means of repressing it.

A common dysfunctional pattern is as follows: When white women feel guilty, their ears hear criticism not as an invitation to dialogue but as blame, and because an individual white woman knows that she is not personally responsible for the history of the social realm in which we all dwell, she can refuse guilt and blame and, as a result, dismiss the initial criticism that triggered this narcissistic foray. As this silence continues, opportunities for dialogue are missed and possibilities for critiquing unearned racial privileges are occluded. In the process, opportunities for debating the initial criticism's validity is lost, which is too bad . . . because sometimes such criticisms are valid, and sometimes they are not. But until our culture makes public spaces for such discussions, such distinctions will never be made, and guilt/blame will be perpetuated within a rhetoric of dysfunctional silence.

Function 4: A rhetoric of dysfunctional silence proceeds via the interpretive trope of reading metaphorically. Because metaphor assumes that two unlike objects share a substance that marks them for comparison, the trope of reading metaphorically assumes that a text or person shares substance with all other members of its/his/her associated cultural group. In other words, this trope invites readers to assume that one member of a group represents (i.e., is practically identical to) all other members; further, it invites readers to commence down the slippery slope to unfair generalizations and, worse, to stereotyping. In the Lorde-Daly debate, reading metaphorically enables readers to agree with Lorde's assumption that *all* white women will react negatively to questions of race (again, it is precisely this trope that Lorde tries to interrupt when she reaches out to Daly). Reading metaphorically also enables readers to agree with Daly's assumption that *all* women suffer similarly under patriarchy. By focusing on substances that are similar, the trope of reading metaphorically inadvertently masks differences.

More generally, reading metaphorically enables someone functioning with a patriarchal logic to conclude, oxymoronically, that *all* women are too emotional to be effective CEOs *and* that one successful woman proves that there is no glass ceiling. Such generalizing and tokenizing both perpetuate patriarchy. When the assumption that all members of a group are practically identical is coupled with the assumption that one's own stance represents the only true knowledge, then the stage is set, so to speak, for the performance of denial ("There is no glass ceiling"), defensiveness ("Why are you talking to me about this anyway?"), and guilt/blame ("I've never personally stood in the way of any woman's advancement"). In such a metaphorically driven interpretive trope, self-other communication cannot escape the violence of identification, and the communicative excess that is not approved by dominant speakers is often expelled from consideration and, hence, erased . . . or silenced (even if "others" continue to speak it). What is also erased is a consideration of systematic sexism, racism, and unearned privileges—as well as accountability for such privileges.

So what are the limits of this rhetoric of dysfunctional silence? Quite simply the limits are lost opportunities, that is, an absence of claims about the commonality-difference debate and an absence of viable tactics for communicating across differences. Within this rhetoric, all women are hesitant to *speak* about differences and, perhaps more tragically, are often unable to *hear* them when they are spoken. As such, this rhetoric of dysfunctional silence is unacceptable: It too often assures the status quo and sets in motion the all-too-common plot of white women's priding themselves on doing the right thing (such as, Daly's deciding not to speak publicly) and non-white women feeling further marginalized (such as, Lorde's feeling that Daly refused to engage her ideas). Obviously, we need new plots and new hearings. So while I agree with Daly that women's wrangling over the question of who is more oppressed is probably a counterproductive political move, I do not agree that Lorde need be interpreted as inviting only that question. Rather, if we listen closely, Lorde may be heard as inviting questions about methodology, terminology, cultural logics, rhetorical stances, tropology, and . . . heartbreak. The question, of course, is: What ears make such a hearing possible? One response might be: ears positioned within a rhetoric of listening.

Places In-Between . . .

Moving from a rhetoric of dysfunctional silence does not mean walking from one end of a continuum to the other end where there exists an idyllic rhetoric of listening. For listening is not the polar opposite of silence, nor is it the perfect solution to all differends. Rather, as was argued in chapter 1, listening (like reading, writing, speaking, *and* silence) is a rhetorical art, a tactic of interpretive invention. And as was argued in chapter 2, if rhetorical listening is to be practiced, then new ground for this praxis must be imagined, such as, a place of non-identification that functions as a place of pause and reflection.

As T. Minh-ha Trinh has argued, this new ground must be imagined within the time and space that we live but also as a "ground that belongs to no one, not even to the creator" (932). As Gloria Anzaldúa has argued, this new ground must be imagined as *nepantla*—"an Aztec word meaning 'torn between ways,' . . . that contains in-between spaces as well as the borders of those spaces and agreed upon realities, . . . [and] involves the process of moving through these spaces from the unknown to new understandings [and identifications] and identities" (qtd. in Foss and Griffin 108–9).

This new ground emerges as a synthesis that is greater than its parts. As a result, what is rendered "excess" within a rhetoric of dysfunctional silence may become audible within a rhetoric of listening, and what is heard within a rhetoric of listening may find space to flourish. Moving from a rhetoric of dysfunctional silence to a rhetoric of listening requires, finally, a belief that such movements are worth the efforts. Though individually we may each have moments when listening appears too great an effort to imagine or enact, culturally we have no such excuse. Lives and psyches, indeed fates of nations, frequently depend on such efforts.

A Rhetoric of Listening

A rhetoric of listening is actually suggested by Daly and Lorde, with a little help from Toni Morrison. Daly implies the importance of listening when she concludes *Gyn/Ecology* by stating: "In the beginning was not the word. In the beginning is the hearing. . . . We can spin only what we hear, because we hear, and as well as we hear" (424). Complicating Daly's gendered focus on listening with race, Morrison claims that as a writer "struggling with and through a language that can powerfully evoke and enforce hidden signs of racial superiority, cultural hegemony, and dismissive 'othering' of people and language," she is forced to consider not just speaking but also listening (*Playing* x). And Lorde claims that although "[t]he white fathers told us: I think, therefore I am, [the] Black mother within each of us—the poet—whispers in our dreams: I feel, therefore I can be free" ("Poetry" 38). Yet, if the poet whispers, we must be ready and able to hear. Building on these claims, I argue that a rhetoric of listening may emerge via the following functions: (1) it is driven by an openness to terms, both negative and positive; (2) it is motivated by a cultural logic that recognizes differences as well as commonalities; (3) it offers functional rhetorical stances of recognition, critique, and accountability; and (4) it proceeds via the interpretive trope of listening metonymically.

Function 1: A rhetoric of listening focuses openly on terms (both positive and negative) in order to engage them. In terms of the Lorde-Daly debate, such an engagement might enable listeners to hear the debate's terms differently. Instead of reading the terms only as negative, listeners might also hear the terms as offering honest and painful claims that deserve further consideration. For example, Lorde's discourse might be heard as publicly laying her cards on the table, risking rejection and pain—and yet potential gain. Daly's discourse might be heard as politely declining public debate, which is not all that surprising given that U.S. culture has few terms and even fewer protocols for discussing race, especially as it intersects with gender. Perhaps listeners could then engage the debate, not by taking sides and blaming one woman or the other but rather by recognizing the potential gains and deciding to help construct more terms and protocols to foster public debates even while recognizing the uphill battles of such moves.

The dearth of such terms and protocols for public debate about race and gender is painfully obvious in dominant U.S. discourses. Consider, for example, the 13 April 2001, "debate" on *Good Morning America* between NAACP President Kweisi Mfume, who is African American, and Cincinnati Police Chief Thomas Streicher Jr., who is white. They were trying to debate publicly the protests and curfew resulting from the then recent shooting of an unarmed African American male in Cincinnati ("Cincinnati Cools"). Being open to terms (both positive and negative) will not compensate for a dearth of terms and protocols, and developing terms and protocols will not guarantee happy-ever-after endings. But combining these two moves will ensure more productive moments of debate.

Function 2: A rhetoric of listening proceeds via a cultural logic that recognizes simultaneous commonalities and differences. A rhetoric of listening interrupts the emphasis of Western logic to perpetrate either-or reasoning, for instance, to recognize commonalities or to recognize differences. Such simultaneous recognitions are important because they afford a place for productively engaging differences, especially those differences that might otherwise be relegated to the status of "excess." *Excess* refers to that which is discarded in a culture's dialogue-as-Hegelian-dialectic; that is, when the thesis and antithesis are put into play, the excess is what is left out of the resulting synthesis. An engagement with differences-as-excesses is important, for as Lorde asserts: "It is not those differences between us that are separating us. It is rather our refusal to recognize those differences, and to examine the distortions which result from our misnaming them and their effects upon human behavior and expectation" ("Age" 115).

In terms of the Lorde-Daly debate, a focus on simultaneous commonalities and differences may sidestep the binary opposition of who's right and who's wrong and, instead, translate into moves that foster win-win propositions. For example, a simultaneous focus on commonalities and differences might offer the following three moves: (1) Daly's focus on a general method, the Sado-Ritual Syndrome, may be imagined as *one of many means* of explaining both African genital mutilation and nineteenth-century American gynecology; (2) Lorde's focus on particular African women may be imagined as *one of many means* of recognizing multiplicity and explaining both African genital mutilation and nineteenth-century American gynecology; and (3) each women's focus may be laid side by side not to silence one another but to inform and challenge one another, rather like Paul D's implicit plea in Toni Morrison's *Beloved* for readers to lay our stories alongside one another. Together, these three moves expose that each of our stories—and each of our theories—are only a synecdoche, a part of something larger.

Function 3: A rhetoric of listening offers listeners three functional rhetorical stances—recognition, critique, and accountability. First, instead of the denial associated with a rhetoric of dysfunctional silence, a rhetoric of listening fosters recognition (or re-cognition as Daly might say). Such recognition does not imply a simple reversal of racist and patriarchal binaries—wherein all things white are seen as bad and all things other-than-white are seen as good or wherein all things male are seen as bad and all things female are seen as good. Such false simplicity benefits no one. Rather, recognition implies a complex understanding of how gender and race become embedded within our bodies via cultural socialization and identifications and also of how they intersect with other cultural categories, such as nationality and age, at particular historical moments to construct our personal and cultural functions and dysfunctions.

As such, recognition offers the opportunity for merging reflection with praxis, in hopes of not only reinforcing the positive personal and cultural functions but also revamping the dysfunctions. In terms of the Lorde-Daly debate, adopting the rhetorical stance of recognition might mean moving beyond the simple interpretation that Lorde speaks publicly and Daly does not. Instead, a stance of recognition might encourage listeners to examine the subject positions of Lorde and Daly as well as the 1979 historical contexts of the U.S. and feminisms that made speaking and silence (im)possible and/or (un)desirable. A stance of recognition might encourage listeners also to question which patterns of speaking and silence seem particular to the debate and which seem illustrative of more general cultural patterns in the U.S.—and why.

Recognition assumes that publicly discussing issues, such as those in the Lorde-Daly debate, might actually benefit feminism and U.S. culture at large. For as hooks claims, "I have gone back to 'confession' not as a need to tell my own story in public or to be narcissistic, but because I now realize that people really learn from the sharing of experience" (Childers and hooks 77). Realistically, recognition leaves open the possibility that silence may sometimes be the better option. But when debate is warranted (and it is warranted much more frequently than it is practiced), recognition means neither underestimating the level of preparation needed (in terms of understanding the issues and their histories) nor underestimating the trust needed for productive public debates to occur. Yet it also means acknowledging along with Adrienne Rich that "we can't wait to speak until we are perfectly clear and righteous. There is no purity, and in our lifetimes, no end to this process" ("Split" 123).

A second rhetorical stance afforded by a rhetoric of listening is critique. At our current scholarly moment, the term *critique* is under attack.[10] Associated with the dialectical tradition of Marxism, it often signifies an activity of "demystifying . . . an apparent static surface and . . . disclosing . . . an underlying process whose emergence negates, preserves, and transforms this surface" (West 143). Poststructuralism's suspicion of surface/deep structure has called that process and, hence, the term *critique* into question—and rightly so. But as poststructuralists know, a term does remain static. Thus, as I engage it here, *critique* signifies an evaluation that moves beyond easy, common-sensical interpretations (or the sense that a dominant culture holds in common); it is an evaluation that makes audible the echoes of that which is commonly rendered "excess."

Despite its troubled history, the term *critique* affords opportunities for negotiation, for questioning not just others' claims, assumptions, and conclusions but also our own. Instead of the defensiveness associated with a rhetoric of dysfunctional silence, critique puts all the claims, assumptions, and conclusions into play while continually asking: What's at stake? For whom? And why? In terms of the Lorde-Daly debate, the rhetorical stance of critique might encourage feminists, for example, to ask questions such as: "Do I understand Daly's desire for a transcultural and transhistorical method in *Gyn/Ecology*? Do I understand why Lorde was so troubled by this method? What historical conditions, other than Lorde's and Daly's good intentions, were in play in this debate? Do I cite non-white feminists' texts only when I'm discussing race? What different answers might there be to the aforementioned questions? and What cultural logics might undergird the different answers?

Such critique assumes the existence of multiple questions, multiple answers to each question, and multiple places from which to speak and listen. It assumes places of identification, disidentification, and non-identification, wherein subject and cultural positions are always already in play just as they are always already weighted with history and culture. Such critique may seem scary to people occupying traditionally privileged cultural positions because they may feel their unearned privileges threatened; such critique may also seem scary to people occupying traditionally nonprivileged cultural positions because they may not be able to pull on the power of tradition to model their efforts. But what both sides may draw on is a concept of fair play and equal opportunity, both deeply engrained concepts in U.S. culture. For as exemplified by the women's movement, such fears need not prevent action: Women's entering the workforce in greater numbers during the past thirty years in the U.S. has not destroyed the family, men's power, or the economy; neither has lack of a dominant workplace tradition kept women from making inroads in the workplace.

A third rhetorical stance engendered by a rhetoric of listening is accountability. Instead of the backward-looking stance of guilt/blame, which is so often associated with a rhetoric of dysfunctional silence, accountability offers forward-looking ways to address not just individual errors but also unearned structural privileges, which are grounded in the-past-that-is-always-present. As discussed in chapter 1, accountability means *recognizing* the complex interweavings of gender, race, and other cultural categories within a culture and *critiquing* these interweavings so as to determine the most expedient, productive praxes for the many, the few, and the one. Determining who should be given priority—the many, the few, or the one—depends on each situation, and listeners must be accountable for such prioritizing. In terms of the Lorde-Daly debate, my stated purpose is not to hold these two women guilty or innocent for their actions, as if I were some all-knowing judge or jury. Instead, my purpose is to hold myself accountable for how I listen to their debate and for what I choose to offer (or not offer) in return.

Function 4: A rhetoric of listening proceeds via the interpretive trope of listening metonymically. Metonym signifies figurative juxtaposition; it assumes that two objects do not share a common substance but are rather merely associated, hence its prominence in poststructuralist theory. For example, metonym occurs when we say, "The chair speaks." Literally, of course, a chair does not speak; the person who is head of a committee does. In such figuration, the chair and the person do not share a substance but are merely associated with one another. Thus, the trope of listening metonymically assumes that a text or person does not share substance with all other members of its/his/her cultural group but, rather, is associated with them. In other words, this trope invites listeners to assume that one member of a group (say, one woman) does *not* speak for all other members (say, all women); as such, this trope helps listeners avoid the trap of unfair generalizations and stereotyping.

In the Lorde-Daly debate, listening metonymically enables listeners to hear Lorde's claim that white women react negatively to questions of race and understand that Lorde may be illustrating a general cultural pattern, not necessarily describing the actions of each and every white woman in the U.S. Listening metonymically also enables listeners to hear Daly's claim that women suffer similarly under patriarchy and understand that Daly may be illustrating a general transcultural pattern, not necessarily claiming that all women suffer identically under patriarchy. In this way, general cultural patterns may be recognized, critiqued, and accounted for without sliding down the slippery slope to stereotyping. By focusing on common patterns as well as acknowledging differences within these patterns, the tactic of listening metonymically assumes the presence of commonalities and differences and actively engages both.

As becomes evident, a rhetoric of listening with its terms, cultural logic, rhetorical stances, and interpretive trope is not a step-by-step developmental model, like Jean Piaget's or Elisabeth Kubler-Ross's. Instead, the terms, cultural logic, stances, and trope are recursively intertwined, emerging from and also (re)constructing a rhetoric of listening within which feminists and others may unite reflection and praxis. Within such a rhetoric lies the potential to turn denial into recognition, defensiveness into critique, and guilt/ blame into accountability.

Implications for Rhetoric and Composition Studies

The implications of listening metonymically within a rhetoric of listening are many. It allows feminist methodologies of commonalities and differences to coexist; it provides *a,* not *the,* model for feminists and others to communicate across differences; it allows feminist reflective practice to be just that, an interanimation of reflection and praxis; it foregrounds how race and gender intersect in feminist analyses; and it provides another possible interpretation for the Lorde-Daly debate, an interpretation that respects speaking as well silence, an interpretation that posits listening as both prior to and subsequent to speaking. Finally, it allows listeners to model scholarship on Daly's method while learning from Lorde's critique, and just as importantly, it allows listeners to model scholarship on Lorde's method while learning from Daly's critique.

Within our particular cultural moment, feminists have come to terms with the facts that *all* our bodies are marked by all kinds of intersecting cultural categories. In terms of how gender and race are marked on bodies, some particularly useful critiques are Elizabeth Abel's "Black Writing, White Reading: Race and the Politics of Feminist Interpretation," Ana Castillo's *Massacre of the Dreamers,* Helen Fox's *When Race Breaks Out,* Ruth Frankenberg's *White Women, Race Matters: The Social Construction of Whiteness,* Toni Morrison's *Playing in the Dark: Whiteness and the Literary Imagination,* and Lynn Worsham's story of Blue Betty in "After Words." But I want to give the last word to Lorde, for in "Poetry Is Not a Luxury," she quite lyrically sums up the potential of a rhetoric of listening:

> Sometimes we drug ourselves with dreams of new ideas. The head will save us. The brain alone will set us free. But there are no new ideas waiting in the wings to save us as women, as human. There are only old and forgotten ones, new combinations, extrapolations and recognitions from within ourselves—along with the renewed courage to try them out. (38)

4

Eavesdropping: A Tactic for Listening to Scholarly Discourses

> —what's taught, what's overheard.
> > —Adrienne Rich, "Inscriptions"

> There are some things I can't explain to white people. Words aren't enough.
> > —Annawake Fourkiller in Barbara
> > Kingsolver's *Pigs in Heaven*

> What would I do white?
> I would do nothing.
> That would be enough.
>
> > —June Jordan, "What Would I Do White"

> Nothing has trained me for this.
> > —Adrienne Rich, "Split at the Root"

To continue the project of conceptualizing and defining tactics of rhetorical listening, this chapter offers a second tactic: eavesdropping. Recovered from its negative connotations of busybodiness, *eavesdropping* is posited here as an ethical tactic for resisting the invisibility of a gendered whiteness in scholarly discourses within rhetoric and composition studies. Why recover eavesdropping? After completing *Anglo-American Feminist Challenges to the Rhetorical Traditions: Virginia Woolf, Mary Daly, Adrienne Rich,* I was left wondering how whiteness informs these three feminist theories of rhetoric as well as how a gendered whiteness plays out more generally in rhetorical studies? These questions, combined with a fortuitous overhearing at a 1997 4C's cocktail party, led me to a consideration of eavesdropping.

At the cocktail party, I overheard an unidentified male voice behind me say, "I guess it's hip to be a white guy again, huh?" I immediately wondered,

"How did whiteness become a hip topic at cocktail parties? And does he think it's hip to be a white 'gal,' too?" After returning home, I wondered some more: "How does history function so as to make such comments possible? What exactly does it mean to be a *white guy*? And how does all of this inform rhetoric and composition studies?" My overhearing of the cocktail-guy's comment and my subsequent questions have haunted me ever since, ultimately compelling me to propose eavesdropping as a one tactic of rhetorical listening that may be employed to investigate intersections of history, whiteness, and rhetoric in scholarly discourses.

In the U.S., scholarly discussions of history and rhetoric have rarely included whiteness. Instead, when rhetoric was first recovered for composition studies, rhetorical theories were presented as a/historical structures that may lifted from fourth and fifth century B.C.E. Greece and dropped into, say, twentieth-century U.S. politics in an effort to persuade, say, Southern Democrats to vote for Richard Nixon circa 1968 and George W. Bush circa 2000. The idea was that rhetorical theories are timeless—their applications, time-bound. This idea has been challenged by scholars, such as James Berlin, who argue that rhetorical theories are not timeless but, rather, always grounded in the sites of their origins ("Revisionary" 115). This idea has also been challenged by scholars, again such as Berlin, who argue that rhetorical theories are always grounded in their sites of usage in ways that remake, not simply lift, the theories (116).

Often remaking is posited as a potentially positive move. And rightly so. Note Susan Jarratt's feminist transformations of sophistic rhetorical theory in *Rereading the Sophists* and Cheryl Glenn's feminist transformations of classical rhetorical theory in *Rhetoric Retold*. But what happens when remaking is not a positive move, when it is what John Poulakos calls "dysfunctional"? (90). For example, what happens when remaking denies the influence of cultural categories, such as whiteness? One answer is that such remakings circumscribe the possibilities of rhetorical theories and rhetorical usages.[1]

To heed Adrienne Rich's advice "*[t]o come to terms with the circumscribing nature of (our) whiteness,*" rhetoric and composition studies needs to factor whiteness into its theories and praxes ("Notes" 219). Given the absence of whiteness in many of our disciplinary conversations, however, we may first need to define the term. In the past decade, whiteness studies has emerged as an academic enterprise attempting to articulate such a definition by analyzing and critiquing how *whiteness* functions in U.S. culture, both productively and dysfunctionally.[2] Despite its antiracist agenda, whiteness studies has been questioned by scholars of both feminist and critical race studies: Is it really a forum for laying all our cultural cards on the table in order to facilitate more honest negotiations about and across differences, *or* is it just a forum for rechanneling money and attention to whitefolks, particularly the boys? (Talbot 118). In its best efforts, whiteness studies questions the dominant culture's tendency to define *race* in terms of a black/white binary while only articulating blackness. This field acknowledges that whiteness speaks as does the slash mark. And it argues that because whiteness is impossible to understand apart from its intersections with gender, class, age, and other factors (Thompson 94), whiteness functions differently not just for whites and non-whites[3] but for particular people within each category and for multiethnic people straddling these categories.

Despite the recent emergence of whiteness studies, whiteness is hardly a new topic. Out of necessity, non-whites have been quite savvy in articulating the power, privilege, and violence of whiteness throughout U.S. history. Out of privilege, many whites have refused to see it, let alone critique its dysfunctions. But not all whites. In the 1940s, Lillian Smith named and critiqued whiteness in *Killers of the Dream* (her 1949 autobiography of growing up white and female in the South) and kissed a writerly reputation goodbye, at least for that particular moment; in the 1960s, *Killers* was embraced by the civil rights movement and reprinted; in the 1970s, the book was celebrated by the white feminist movement; and in the midst of the whiteness studies explosion of the 1990s, it was again reissued. What accounts for these different receptions? Not the "rhetorical stance" of Smith (Booth 111), not the "rhetorical situation" of her audiences (Bitzer 6), not even their respective "discourse communities" (J. Harris 101–2). Rather the difference lies in the circling of time, that is, when bodies, tropes, and cultures converge, making possible moments of rhetorical usage. Only in these moments of convergence, when bodies are troped and tropes are embodied, may personal and/or cultural change be effected.

As I listen to echoes of the cocktail guy's comment, it strikes me that one way to make possible these moments of convergence is by eavesdropping. As a result, this chapter (1) redefines *eavesdropping* as an ethical rhetorical tactic and posits it as a means for investigating history, whiteness, and rhetoric; (2) offers eavesdropping as a mode of historiography, or thinking about history, that shifts our emphasis from origins to usage, foregrounding how we may circle through history even as history circles through us; (3) employs eavesdropping to trace the trope of whiteness in the U.S., not to provide a comprehensive definition but to expose its dysfunctions; and (4) uses eavesdropping to circle through history to argue that, within the U.S., the dysfunctions of whiteness have remade rhetorical theory in ways that circumscribe available agencies.

Eavesdropping: Rhetorical Tactic, Tactical Ethic

As Lynn Worsham mused in an e-mail response to an early draft of these ideas, differences exist between accidental overhearing and purposeful eavesdropping. Her musings started me thinking: If my overhearing of the cocktail guy's comment was accidental yet productive, perhaps such productivity could be more systematically tapped if purposeful overhearing, or eavesdropping, were imagined as a rhetorical tactic. Given the negative connotations linked with *eavesdropping,* such a claim begs, at the very least, questions of definition, justification, ethics, and pragmatics. In this section, I explore these questions in order to demonstrate that eavesdropping may be employed effectively not only as a rhetorical tactic but also as an ethical choice, or tactical ethic.

To define *eavesdropping* for rhetoric and composition studies, I invoke one aspect of Mary Daly's method of "gynocentric writing"—that is, uncovering gender potentialities in words by studying their dictionary definitions, reworking them, and excavating their etymologies (24). The goal of Daly's method is to expose gendered dismissals of words and mine their "'obsolete' meanings" (24). For *eavesdrop,* a common dictionary definition is "to listen secretly to the private conversations of others" (*Webster's New World*). At first glance, this definition connotes a gendered dismissal of the term, a dismissal accomplished by associating *eavesdropping* with a feminine busybodiness—remember, for example, Gladys Kravitz, the nosy neighbor on the television series *Bewitched*? But at second hearing, this definition resonates with Daly-esque possibilities. I found Old English etymologies of *eaves* suggesting "edge" and "margin" and "border" (*Webster's New World; New Shorter OED*); I found an archaic definition of *eavesdropping* suggesting "to learn or overhear" (*Webster's Third*); and I found a Middle English definition of *eavesdropper* suggesting "one who stands on the eavesdrop [the spot where water drops from the eaves] in order to listen to conversations inside the house" (*Random House*).

Together, these lexical threads weave a composite of *eavesdropping* that signifies an effective rhetorical tactic. Its moves include: choosing to stand outside . . . in an uncomfortable spot . . . on the border of knowing and not knowing . . . granting others the inside position . . . listening to learn. From such a composite, *eavesdropping* emerges not as a gendered busybodiness but as a rhetorical tactic of purposely positioning oneself on the edge of one's own knowing so as to overhear and learn from others and, I would add, from oneself.

Such a tactic is needed because in our daily exchanges we are too often positioned like viewers of *Bewitched,* seduced into identifying with the main characters of cultural discourses just as viewers are charmed into identifying with Samantha and Darrin. In *The Other Side of Language: A Philosophy of Listening,* philosophy professor Gemma Corradi Fiumara contends that the "bewitchment of these authoritative voices appears to persist as long as they address us directly" (58). But what if we position ourselves so that these "authoritative voices" are not addressing us directly? What if we position ourselves as the eavesdropper? In other words, what if we align ourselves with Gladys Kravitz, granting her the presumption of truth instead of laughing at her? (She was right, you know, at least most of the time.) When we choose to position ourselves thusly, we hear differently. And the results may just be worthwhile. According to Fiumara, "listening creates a minimal but fertile logical passage which will then allow our minds to move with greater freedom and envisage still further ways of approaching reality" (161). Moreover, Fiumara claims, "the more one listens the more one is absorbed by an awareness of the fragility of our [own] doctrines" (191). In other words, eavesdropping is a tactic for listening to the discourses of others, for hearing over the edges of our own knowing, for thinking what is commonly unthinkable within our own logics.

A process for listening to the discourses of others is described in chapter 1 as "first, acknowledging the existence of these discourses; second, listening for the (un)conscious presences, absences, unknowns; and third, consciously integrating this information into our world views and decision making" (see p. 29). This claim about rhetorical listening benefits from being considered alongside rhetorical eavesdropping. For eavesdropping, as one kind of rhetorical listening, more sharply tunes listeners into "private conversations of others," conversations in which eavesdroppers are not directly addressed (*Webster's New World*). But such eavesdropping demands an accompanying ethic of care.

Eavesdropping as rhetorical tactic raises questions of ethics because it demands a consideration of how the self and other find a way of being together in the world. The first ethical issue to consider is the belief that eavesdropping is an invasion of privacy. Within the common definition, this belief is valid. But within my reworked definition, this claim is groundless. For rhetorical eavesdropping entails positioning oneself to overhear both oneself and others, listening to learn, and most importantly, being *careful* (i.e., full of care) not to overstep another's boundaries or interrupt the agency of another's discourse. The second ethical issue to consider is the danger of romanticizing the outsider's position. Rhetorical eavesdropping is not the rhetorical version of "slumming," which condescendingly reinscribes existing cultural positions. Rather, without denying the very real power differentials of existing cultural positions, rhetorical eavesdropping assumes that *all* cultural positions possess an inside and an outside, the trick for eavesdroppers being to find an outside position where they are not directly addressed. The third ethical issue to consider is one's own willingness not just to eavesdrop but to hear. For, as Fiumara asserts,

> [I]n our basic logic it is only possible to advocate an ethical attitude with regard to something or someone who can *say something to us,* someone who can make himself heard. And yet the point at issue is whether we are capable of hearing a message and whether we select or predetermine what we hear. (61–62)

This claim warrants further reflection on all our parts because it challenges us to question our defensiveness. Given all these ethical issues, an eavesdropper must take care, at all times, not to fall into old patterns but to eavesdrop with care, respect, and reflection.

One path of reflection leads to the pragmatic: How does rhetorical eavesdropping play out in daily life? A person may eavesdrop on him- or herself, on other people's conversations, on written texts, on TV advertisements. The possibilities are endless. For example, when I am talking to my daughter in my mother's voice (double meaning intended), perhaps I should mentally shift my rhetorical positioning and eavesdrop on myself from my daughter's point of hearing. When my students are talking before class about one of our readings (when they know I am in the room and can hear them even though they are not directly addressing me), perhaps I should eavesdrop and use their questions, concerns, and applications as a way into class discussions. When I am reading a scholarly text on an unfamiliar subject, perhaps I should approach the text by trying to weave the edges of my knowledge into the article's claims. And when I am viewing a TV ad for a political candidate I dislike, perhaps I should heed why its addressed audience finds it so compelling. In each instance, eavesdropping enhances critical thinking, helping me better assess the situation.

Will eavesdropping work well in all situations? Will it work equally well for people in all cultural positions? Will it expose that the unthinkable is always a better way of thinking? The answer to all these questions is obvious: of course not. As with all rhetorical tactics, *kairos* factors into usage. But eavesdropping as a rhetorical tactic possesses potential for mapping places of identification, disidentification, and non-identification. In this way, eavesdropping may be employed generally as a tactical ethic; it may also be employed specifically here as a rhetorical tactic to intervene in scholarly debates about the structuring of history, whiteness, and rhetoric.

The Uses of History, History as Usage

In the U.S., the dominant narrative mode for thinking about history at this century's beginning is an origins mode, one that begins at the beginning (which is assumed to be obvious) and moves in a linear, evolutionary progression. Despite journalistic warnings about Gen-X's and Gen-Y's economic regression, many undergraduate students deeply desire and defend the origins mode. So does mainstream U.S. culture. So, too, do some of our histories of rhetoric, as Berlin explains:

> Our "official" histories of rhetoric—the formulations of George Kennedy (1980a) and Edward P. J. Corbett (1990) and Brian Vickers (1990) and Wilbur Samuel Howell (1971)—for example, depict rhetoric's historical trajectory as a march of ideas, ideas characterized as unified, coherent, and rational. ("Revisionary Histories" 112)

The appealing features of the origins mode are obvious; the unappealing ones, less so. What gets displaced in the origins mode is the presence of the past in the present, that is, the *then-that-is-now;* what gets further displaced is people's sense of accountability for the *then-that-is-now.*

Although rhetorical theorists have challenged the origins mode in order to rethink rhetorical history (e.g., Victor Vitanza's excellent 1994 collection *Writing Histories of Rhetoric*),[4] I offer yet another challenge to the origins' mode of historiography, one that foregrounds our accountability for the *then-that-is-now* in our daily lives. By invoking Martin Heidegger, W. E. B. Du Bois, and Toni Morrison, I offer a mode of historiography that not only shifts our focus from origins to usage but demonstrates how we may eavesdrop on history, circling through time in order to expose the circling of time. Such a mode will help us analyze in the next section our accountability in terms of whiteness.

In *What Is Called Thinking?* Heidegger ponders the connections among the movement of time, the movement of thinking, and the sphere of language (what we might today call discourse). For Heidegger, sometimes the "only way to go forward is to return to the origins and seek a new beginning" (Gray xxv), and he believes that the vehicle for circling through time is language—"that sphere in which man can dwell aright and make clear to himself who he is" (xix). Heidegger is obviously not imagining time travel but mind travel—circling back to "the origins" to trace how a historical moment emerges, how it gets constructed, how it becomes not just a past fact (something that happened) but a historical fact (something that happened and is preserved within cultural discourses) (E. H. Carr 10).

Heidegger's circling through time is exemplified in Du Bois's "Dialogue with a White Friend" in which Du Bois replies to a fictional white friend's claim of white superiority:

> You are obsessed by the swiftness of the gliding of the sled at the bottom of the hill. You say: what tremendous power must have caused its speed, and how wonderful is Speed. You think of the rider as the originator and inventor. You admire his poise and *sang-froid*, his utter self-absorption. You say: surely here is the son of God and he shall reign forever and ever.
>
> You are wrong, quite wrong. Away back on the level stretches of the mountain tops in the forests, amid drifts and driftwood, this sled was slowly and painfully pushed on its little hesitating start. It took power, but the power of sweating, courageous men, not of demigods. As the sled slowly started and gained momentum, it was the Law of Being that gave it speed, and the grace of God that steered its lone, scared passengers. Those passengers, white, black, red and yellow, deserve credit for their balance and pluck. But many times it was sheer luck that made the road not land the white man in the gutter, as it had others so many times before, and as it may him yet. He has gone farther than others because of others whose very falling made hard ways iced and smooth for him to traverse. His triumph is not a triumph of himself alone, but of humankind, from the pusher in the primeval forests to the last flier through the winds of the twentieth century. (36–37)

This passage not only exemplifies Heidegger's concept of circling through time but also exposes this concept's danger and difficulty. The danger lies in embracing false origins, such as the sled at the bottom of the hill; in this instance, embracing false origins erases our knowledge of common effort and, hence, undermines our imperative for common good. The difficulty lies in establishing true origins, such as the sled in the primeval forest. If (and let me stress *if*) true origins exist as single, causal phenomena, they may have occurred within our past but outside of our history, in which case they are either forgotten or remembered today as myths, legends, folklore, or speculation; as such, they may challenge the limits of our historical knowledge, but often they do not receive the same respect as historical knowledge. If (and let me again stress *if*) true origins exist as complicated, interwoven webs of phenomena, then they may be impossible to pinpoint exactly (read: *empirically*) (Mountford, par. 4).

So to sidestep this danger and this difficulty, let us shift our thinking about history from origins to usage. Let us heed Heidegger's advice and mind travel . . . but with a twist: Instead of focusing on traveling back *to* a moment of origin, let us focus on traveling back *from* a particular moment of usage. From a moment of usage, we may find ourselves circling back through/out historical narratives, finding pertinent threads (not origins in the traditional sense), and weaving our way forward to our current moment.[5] This shift from origins to usage is more than the rhetorical sophistry denigrated by Plato; it is the rhetorical sophistry defined by Jarratt, a sophistry that links history to bodies, tropes, and cultures (*Rereading* 11–12), a sophistry that does not forsake truth and ethics but demands their continual negotiation within different moments of usage.

What emerges if we lay this usage-based mode of historiography (circling through time) alongside Morrison's concept of rememory (the circling of time)? In *Beloved*, *rememory* signifies the embodied circling of time via identifications and disidentifications. It is an insidious embodiment for Sethe Suggs, the escaped slave who kills her two-year-old daughter rather than let her be taken back to the horrors of slavery on a farm called Sweet Home. According to Morrison's narrator, rememory is triggered for Sethe by a smell, a sound, a touch: "and suddenly there was Sweet Home rolling, rolling, rolling out before her eyes, and although there was not a leaf on that farm that did not make her want to scream, it rolled itself out before her in shameless beauty" (6). In this way, rememory has an agency all its own. It returns whether or not Sethe wants it to (14)—sometimes falsely (6), sometimes releasing repressed memories (61–62) but always serving as a testament to her seemingly infinite capacity to hear bad things (70).

Despite these inescapable identifications, Sethe and other characters assert some agency over rememory, at least for a while, via these coping strategies: Sethe can "[beat] back the past" by kneading dough every morning (73), by folding and doublefolding sheets (61), or by rubbing the leg of someone she loves (72); Paul D can "leave it alone" (71). But denial and forgetfulness are ultimately not only not possible, they are dangerous. For as Sethe warns her daughter Denver, "[I]f you go there—you who never was there—if you go there and stand in the place where it was, it will happen again; it will be there for you, waiting for you" (36). Ultimately, the characters (and the readers) must wrestle with the past just as Sethe wrestles with Beloved, who represents not only the ghost of Sethe's long-dead daughter but also the "Sixty Million and more" slaves to whom Morrison dedicates her book. Readers learn what Paul D and Sethe learn: to put our stories next to someone who "is a friend of [our] mind" (272–73) and to realize that we are our own "best thing" (273).

This love ethic—both love of others and love of self—tenders us the agency for escaping the repetitive circling of denial and the idealized dream of forgetfulness. It offers a means for telling our rememories as stories, using them as a means for getting on with our lives. As represented in this novel, Morrison's concept of rememory exposes that the past is not simply a series of fixed points on an abstract historical continuum but rather a series of inscriptions not just in discourse but in our material bodies, inscriptions that continually circle through our present and inform our identities, inscriptions that will control us if we do not acknowledge them and pass them on.

What emerges from laying a revised Heideggerian circling through time alongside Morrison's circling of time is a concept of the past that haunts the present. This past is both a cultural structure and an individual embodiment of that structure, with the embodiment being different in different people depending upon their experiences and identifications with/in the cultural structure. Within this usage mode of historiography, when we deal with the past, it strengthens us (like Denver, we can walk off the porch). When we do not deal, it saps our strength, relegating us either to emotional prisonhouses (like Paul D's rusty tin box of a heart) or to endless repetitions of the moments that landed us here (like Sethe's rememories of Sweet Home). When we shift narrative modes of historiography—that is, when we reject the dominant (and oh-so-desired) origin-to-happily-*ever-after* mode and embrace a not-so-dominant (and let's be honest, not-so-desired) usage-as-*ever-present* mode—we recognize that narratives of history refuse to give up the ghost, so to speak, until (like Denver, Paul D, and Sethe) we refuse to pass on them so that, in turn, we can garner the strength to pass them on. Within such a recognition of history, when we eavesdrop, circling through time to expose the circling of time, we not only identify some of our identifications but also find ourselves accountable to ourselves and to others not for the *then* but for the *then-that-is-now.*

The Trope of Whiteness, Whiteness as Embodied Trope

In the U.S., one site of usage (and accountability) for the *then-that-is-now* is the trope of whiteness. In this section, I first define the terms *trope* and *whiteness;* then I circle through history, eavesdropping, to expose how this trope resonates at *this* particular moment of usage. When tracing the trope of whiteness, I focus only on its dysfunctions as they are articulated by non-whites and by whites. Though by no means a comprehensive definition, what follows may help us analyze in the next section how these dysfunctions help remake rhetorical theory.

Simply put, tropes are figures of speech. They influence signification, or how meanings are made within discourse(s). Most commonly, tropes are defined as rhetorical figures, such as metaphor, metonymy, analogy, and aposiopesis. Although such tropes are sometimes defined as the dressing of thought or as a deviation from ordinary expression, they are much, much more (Corbett 459). Tropes designate the movement of a text, as when a prosecuting attorney employs a one-two-three domino analogy to simplify a complex web of causation. Indeed, tropes designate the very movement of language itself. Because all language is inherently figurative (i.e., because a term always signifies something other than the term itself), all terms are tropes.

Although tropes are terms within discourse, the socially constructed attitudes and actions associated with these terms become embodied in all of us (albeit differently) via our cultural socialization; for example, in the U.S., we are born into discourse communities wherein the term *student* signifies certain attitudes and actions about learning and classroom behavior. Once embodied, these tropes with their associated attitudes and actions may (un)-consciously inform our own attitude and actions. This chicken-and-egg cycle continues in perpetuity, with discourse socializing people and people accepting, resisting, and/or revising this socialization via discursive practices.

Because socially constructed categories (*student, teacher, dean, gender, race, class*) are terms and because all terms are tropes, it stands to reason that the term *whiteness* is a trope. Further, because all tropes are embodied, it stands to reason that whiteness with its associated actions and attitudes is embodied in all of us (albeit differently) via our socialization. But the real issue is: What do we do with this trope and its embodiment, both culturally and individually? Academic whiteness studies attempts to answer this question. For example, in *How the Irish Became White,* Noel Ignatiev explores whiteness in terms of Irish immigration and assimilation in the nineteenth-century United States: "This book looks at how one group of people became white. Put another way, it asks how the Catholic Irish, an oppressed race in Ireland, became part of an oppressing race in America" (1). The productive side is that, in becoming white, the Irish could "sell themselves piecemeal instead of being sold for life, and later they could compete for jobs in all spheres instead of being confined to certain work"; indeed, the Irish men (if not women) could begin taking advantage of the full rights of citizenship (2–3), thus extending the cultural map of privilege. The dysfunctional side (in addition to the aforementioned gender bias) is that in becoming white, the Irish did not alter the cultural structure of oppression but simply managed to literally work themselves into the white category, inadvertently reinforcing already existing oppressive cultural patterns for those still categorized as non-white (e.g., American Indians, Chicanos/as, African Americans). Is Irish assimilation more complicated than simply a focus on economics and whiteness? Yes, absolutely. It is complicated by factors such as the nation's industrial status, religion, regional politics, and other factors. But Ignatiev's point is this: Whiteness is a factor.

As a trope, whiteness designates both people and practices.[6] Yet as AnnLouise Keating reminds us, a "conditional" relationship exists between white people and white practices: That is, while not everyone can be classified as a white person, everyone can perform white practices (907). Performing whiteness is often a very visible practice for non-white people. "Acting white" on the job or in school may garner promotions or good grades (or in the case of a comedy routine by Paul Rodriguez or Chris Rock, lots of laughter), but it may also garner charges of betraying one's roots, as Milwaukee high school student Brandle Morrow discovered when "some of his classmates equat[ed his] good grades, studiousness and proper speech to 'acting white'" (Thomas-Lynn). Sadly, such accusations position students like Morrow in a double-bind: damned by some of their peers if they identify with school success, damned by the school if they identify with some of their peers.

Conversely, performing whiteness is often an invisible practice for white people, many of whom assume that not thinking about whiteness is the norm. Like any trope, *whiteness* is historically and locally grounded (gaining linguistic currency in the North American colonies in the seventeenth century), always already evolving, and open to multiple interpretations. But as American studies professor Ruth Frankenberg reminds us, in the U.S., whiteness has consistently signified privilege—a privilege that fosters stasis by resisting and denying differences (*White* 236–37).[7]

When defining privilege, Stephanie M. Wildman and Adrienne D. Davis name three of its elements: (1) "the characteristics of the privileged group define the social norm"; (2) "privileged group members can rely on their privilege and avoid objecting to oppression"; and (3) "privilege is rarely seen by the holder of the privilege" (658). This latter unseen feature of white privilege is explained by historian David Roediger: "Whiteness describes, from Little Bighorn to Simi Valley, not a culture but precisely the absence of culture. It is the empty and therefore terrifying attempt to build an identity based on what one isn't [whiteness is often defined in terms of what it is not—*not* African American, *not* Latina, *not* Chippewa, etc.] and on whom one can hold back" (qtd. in Talbot 118). My hope is that, if white privilege cannot be seen, perhaps it can be heard via rhetorical listening.

In the previous two paragraphs (and in subsequent paragraphs), I examine the trope of whiteness as practiced by non-whites and whites, a questionable method in that it establishes a too-simple binary between whites and non-whites. Joyce Middleton argues this very point in "Kris, I Hear You," a *JAC* reader response to an earlier published version of this chapter that classified responses in terms of whites and people of color: "The repetitive pattern of 'white people' and 'people of color' . . . reinforces a reductive binary of 'white' and 'Other'—as if white is not a color" (439). Although erasing color from whiteness was not my intent, I acknowledge that it may be an effect (for as we all know, it is the gap between intent and effect that gives rise to the need for rhetorical negotiation). As an alternative, Middleton turns to the work of Richard Dyer and suggests the terms *white* and *non-white* (439). Initially suspicious of these terms because they position *white* as the central term, I decided after careful consideration that such a move may be effective in making whiteness visible, especially in a culture in which whiteness is dominant yet too often rendered invisible.

But while Middleton's suggested usage may address her concern about foregrounding white as a color, it does not really address her "reductive binary" issue. For the non-white/white binary continues to elide differences, specifically multiethnic people who have a foot in each category or who have a foot in multiple subcategories. Still, given the history and power dynamics associated with racial categories in the U.S., I find it useful to analyze how whiteness (as a dominant term) has functioned similarly and differently for those marked as white and for those marked as non-white. My purpose is neither to reinscribe these categories nor to presume a biological grounding for their existence. Rather, my purpose is, first, to demonstrate how the categories have both changed over time and place and/or resisted change and, second, to explore how this change and/or resistance has informed rhetorical studies in the U.S.

As a trope that fosters stasis by resisting and denying differences, whiteness has very real implications in everyone's daily life. Non-whites and whites have astutely articulated these implications—sometimes as survival strategies, sometimes as political and/or ethical moves, sometimes as both. One example of white privilege in U.S. culture is that people marked as non-white have often been forced to articulate whiteness as a survival strategy while people marked as white have had some choice in the matter. As a result of this choice, when many whites are asked what it means to be white in the U.S., they simply stare blankly. Either they have never thought about it (because they don't have to) or they are afraid of answering for fear of being associated with extremist racist organizations, such as the KKK, who have for too long claimed whiteness as their own turf and defined it in their own terms. Notable exceptions are Frankenberg, Roediger, Smith, and Dalton Conley, whose 2001 autobiography *Honky* provides a witty yet searing commentary on the intersections of whiteness and class.

Non-whites claim that in the U.S., whiteness signifies a myriad of things, ranging from acting white to terror. The core of this terror—white violence and its effects on everyone—is captured in Claude McKay's 1922 poem "The Lynching": a lynched African American man is described as a "swinging char," a "ghastly body swinging in the sun" (335.8, 10); white observers are described as

> never a one
> Showed sorrow in her eyes of steely blue;
> And little lads, lynchers that were to be,

Danced round the dreadful thing in fiendish glee.

$$(335.11-14)$$

In this poem, the effects of white violence are shown to be marked both on the terrorized (those who are lynched) and on the terrorizers (those who lynch). The power of McKay's poem is that it speaks a very real social trauma that was either unspoken or unheard in the public sphere until Ida B. Wells and others launched public antilynching campaigns. The risks of McKay's poem are, first, that it may be read as reducing all African American men as victims and all white men as lynchers and, second, that it may be dismissed because exceptions to these claims can be named.

To counter these risks, bell hooks offers two useful tactics that both speak the terror and its exceptions. First, in "Representing Whiteness in the Black Imagination," hooks argues that representations of terror (like McKay's) emerge not from African Americans' stereotypes about all white people but rather from African Americans' ethnographic observations of some white people, that is, those who perpetuate the violence as well as those who enable the violence by standing silently by. Ethnographic observation of white people has often functioned as an African American survival mechanism throughout U.S. history—from centuries of slavery to contemporary prison demographics, welfare reforms, corporate glass ceilings, even unwelcoming classrooms (338–40). This is a survival strategy all too familiar to marginalized groups. Second, to deal with this *then-that-is-now* terror, hooks offers a simple yet difficult tactic that we would all do well to adopt: understanding how whiteness functions culturally without resorting to an essential us-versus-them mentality that plays into the white desire for stasis. Her strategy is one that both she and a white male friend have employed: "Understanding how racism works, he can see the way in which whiteness acts to terrorize without seeing himself as bad, or, all white people as bad, and black people as good" (346). Such an understanding recognizes resonances of cultural tropes—in this case the resonance of *terror* with *whiteness*—without stereotyping all white people as equally guilty of perpetuating terror or all non-whites as equally victimized by it.

Non-whites also claim that whiteness in the U.S. signifies the drive to consume others' lands and cultures. In his 1860 "What Shall We Do with the White People?" William J. Wilson describes how white consumption functions in the U.S.: "Restless, grasping, unsatiated [whites] are ever on the lookout for not what is, or ought to be theirs, but for what they can get" (59). Although consumption (as an economic term) initially appears more closely aligned with class issues of capitalism than with race, the history of U.S. capital flowing mainly through white men (and off the backs and lands of non-white men and women) renders some *then-that-was-now* effects today even as these effects are changing.

In addition, Alice Walker exposes that white consumption has some *then-that-was-now* effects that are not just economic but cultural: She believes that implicit in a "melting pot" mentality is actually a way of normalizing difference in terms of whiteness. Walker specifies this claim in her 1981 "The Dummy in the Window: Joel Chandler Harris and the Invention of Uncle Remus," wherein she argues that, by inserting Uncle Remus into the African folktales of Brer Fox and Brer Rabbit, Harris robbed Walker of her heritage:

> How did he steal it? By making me feel ashamed of it. In creating Uncle Remus, he placed an effective barrier between me and the stories that meant so much to me, the stories that could have meant so much to all of our children, the stories that they would have heard from their own people and not from Walt Disney. (239)

Because whiteness is a trope that influences all people in the U.S., the economic and cultural consumption associated with whiteness is not limited to white bodies. This consumption is embodied in Lyman Lamartine, a Chippewa entrepreneur in Louise Erdrich's *Love Medicine*. It drives him to turn the tables on white people by opening a bingo palace: "He'd . . . teach Chippewas the right ways, the proper ways, the polite ways to take money from retired white people who had farmed Indian hunting grounds, lived high while their neighbors lived low, looked down or never noticed who was starving, who was lost" (327). Lamartine performs a recycled notion of white consumption in order to counter white peoples' consumption of his ancestors' land and culture, and he justifies his own consumption in terms of prior ownership privileges and fairness. Rewards of such embodied white consumerism include financial gain, cultural power, and revenge; costs include the risks of a consumer's being culturally and spiritually consumed.

Non-whites have associated whiteness with hypocrisy, especially religious hypocrisy, as when white people have professed Christian principles yet practiced racism. In "The Color of Heaven," historian Mia Bay exposes this hypocrisy when researching nineteenth-century white slaveowners' conceptions of heaven and finding it to be a "racially divided place" (69). This pervasive hypocrisy is what Martin Luther King Jr. names and challenges a hundred years later in his 1963 "Letter from Birmingham Jail," addressed to eight white fellow clergy in Alabama:

> I have almost reached the regrettable conclusion that the Negro's great stumbling block in his stride toward freedom is not the White Citizen's Council or the Ku Klux Klan, but the white moderate, who is more devoted to "order" than to justice; who prefers a negative peace which is the absence of tension to a positive peace which is the presence of justice. (892)

The brilliance of King's rhetoric, of course, is that he challenges this hypocrisy via the Christian terms of the white clergy, thus interrupting their white desire for stasis in spiritual and political matters.

Non-whites have also associated whiteness with a denial of race issues, a denial stemming from fear and guilt. In his 1965 "White Man's Guilt," James Baldwin maps the interrelated web of denial, fear and guilt: It

> is heard nowhere more plainly than in those stammering terrified dialogues which white Americans sometimes entertain . . . the black man in America. The nature of this stammering can be reduced to a plea. Do not blame me. I was not there. I did not do it. (321–22)

Yet, according to Baldwin, "on the same day, in another gathering and in the most private chamber of his heart always, the white American remains proud of that history for which he does not wish to pay, and from which, materially, he has profited so much" (322). For Baldwin, this denial abates the white person's fear and guilt and, thus, creates a safe space in which white America may live without having to confront its past or *the-then-that-is-now*.[8] Although Baldwin's text does cite a common cultural pattern of denial that still echoes among white America, it fails to acknowledge that some people of good will believe (mistakenly in my opinion) that color blindness is the best tactic for overcoming racism; in such a case, denial is not always driven by fear and guilt but rather by a desire for social justice based on egalitarian treatment. Nevertheless, the main contribution of Baldwin's text lies in exposing the dominant either/or logic haunting whiteness in the U.S. That is, either whiteness has perpetuated great violence, or it has fostered great accomplishments. There is little room in his essay or in U.S. culture at large for a both/and logic, even though this logic may be just the grounds needed for initiating genuine cross-cultural dialogues.

Non-whites have also linked whiteness with an ignorance of other cultures although they may differ in their ideas of what this ignorance signifies. In *The Joy Luck Club,* Amy Tan demonstrates that whites are often well-intentioned but unconsciously ignorant not just of other cultures but of their own ignorance. For example, Rich (the good-hearted white boyfriend of Chinese American Waverly Jong) goes home with her to dinner and not only brings a French wine to her parents (who do not own wine glasses) but also calls them Tim and Linda (their names are Tin and Lindo) (196, 198). In *Playing in the Dark,* Morrison argues that this ignorance manifests itself in literary studies not so much as an unconscious phenomenon as a "willful critical blindness" (18), and she makes her case convincingly via her analysis of how whiteness functions in American literature. In *Massacre of the Dreamers,* Castillo (Chicana poet, fiction writer, and theorist) does not let whites off so easily: "The ignorance of white dominant society about [Chicana] ways, struggles in society, history, and culture is not an innocent and passive ignorance, it is a systematic and determined ignorance" with systematic, discriminatory effects (5). These three differing theories of ignorance are productive in that they posit not simply *the* one right answer about white ignorance but, rather, a range of possibilities for analyzing how whiteness may function in particular situations, literary or otherwise.

Non-whites have not always been alone in defining whiteness. In *Killers of the Dream,* Smith makes visible the convergence of bodies, the tropes, and U.S. cultures. She also makes visible the intersections of multiple tropes (race, gender, class, region, sex, etc.), a move much heralded by 1990s feminists of all "colors":

> I shall not tell, here of experiences that were different and special and belonged only to me, but those most white southerners born at the turn of the century share with each other. Out of the intricate weaving of unnumbered threads, I shall pick out a few strands, a few designs that have to do with what we call color and race . . . and politics . . . and money and how it is made . . . and religion . . . and sex and the body image . . . and love . . . and dreams of the Good and the killers of the dreams. (27)

As tropes, Smith's ellipses are just as important as her terms. The ellipses invite readers to pause and contemplate each term individually (e.g., "color and race," then "politics," then . . .); they invite readers to link the terms together metonymically; and they invite readers to fill the gaps with their impressions of "white southerners born at the turn of the [twentieth] century" as well as with their own experiences and definitions.

From her standpoint as a mid-twentieth-century, upper-middle class, Southern white female, Smith names the white "TERRORS" as not just "the Ku Klux Klan and the lynchings I did not see" but also "the gentle back-door cruelties of 'nice people'" (12). Smith in no way implies that her experiences of white terror are comparable to the experiences of those lynched; however, she does analyze its influence on her own body and moral consciousness:

> The mother who taught me what I know of tenderness and love and compassion taught me also the bleak rituals of keeping Negroes in their "place." The father who rebuked me for an air of superiority toward schoolmates from the mill and rounded out his rebuke by gravely reminding me that "all men are brothers," trained me in the steel-rigid decorums I must demand of every colored male. They who so gravely taught me to split my body from my mind and both from my "soul," taught me also to split my conscience from my acts and Christianity from southern tradition. (27)

Indeed, Smith stresses the importance of analyzing this white-terror's influence on everyone's body and moral consciousness and on the cultures they all share:

> Something was wrong with a world that tells you that love is good and people are important and then forces you to deny love and to humiliate people. I knew, though I would not for years confess it, that in trying to shut the Negro race away from us, we have shut ourselves away from so many good, creative, honest, deeply human things in life. I began to understand slowly at first but more clearly as the years passed, that the warped, distorted frame we have put around every Negro child from birth is around every white child also. (39)

Such a move makes redressing racial inequality an imperative for everyone.

In her analysis, Smith employs a usage-based circling through time to expose the circling of time in her own body: "I am afraid this book has played tricks on me: I am caught again in those revolving doors of childhood" (13). When writing, she grounds herself in her current moment, picking out "threads" from the past (identifications and disidentifications) that still haunt her in order to explain her present. Her circling of time exposes her, and our, accountability for the *then-that-is-now*:

[W]e know White Supremacy is indefensible in today's world, we know that as an idea it is dead, but the bitter struggle goes on . . . wasting minds and time and hearts and economic resources, tying us to a past where ghost battles ghost. And while this happens the human spirit sits on the rim of things, waiting. (235)

This ghostly battle represents the dichotomy of real and ideal that pervades racialized (and gendered and classed . . .) discourses in the U.S.: "And so we stand: tied to the past and clutching at the stars!" (253).

Before people in the U.S. can untie ourselves from the dysfunctional realities of the past and the dysfunctional idealizations of the present, we need to make (at least) two moves. First, we need to make visible and/or audible the reality of the *then-that-is-now*. Smith tried to do this in 1949. Academic whiteness studies is attempting to do it now. For example, Lynn Worsham's "After Words" to *Feminism and Composition Studies* weaves her personal stories of performing whiteness into a critique of the discourses and cultures surrounding us. Second, we need to stop hiding behind the ideal of color blindness. In addition to multicultural studies and whiteness studies, some popular publications are attempting to do this, too. For example, in the 1999 biography of Vince Lombardi, which lauds his antiracist work while he coached the Green Bay Packers, author David Maraniss claims: "It has always been easy for whites to claim [the ideal of] color blindness in the United States since white is the dominant color in American society, but the claim often serves as a ruse for not recognizing the [real] obstacles faced by non-whites" (8). In other words, in academic and popular discourses, we need to investigate whiteness by eavesdropping within history so that bodies, tropes, and cultures may converge in moments of productive rhetorical usage, moments when personal and/or social change may be effected.

The Agencies of Rhetoric, Rhetorical Agents

Discussions of history and whiteness are significant for rhetoric and composition studies because they invite, among other things, questions of ethics and agency. According to Lawrence Buell, "[E]thics" has gained a new resonance in literary studies" (7), and, consequently, literary scholars are rethinking agency in its various guises—discursive agency, authorial agency, readerly agency, and sociopolitical (or cultural) agency (12–14). I would extend Buell's claim to rhetoric and composition studies. (I would also claim that, for feminists, ethics never ceased to resonate [but I digress . . . or maybe I don't]). Regardless, rhetorical studies is the site where discursive, authorial, readerly, and sociopolitical agencies have been kept in play and their intersections, duly noted—even when biographical criticism privileged the author, New Criticism privileged the work, deconstruction privileged textuality, reader response privileged the reader, and cultural studies privileged class. Indeed, if we associate discursive agency with tropes, authorial and readerly agencies with the body, and sociopolitical agency with culture, what emerges is *not* a battle for which site possesses agency but *rather* a question of how the agencies of different sites converge to effect moments of rhetorical usage.

When I circle through history, at *this* moment, eavesdropping to trace how dysfunctions of whiteness in the U.S. remake rhetorical theory and usage, I find that these four agencies are not simply concepts lifted from classical times and dropped into our lives but rather are concepts remade in the image of their moments of usage. In the late-twentieth- and early-twenty-first-century U.S., for example, the whiteness-that-fosters-stasis has worked to circumscribe all four of these agencies. Granted (and this is an important point), whiteness is not the only force at work in this circumscription, but it has definite vested interests. What follows is an attempt to articulate some of these interests. Inspired by Jacqueline Jones Royster's "When the First Voice You Hear Is Not Your Own" and Kathleen Welch's "Interpreting the Silent 'Aryan Model' of Histories of Classical Rhetoric," what follows is also an invitation for more such work to be done.

In terms of discursive agency, whiteness in the U.S. (in its desire for stasis) encourages the denial of language play. Castillo describes the performance of this denial:

> Word-play for the Mexican Spanish speaker is contagious, a reflection of our sense of irony and humor about life. . . . In attempting to do this with English dominant speakers—especially, but not exclusively white people—I am always disappointed to see that the unimaginative way they have been taught to hear language makes a complete disaster of my attempt at "word-play." (168)

This denial backgrounds the tropological functions of language, and, by extension, it constrains the ways bodies, tropes, and cultures are imagined to converge. Here are just four examples.

First, the whiteness-that-denies-language-play signifies an un/conscious desire for closure in mythmaking and storytelling. As Leslie Marmon Silko says in an interview, white culture foolishly tries to freeze-frame stories to preserve them forever:

> The folks at home [Laguna Pueblo] will say, "If it's important, if it has relevance, it will stay regardless of whether it's on video tape, taped, or written down." It's only the western Europeans who have this inflated pompous notion that every word, everything that's said or done is real important, and it's got to live on and on forever. And only Americans think that America . . . [will] just continue on. (qtd. in Barnes 52)

Though Derridian deconstruction might serve as a counterexample to Silko's claim about language play, she does put her finger on a dominant means of performing language in the U.S. And this performance of whiteness-that-denies-language-play reinforces a separation of whites from non-whites, story from history, poetics from rhetoric and, hence, politics.

Second, the whiteness-that-denies-language-play erases how blackness participates in the formation of whiteness. In "What America Would Be Like Without Blacks," Ralph Ellison explains:

> Much of the sound of [U.S.] language is derived from the timbre of the African voice and the listening habits of the African ear. So there is a de'z and a do'z of slave speech sounding beneath our most polished Harvard accents, and if there is such a thing as a Yale accent, there is a Negro wail in it—doubtlessly introduced there by Old Yalie John C. Calhoun, who probably got it from his mammy. (164)

This manifestation of whiteness-that-denies-language-play reinforces the dominant culture's tendency not to hear or listen to other cultures (not to mention women's voices) as well as its tendency to inflate its own autonomy and importance.

Third, the whiteness-that-denies-language-play also erases how whiteness participates in the formation of blackness.[9] In *Beloved*, Stamp Paid brilliantly articulates for Paul D how whiteness inscribes blackness in the U.S.:

> It wasn't the jungle blacks brought with them to this place from the other (livable) place. It was the jungle whitefolks planted in them. And it grew. It spread . . . until it invaded the whites who had made it. . . . Changed and altered them. Made them bloody, silly, worse than even they wanted to be, so scared were they of the jungle they had made.

The screaming baboon lived under their own white skin; the red gums were their own. (198–99)

As Stamp implies, this manifestation of whiteness-that-denies-language-play essentializes blackness and whiteness as biological destiny, obscuring their status as tropes and ignoring power differentials between definers and defined as well as the potential of language use for personal and social change.

Fourth, the whiteness-that-denies-language-play not only effaces "colors" other than black and white but also hides the slippage of these "color" categories. Cherríe Moraga's commentary on "light-skinned breeds" astutely exposes these effaced colors and their categorical slippage:

> With a Black lover in apartheid Boston I was seen as a whitegirl. When we moved to Brooklyn, we were both Ricans. In Harlem I became "Spanish." In México, we were both Cubans. With my brown girlfriends we be brown girls sitting on brownstones. We be family. Among Indians in the States I'm a half-breed who looks like every other breed, colored mixed with cowboy. Among Chicanas, I am everybody's cousin Carmen. Whitegirls change my shade to a paler version. People think I'm Italian, Jewish. ("Breakdown" 233)

Such slippages make visible the nonessentialist, context-dependent functions of racial and ethnic categories.

Finally, despite such slippages, the whiteness-that-denies-language-play blinds and blindsides people by offering them socially constructed concepts, such as race and gender, presented as The Truth. Smith concretizes this claim when discussing the politicians of her childhood:

> The singsong voices of politicians . . . [were] telling us lies about skin color and a culture they were callously ignorant of—lies made of their own fantasies, of their secret deviations—forcing decayed pieces of their and the region's obscenities into the minds of the young and leaving them there to fester. (12–13)

According to Smith, these festering obscenities exist both on "semantic" (130) and "somatic" levels (161); in other words, bodies are troped, and tropes are embodied.[10]

Fighting these festering obscenities is doubly difficult when tropological functions of language are backgrounded. For then, Plato wins the theory war. Language becomes literal, in the service of The Truth. Language play becomes suspect; rhetorical negotiation, dubious; the possibilities of discursive agency, limited. Also limited are possibilities ascribed to authorial, readerly and cultural agencies. To counter such limitations, teacher/scholars in rhetoric and composition studies need to think seriously about how the tropological functions of language connect to our concepts of truth/ Truth, knowledge, and belief; then we need to implement our thinking *consciously* into our theories and praxes, including pedagogy. Too often these concerns hover at the edges of our thinking and doing, unspoken and unheard. For example, consider our injunction to students to "write clearly"; as a trope, *write clearly* needs to be interrogated. Scholars, teachers, and students all need to ask: (1) what writerly and cultural attitudes and actions are associated with the trope *write clearly*? (2) what benefits are associated with it? (there are many); and (3) what gets lost in our stated and implied definitions of it? (*clearly* signifies differently in different discourse communities). Such attention to language provides a means for questioning discursive agency and an opportunity for articulating authorial agency.

In terms of authorial agency,[11] whiteness in the U.S. (in its desire for stasis) encourages what Nedra Reynolds calls the reduction of *ethos* to individual ethical appeal ("*Ethos*" 327–29). According to Reynolds, Aristotelian *ethos* is not merely the "ethical appeal" of an individual but "a shared enterprise among members of the community" with the community's deciding "what constitutes justice, temperance, bravery or ethics" (328). In the U.S., reducing *ethos* to individual ethical appeal is metonymically linked to a rugged-individualist ideology. This ideology is haunted by the ghost of J. Hector St. John de Crèvecoeur's 1782 American, a white male of European ancestry who succeeds on the basis of individual will and toil (7, 9). De Crèvecoeur's description, along with other U.S. texts (both legal and literary), leads Morrison to conclude that while *American* has been presented as an inclusive term, it has often played out as a code for *white male* (*Playing* 39–44); this coding is why Frederick Douglass and Martin Luther King Jr. both argue that the U.S. must extend the promise of its founding documents to all its peoples. Following Morrison's logic, the reduced *ethos* of the rugged individualist in rhetorical theory translates as the reduced *ethos* of the rugged white male individualist.

Reducing *ethos* to this individual ethical appeal may work for de Crèvecoeur's American because it is tailor-made in his own image (to identify the *then-that-is-now*, we need look no further than entrepreneur and presidential wanna-be Donald Trump). But this reduced *ethos* does not always work for those falling outside de Crèvecoeur's category. For within this reduced concept of *ethos*, which celebrates individual will and toil, "falling outside" can be interpreted in only one way: as failure of individual will and toil. Sometimes it is. But not always. Note, for example, the effects of falling outside Milwaukee Public Schools' integration plan. A former MPS board member recently—well, finally—admitted that the court-ordered school integration plan of the late 1970s "was set up for 'white benefit' at the expense of African-American children" and their communities (J. Williams A-1). In practical terms, this admission means that white students stayed in their home communities unless they chose to attend magnet schools in African American neighborhoods but African American students were compelled to attend outlying area schools. NAACP volunteer and later school-board member Joyce Mallory explains the consequences:

> What really hurts now is when I look at all these kids in prison, a lot of that is the result of thousands of kids not getting a good education and being forced, pushed and dropped out of MPS in the last 20 years. . . . A lot of them dropped out because going to the Pulaskis, the Bay Views, the Hamiltons and the Madisons of this community weren't places where they could be educated in a climate and an environment that valued who they were as individuals. (qtd. in J. Williams A-8)

When, as in the MPS example, the actual individual does not mesh with the existing cultural category of individual, "falling outside" may result from factors other than individual will and toil. But reducing *ethos* to individual ethical appeal occludes these other factors—what Reynolds calls the "spatial and social" dimension of Aristotelian *ethos* ("*Ethos*" 327),[12] what Buell calls readerly, discursive, and sociopolitical agencies (12–14), and what I call the convergence of bodies, tropes, and cultures. To combat this reduction, we need to foster an expanded concept of *ethos*.

The possibilities of an expanded *ethos* may be seen by returning to the receptions of Smith's text. As mentioned earlier, in 1949, *Killers* was given a decidedly chilly reception, which disciplined not just Smith but other white writers;[13] in 1994, *Killers* was received more favorably.[14] If we function within a reduced concept of *ethos*—one that posits it as individual ethical appeal—we might argue that only individual writers and speakers are responsible for their own receptions (e.g., we might blame Smith for the chilly 1949 reception and praise her for the warmer 1994 one). But if we function within an expanded concept of *ethos*—one that acknowledges its individual, discursive, and cultural components—we might argue that negative receptions, such as Smith's 1949 one, may represent a convergence of bodies, tropes, and cultures for an individual author but a failed convergence for the dominant white culture. We might also argue that successful receptions, such as Smith's 1994 one, represent a more successful convergence within the dominant white culture, a convergence made possible in part by her 1949 interruption of the status quo. While this expanded *ethos* rejects the possibility that *ethos* functions only as an individual enterprise, it retains the possibility that *ethos* emerges as a result of rhetorical negotiation in which speakers and writers are active agents, albeit with discursive and cultural limitations, in the dance of bodies, tropes, and cultures.

In terms of readerly agency, whiteness in the U.S. (in its desire for stasis) reinforces rhetorical theory's tendency to relegate readers to secondary importance in the making of meaning. But wait, you may be thinking. Aristotle's rhetorical theory uses audience as its foundational category for classifying speeches and audience members (*On Rhetoric* 1.3.1358b.1–5), and his enthymeme invites the audience to insert their own ideas into the orator's gaps (2.23.1400b.25–35). My response is: "Yes . . . but." Enthymemic gaps are purposely employed by a speaker/writer so that audience members will fill in the gap and, thus, feel smart, concur with the speaker/writer, and believe they are full partners in the making of meaning so that the speaker/writer's will may be implemented without (too much) resistance. But as Michelle Ballif claims, rarely do rhetorical theories [or speakers or writers] ask: "What is it that the audience wants" or desires or demands or needs? ("What" 51).

Because whiteness is embodied differently in white people and non-whites, whiteness socializes them into *different* secondary positions of readerly agency. According to Castillo, whiteness socialization gives white readers certain expectations: They expect to be included in a text "in a direct way, if not as subjects, then emotionally. Otherwise they are disinterested and even feel threatened when excluded" (17). Whether white readers accept or resist this socialization is for each to negotiate. According to Royster, whiteness socialization gives non-white readers different expectations, especially of white speakers and writers:

> I have been compelled to listen to speakers, well-meaning though they may think they are, who signal to me rather clearly that subject position is everything. I have come to recognize, however, that when the

subject matter is me and the voice is not mine, my sense of order and rightness is disrupted. In metaphoric fashion, these "authorities" let me know, once again, that Columbus has discovered America and claims it now, claims it still for a European crown. ("When the First Voice" 31)

Without downplaying or denying Royster's very real and very painful experiences, it is important to remember that, just as European crowns may be overthrown, readerly agencies haunted by whiteness may be circumnavigated. But such work takes a concerted effort by everyone, that is, by people marked white and non-white, to articulate and negotiate the stakes, the processes, and the rewards.

Castillo, Royster, and Smith all offer critical readerly agencies for circumnavigating readerly agencies haunted by whiteness. Castillo's is the most radical in that she purposely does not accommodate white readers. That is, as an author she chooses not to address white people directly as in *Massacre of the Dreamers:*

> I AM A BROWN WOMAN. . . .
> Throughout the history of the United States "I" as subject and object has been reserved for white authorship and readership. However, when I speak of woman within these pages, I speak very specifically of the woman described above. (This also holds true for the use of the word men, children, people, and so on. I refer at all times to Chicanos/as-mejicanos/as unless otherwise specified). (1)

The readerly agency that Castillo offers brown women is: at last, you are the subject, enjoy. But she stipulates this enjoyment:

> [N]on-white readers in the U.S. . . . are not asserting that our perspective is the only legitimate one, that it is superior to or should replace, repress, or censure others. What we are conscious of is that our reality is vastly different from that of the dominant culture. (5)

The readerly agency that Castillo offers white readers is simply this: Get over not being addressed, but keep reading (eavesdropping), for Chicana struggle "is relevant to anyone trying to understand the world he or she lives in" (17). Because Castillo does not position whites as subject or even invite them in emotionally, she potentially proves her point about white readers' expectations each time one resists her. In this way, white readers are challenged when reading Castillo to critique not just her claims but also their own reactions to her claims. The risk of this strategy, however, is that white readers will neither read nor listen to her.

Royster's model of critical readerly agency offers all readers a more rhetorically (and emotionally) complicated positioning, a positioning that may be more successful than Castillo's in fostering cross-cultural negotiation. In "When The First Voice You Hear Is Not Your Own," Royster demonstrates how two or more people may interact so as to approximate equal positioning:

> My experience tells me that we need to do more than just talk and talk back. I believe that in this model we miss a critical moment. We need to talk, yes, and to talk back, yes, but when do we listen? How do we listen? How do we demonstrate that we honor and respect the person talking and what that person is saying, or what the person might say if we valued someone other than ourselves having a turn to speak? How do we translate listening into language and action, into the creation of an appropriate response? How do we really "talk back" rather than talk also? The goal is not, "You talk, I talk." The goal is better practices so that we can exchange perspectives, negotiate meaning, and create understanding with the intent of being in a good position to cooperate, when, like now, cooperation is absolutely necessary. (38)

This listening model of readerly agency imagines a readerly agency inextricably intertwined with discursive, authorial, and cultural agencies. Instead of submitting to traditional rhetorical moves in which authorial agency tries to control readerly agency by dictating the terms of identification, Royster offers the possibility of both agencies functioning as subject positions, with everyone rotating in and out of each agency, assuming respect for the process, the people, and each other's subject positions.

Finally, Smith posits a model of critical readerly agency that demonstrates the interactions of one person's many voices. Her readerly agency is also intertwined with discursive, authorial, and cultural agencies: "I was in dialogue with myself as I wrote, as well as with my hometown and my childhood and history and the future, and the past" (13). And this readerly agency has ethical dimensions:

> Our big problem is not civil rights or even a free Africa—urgent as these are—but how to make into a related whole the split pieces of

the human experience, how to bridge mythic and rational mind, how to connect our childhood with the present and the past with the future, how to relate the differing realities of science and religion and politics and art to each other and to ourselves. Man is a broken creature, yes; it is his nature as a human being to be so; but it is also his nature to create relationships that can span the brokenness. This is his first accountability; when he fails, he is inevitably destroyed. (21)

Though Smith's vision may seem utopian (even as it is haunted by apocalypse), it is a possible ethical choice with material consequences. Note its *then-that-is-now* echo in Victor Villanueva's *Bootstraps:*

Change is possible, I believe. Language used consciously, a matter of rhetoric, is a principal means—perhaps *the* means—by which change can begin to take place. . . . It's a utopian hope. . . . The utopian, I know, drives me, even when tempered by the practical. (121)

And mention of "the practical" leads us directly to issues of cultural structures that must be negotiated.

In terms of cultural agency, whiteness in the U.S. (in its desire for stasis) occludes the influence of cultural structures (such as race, gender, class, etc.) on everyone's life, rendering these structures either invisible or unimportant or both. By now, we can all rehearse the Marxist maxim that the most ideologically entrenched position is the one that appears invisible, unimportant, or natural. Smith concretizes this naturalizing process of occlusion in terms of the cultural structures of her own life and times:

Southern Tradition taught well: we learned our way of life by doing. You never considered arguing with teacher, because *you could not see her.* You only felt the iron grip of her hand and knew you must go where all the other children were going. And you learned never, never, to get out of step, for this was a precision dance, which you must do with deadly accuracy. (96; emphasis added)

How does whiteness (in its desire for stasis) participate in this occlusion of cultural structures? Through denial. The whiteness that Baldwin claims denies race further complicates that denial with other intersecting denials. For example, in Villanueva's critique of how non-whites are positioned within academia and the dominant white culture, he shows how race and ethnicity are complicated by denials of class:

It's hard to discuss the class system in American, because for so long we believed that ours was a classless society. John Kenneth Galbraith believes that most Americans still hold to the notion and cites George Bush as saying that class is "for European democracies or something else—it isn't for the United States of America. We are not going to be divided by class." (56)

In Shirley Wilson Logan's critique of rhetoric and composition's reception of nineteenth-century African American women, she shows how race is complicated by denials of differences within the category gender: "Marshal Houston reminds us that 'women of color do not experience sexism *in addition to* racism, but sexism *in the context of* racism; thus, they . . . bear an altogether *different* burden from that borne by white women'" ("When and Where" 46).

No doubt we could all list examples of denied and occluded cultural categories, such as age, religion, political affiliation. But the point is this: By denying the role of cultural structures in the construction of identity, whiteness perpetuates a theory and practice of what Villanueva calls "boot-straps" (xiv, 121). Are these denials and occlusions of cultural agency the result of a grand, conscious conspiracy? Not exactly. If they were, they might be easier for insiders to see and for everyone to resist. The denials exist, the occlusions occur, and the status quo remains because, like the segregating signs on the water fountains of Smith's childhood, whiteness is often taken "for granted" (57). And what is granted by whiteness to people marked as "white" is privilege, that is, the privilege of not needing to consider how race informs every aspect of daily life.

One means of resistance is to stop taking whiteness and its privileges for granted. Again, Smith's receptions exemplify this point. In 1949, Smith's authorial agency alone could not guarantee a positive reception of her book. Though body, trope, and culture had converged in 1949 for Smith and other people in terms of whiteness, they had not yet converged in the majority of white bodies or dominant discourses of white culture. As Smith notes, "The quickest way for a writer to be banned as an Outsider . . . was for him to seek new words, new ways of interpreting the earth-shaking hour we live in" (224). No matter how carefully she had crafted her authorial agency, the dominant discursive, readerly, and cultural agencies worked against her. Yet Smith's experience is not the grounds for despair nor the grounds for a retreat into gradualism. It is the grounds—and a model—for how a resisting agency may challenge other agencies haunted by whiteness.

In sum, whiteness (in its desire for stasis in the U.S.) celebrates a discursive agency in which language is made literal, an authorial agency in which *ethos* is reduced to individualism, a readerly agency in which readers are relegated to secondary importance in the construction of meanings, and a cultural agency in which the influence of cultural structures on identity is occluded. Such a whiteness puts authorial agency on a pedestal, subordinates the other three, and denies the intertwining functions of all four. Can the aforementioned dysfunctions be challenged in terms of how they remake rhetorical theory and rhetorical usages? As I have tried to demonstrate, some people have done so, indeed are doing so. As for the rest of us, a pertinent response may be heard in Smith's conclusion (though it obviously does not address my rhetoric question directly): "We have the means, the technics, we have the knowledge and insight and courage. All have synchronized for the first time in history. Do we have the desire? That is a question that each of us must answer for himself" (253).

In/Conclusion

What evidence attests that the current convergence of bodies, the trope of whiteness, and mainstream U.S. culture is not a momentary anomaly? Well, within academic culture, there is whiteness studies. Within popular culture, there is Maraniss's biography of Lombardi. There is even the 4C's cocktail guy. Was he being snide or simply jocular when he claimed that it is hip to be a white guy again? To be honest, when I heard him, I could not tell. But whether or not I am able to discern his intent is little cause for concern. For as Reynolds reminds us, Aristotle, in one of his finer moments, says that "'we become just by doing just acts'" (*Nichomachean* 2.10; qtd. in Reynolds "*Ethos*" 328). Perhaps the cocktail guy, when invoking the trope of whiteness, will accidentally overhear himself and, as a result, embody the trope of whiteness in ways that will help him understand his accountability for the *then-that-is-now.* Perhaps he already has. Such are the possibilities of rhetoric.

But whether or not the cocktail guy accidentally overhears or purposefully eavesdrops on himself, *we* should eavesdrop on him—and then act upon our hearings. Such are our challenges as scholars and teachers. As scholars, we need to reflect on the influences of whiteness in our discipline, our professional journals, our conventions, our books and articles, our professional networks, and dare I say even our friendships. As teachers, we need to introduce students to rhetorical tactics with which to reflect on the influences of whiteness in their own lives and cultures.

Many rhetorical tactics are applicable. For example, Jarratt offers rereading (*Rereading* xxiv); Glenn, remapping rhetorical territory (*Rhetoric* 1–17); Roxanne Mountford, resisting empiricism (par. 4); Royster and Middleton, listening (Royster, "When the First Voice" 38; Middleton, "Delivery"); Ballif, speaking as a listener (59); Reynolds, interrupting ("Interrupting" 70–71); Diane Davis, hearing a/new ("Just"); Logan, speaking the unspeakable ("When" 55); Ellen Gil-Gomez, piece-making (204); and Worsham, composing storied cultural critiques (336–46).

To that list of tactics I add eavesdropping. By living and teaching such tactics in ways that are pertinent for particular locales, scholar/teachers in rhetoric and composition studies may remind ourselves and students that even as history, whiteness, and rhetoric encircle and embody us, we have access to agencies (admittedly in varying degrees) for identifying these embodiments and circling through them.

5
Listening Pedagogically: A Tactic for Listening to Classroom Resistance

> When I encounter these checklists, I automatically mark the box that says "Asian/Pacific Islander." How strange it is for a person born in Evanston, Illinois, and raised in the Midwest to claim that *she* is an *"islander."* [emphasis added]
>
> —Carol Sales, Marquette University
> student

> Resistance to change in a person, according to Anzaldúa, is in direct proportion to the number of dead metaphors that a person carries.
> —Sonja Foss, Karen Foss, and Cindy
> Griffin, *Feminist Rhetorical Theories*

> Having high expectations and good intentions is not enough; these intentions and expectations need to be evident to students in observable, or we might say, *audible* behaviors in the classroom. [emphasis added]
> —Arnetha Ball and Ted Lardner,
> "Dispositions Toward Language"

> Listen. To live is to be marked. To live is to change, to acquire the words of a story and that is the only celebration we mortals really know.
> —Orleanna Price, Barbara Kingsolver's
> *Poisonwood Bible*

This chapter conceptualizes and defines a third tactic of rhetorical listening: listening pedagogically. *Listening pedagogically* signifies the rhetorical-listening moves that students and teachers may make in classroom discourses in order to recognize resistance, analyze it, and, when necessary, resist it.[1] Though the import of this tactic potentially extends beyond the classroom, listening pedagogically targets classroom performances of students and teachers. By listening pedagogically, both students and teachers may become more open to hearing one another's metaphors (dead or otherwise) and, perhaps, more willing to celebrate the words of the stories that we all acquire during our lifetimes.

Two words that are threaded through all our stories are *gender* and *race*. In U.S. culture and classrooms, the question is not whether we notice gender and racial differences. We do. Rather, the question is how we deal with those differences. Two popular tactics are gender-blindness and color-blindness—that is, pretending to be blind to gender and to race. The key term in each of these definitions is *pretending*: It highlights that gender-blindness and color-blindness are not norms in the U.S. but are, at best, ideals.

Functioning as if such ideals were reality, many well-meaning people promote gender-blindness and color-blindness as "solutions" to the "problems" of gender and racial differences. But despite good intentions, these blindnesses mostly reinforce the status quo for students and for teachers. For men, gender-blindness means denying not so much their maleness as the privileges often accorded maleness within U.S. culture. For women, gender-blindness means either accepting these male privileges as natural rights or being made to feel that the "problem" is theirs alone to "solve." Likewise, for whites, color-blindness means denying the privileges often accorded whiteness in U.S. culture; it also means denying very real differences faced by whites and non-whites.[2] For non-whites, it means being made to feel, once again, that race is their "problem" to "solve" because they often seem to be the ones noticing that race is in play.

These dynamics represent predominant power differentials in the U.S., but these dynamics are not static. Sometimes they shift. But when shifts occur, the new dynamics emerge not so much as simple reversals of power differentials (as in *reverse discrimination*) but, rather, as messy complications of these differentials. After all, *maleness* and *whiteness* may at times signify obstacles in the U.S. as well as privileges, and *femaleness* and *non-whiteness* may at times signify privilege as well as obstacles. The point is, however, that for *all* students and teachers, gender-blindness and color-blindness obfuscate the existence and, hence, the intersections of gender and race—intersections that are marked differently on each and every body, depending upon each and every body's particular socialization and identifications.[3] As a result of this obsfucation, these intersections and their power differentials are too rarely discussed.

To counter the well-intentioned but ineffectual ideals of gender-blindness and color-blindness, this chapter echoes the work of scholar/teachers, such as Shirley Wilson Logan and Susan Jarratt, and proposes an alternative ideal to strive toward: that is, redefining *gender* and *race* not as problems to be eradicated but as differences to be more successfully defined, negotiated, and celebrated.[4] To approach this ideal, rhetoric and composition scholar/teachers need to focus on the real so as to expose how the field is already gendered and raced. To that end, scholar/teachers may ask students and ourselves to reflect on how gender and whiteness (the most unspoken of all racial categories) inform theories and praxes. The goal is not to discover some transcendent truth about gender and whiteness but rather to lay all gender and race "cards" on the table in hopes negotiating the existing (mis)perceptions about them and their intersections. This goal echoes Logan's goal for field, that is, to "strengthen the links between language and democracy, text and street" ("Changing" 335). This goal also echoes Jarratt's goal for feminist pedagogy, that is, not to force "students to subscribe to a particular political position but rather [to] engag[e] with students on the terrain of language in the gendered world we all currently inhabit" ("Feminist Pedagogy" 118). Such engagements with gender and race, in text and street, begin when we lay the words of our stories alongside one another's.

My motivation for such classroom practices echoes the case made by Danny Weil in *Towards a Critical Multicultural Literacy*. He argues that laying our stories alongside one another generates knowledge:

> One rarely gains a knowledge of others through exposure alone. It requires an examination of the logic of the points of view advanced—both a cognitive and affective exploration into self and others. Without the knowledge of diversity, we lose opportunities to know ourselves, a knowledge that could free us from unexamined biases and psychological and material bondage. Lacking significant opportunities to reason from other cultural points of view, both students and teachers lose any chance to redefine their own individuality thorough [*sic*] a critical dismantling of the myths that define them. (245)

By engaging competing stories laid side-by-side, students and teachers may broaden our world views.

My motivation also arises from a critique of Weil's claim, specifically a critique of the power dynamics that haunt such classroom practices. For when stories are laid side-by-side, not all students are on equal ground. Though all students participate in a dominant culture, they do not participate in identical ways. According to Audre Lorde, a dominant culture assumes a "mythical norm," which in the late-twentieth-century U.S. manifested as "white, thin, male, young, heterosexual, christian, and financially secure" ("Age" 116). Although students represented by this "mythical norm" are indubitably influenced by the multiple stories and logics constituting U.S. culture, they may often choose whether or not to engage such stories and logics, that is, whether or not to develop double consciousness.[5] Given this choice, students may view Weil's pedagogy as an ethical imperative or as a useless classroom exercise or as something in-between. But students not represented by this "mythical norm" rarely possess such choices; for them, double consciousness may be a way of life. Like the modern American Indian women whom Paula Gunn Allen describes, students who are forced—via "a history of invasion, conquest, and colonization"—to straddle competing cultures often feel trapped in a "bicultural bind: . . . vacillat[ing] between being dependent and strong, self-reliant and powerless, strongly motivated and hopelessly insecure" (48). So what are teachers to do?

The challenge for teachers is to challenge *all* students to make the following moves: to recognize how *all* our lives are implicated within cultural diversity; to acknowledge that we *all* possess a responsibility for naming, explaining, and addressing these implications; and to understand that the categories of *dominant, nondominant,* and even *mythical norm* are socially constructed and fluid, changing over time and place, in ways that influence *all* our lives. Given the difficulty of such moves, it is no wonder that discussing issues related to diversity perpetuates student/teacher resistance.

To study such resistance, this chapter takes as its grounds my own pedagogical practices at Marquette University, a private Jesuit university in Milwaukee, Wisconsin, where since 1993, I have taught graduate and undergraduate courses, such as women's literature, introduction to fiction, autobiography, rhetorical theory, composition theory, first-year composition, and advanced composition.[6] To demonstrate how this location has helped me conceptualize and practice the tactic of listening pedagogically, this chapter (1) identifies student/teacher resistance in terms of gender and whiteness, (2) sets the scene for listening pedagogically, (3) defines *listening pedagogically* as a tactic for recognizing, analyzing, and resisting this resistance, and (4) listens pedagogically to students' listening pedagogically within their essays.

Defining Student/Teacher Resistance

As mentioned in chapter 1, a few years ago, one of my undergraduate rhetorical-theory classes read an excerpt from Cornel West's *Race Matters*. In
reaction to West, a young white man said, "I don't see what the big deal is.
I don't wake up every morning, look in the mirror, and say, 'Hey, I'm a white
man.'" In reaction to the student, I said, "Do you think that is West's point?
That you don't have to think about race but he does?" The student was
resisting West's text, but I was resisting the student . . . and pulling rank.
Although I did not regret speaking up and was grateful for the debate that
ensued, I was haunted by two things: (1) the probable ineffectiveness of my
pulling rank for the student and for those who silently agreed with him and
(2) the class's lack of lexicon for talking not just about gender and race but
about their own resistances—and mine. Consequently, I determined to
develop such a lexicon for discussing such resistance.

But defining student/teacher resistance is tricky because the term *resistance* is slippery. It functions as an *antanaclasis*, that is, as a term connot-
ing opposing definitions rooted in competing theories:

> In post-Freudian psychoanalytic theory, "resistance" describes "a sub-
> ject's *refusal* to admit the hidden meaning of his symptom" (Grigg
> 102). This usage has entered pedagogical lore, referring to students'
> refusals to critique their own commonplace assumptions about race,
> gender, class, and other cultural categories. . . . In neo-Marxist theory
> however, "resistance" describes "a personal 'space,' . . . [of] subjective
> agency" from which students may "subvert the process of socializa-
> tion" by contesting our cultural commonplaces (Giroux, *Teachers* 162).
> This critical pedagogy usage most often refers to teachers' helping
> students identify and then employ their own agencies in order to in-
> terrupt their cultural socializations. (Ratcliffe, "A Rhetoric" 105–6)

In the article cited above, I challenge teachers (myself included) to negotiate
students' resistance as well as our own. For as Maxine Greene claimed in 1972
(which accounts for the following pronoun usage): "I believe the teacher who
is sincerely 'radical' has the capacity to move students to do their own kind
of critical learning—at higher and higher levels of complexity. . . . I think he
also has an obligation to present himself to students (fellow human beings)
as a questioning, fallible, searching human being" (qtd. in Weil 135–36).[7]
Whether possessed of a radical agenda or not, teachers may demonstrate
this *ethos* by modeling how to recognize, analyze, and resist resistance.

How is this goal to be accomplished? Because post-Freudian resistance is defined in terms of symptoms and because post-Marxist resistance is defined in terms of agency, I find it productive to lay these two types of resistance alongside one another.[8] My goal is to employ the latter as a means of recognizing, analyzing, and resisting the former. In this way, these two resistances may work together.

Student/teacher resistance comes in many different forms, and it functions differently given different situations, students, and teachers. Still, I find it useful to name and discuss with students general categories of post-Freudian resistance that may sometimes hinder their engaging texts, speaking in class, or writing papers. In my classrooms, the most common types of resistance are the following:

1. *Denial* emerges when students or teachers refuse to acknowledge the existence of an idea or action. Denial also emerges when students or teachers acknowledge the existence of an idea or action but refuse to acknowledge any accountability—individual and/or systemic—for any privileges or obstacles afforded us by (the history of) this idea or action.

2. *Dismissal* emerges when students or teachers acknowledge the existence of an idea or action but deem it insignificant in general, insignificant in our own lives, or too dangerous for class discussion.

3. *Indifferent compliance* emerges when students or teachers go through the motions but do not genuinely engage an idea or action.

4. *Defensiveness* emerges when students or teachers shift conversations from discussions of an idea or action and instead focus on ourselves, that is, on our own guilt/blame—or lack thereof.[9]

5. *Overidentification* emerges when students or teachers see ourselves as so implicated within an idea or action that we can only imagine confessional responses that preclude cultural/systemic analyses; such overidentification may trigger strong emotions (e.g., fear, embarrassment, righteous anger).

6. *Nonproductive guilt* emerges when students or teachers blame ourselves for current privileges afforded us by history and, thus, either adopt a patronizingly "helpful" attitude toward those we

imagine to be less privileged or focus solely on ourselves and our perceived guilt.

7. *Adherence to gender- and/or color-blindness* emerges when students or teachers ignore history, obsess on the present, and demand an ideal egalitarian fairness that treats everyone identically but ignores different daily effects of gender and race and other cultural categories.[10]

8. *Speaking block* or *writing block* emerges when students or teachers lack a lexicon, a conceptual framework, and/or confidence that the classroom is a viable space for speaking and writing about resistance-prone issues, such as gender and whiteness.

Each teacher must, of course, analyze her or his local conditions to identify the most common types of resistance that occur. But naming and discussing such resistance provide choices to students and teachers about whether to perpetuate, revise, and/or resist the resistance.

Although the above resistance may be performed by students or teachers, three other types (all grounded in fear) haunt teachers: (1) fears about job status; (2) fears about losing control of the class; and (3) fears about lacking the authority of lived experience when discussing resistance-prone issues. Although these fears may initially stymie action, they may also be revisioned as sites for instigating productive pedagogical action.

First, teachers may fear that, if students dislike engaging issues such as gender and whiteness, then the teacher's teaching will be judged a failure, which, in turn, may affect a teacher's job status, raise, tenure, and/or promotion. Such teacher resistance is further complicated by the fact that no one method of teaching will succeed in all situations. Pedagogies, such as the one described in the appendix, cannot be adopted wholesale but, rather, must be adapted by teachers for local students within local conditions. While fear of failure may cause teachers to ignore potentially tense issues (and, yes, on occasion such ignoring may be appropriate), this fear may also be revisioned as an invitation for teachers to think creatively about pedagogy.

Second, teachers may fear that if class discussions get out of hand, then they will lose control of the class for a day, a week, or an entire semester. Teachers, especially inexperienced ones, may fear having to deal with sexist and/or racist comments made (unconsciously or not) by students. In such situations, focusing on discourse, historical moments, and cultural logics instead of on an individual student's character works well. While fear of losing a class may cause teachers to ignore potentially tense issues (and, yes, on occasion such ignoring may be appropriate), this fear may also be re-visioned as an invitation for teachers to examine what we mean by "losing control," reflect on its implications, and brainstorm and research strategies for retaining a civil forum during uncomfortable discussions.

Third, teachers may fear that they lack the lived experiences needed to justify discussing issues of gender and/or race. To this fear, I have two re-sponses: (1) everyone is marked by gender and race and (2) lived experience, while valuable knowledge, is not the only kind of knowledge. In terms of the first response, teachers just need to be honest about our own markings and not pretend to speak *as* or *for* others. In terms of the second response, teachers just need to do the work necessary to supplement our lived expe-riences (or lack thereof) with other kinds of knowledge—just as a teacher of any other subject does.

After all, no contemporary teacher of Shakespeare has had to walk the boards of the Globe in 1598 to justify her or his Shakespearean pedagogy, so no one should have to live life as an Asian American to teach Maxine Hong Kingston's *Woman Warrior*. Granted, our current historical moment makes the former example less politically charged than the latter one, but this "charge" is precisely the reason for making the comparison explicit and discussing its politics.

Moreover, lived experience does not guarantee knowledge. A London ped-dler in 1598 may have known little about Shakespeare's writing talents; a Chinese American in 2005 may know little about Chinese political history and even less about Chinese American literary history. What counts in teach-ing resistance-prone issues is doing the work necessary to prepare for discus-sions:[11] such as, research (for definitions, concepts, and history), observation, listening, engaging the issues in daily life, and being honest about lived expe-rience. In the process, teachers who, for example, are not Chinese American may discover that even if they have not lived their lives as Chinese Ameri-cans, their lives and national histories have been informed by Chinese Ameri-can cultures. So while the fear of lived experience may cause teachers to ignore resistance-prone issues, it may also be revisioned as an invitation for teachers to do the work necessary to address such issues responsibly in class.

In terms of all these fears, a teacher must accept, first, that failure is a possibility and, second, that failure may also serve as the site for a teaching moment. If a discussion fails, interrupt it. Ask the class why things are going awry. Ask what can be done better. Ask if this failed discussion is an isolated incident or if it represents a larger cultural pattern. Have students respond in small groups, in writing, in class the next day . . . whatever seems to work for the particular situation. As I am fond of saying to TAs during training sessions, teaching is a lot like jazz—with improvisation being the dominant mode of play. Good teachers must know the tune and have a practiced facility for playing it, but teaching performances are best when teachers listen and respond to the other players in the room (the students). When you hit a sour note (and you will), practice and try again. If the arrangement of a song (a lesson plan) does not suit you, find another one. But do not give up on the song . . . at least not too soon. And do not forget that everyone hears with different ears.

Setting the Scene for Listening Pedagogically

The success of a course can be determined, in part, by what a teacher does before he/she ever walks into the classroom. Before teaching any course, I try to set the scene for listening pedagogically by making the moves described in this section. Each teacher may particularize his or her way of setting the scene for listening pedagogically; these moves simply reflect what has (more often than not) worked for me. Although these moves may apply to many different courses, this section exemplifies the moves with references to the teaching materials provided in the appendix; these materials are from an advanced writing course's third unit, whose rhetorical focus is analysis and style and whose inquiry theme is whiteness.

Move #1: Reflect on the term pedagogy *and its power dynamics.* The term *pedagogy* is usually associated with a teacher's plan for students' learning, but I broaden the term to include students' and teachers' plans for students' and teachers' learning. This move enhances everyone's capacity for learning from self and others: It makes students more responsible for their own learning, and it removes the mastery burden from teachers' shoulders. As Ira Shor notes in *When Students Have Power*, this move may be "transformative" for both students and teachers alike (4).

But make no mistake: Broadening the term *pedagogy* should not be romanticized. It does not erase very real power dynamics between students and teachers in the classroom, nor does it erase the responsibility accorded to teachers within this power dynamic. Teachers still select textbooks, evaluate students' learning, and design activities toward that end (even when students run a portion of the class, the teacher has "given" them authority to do so). Yet, because such power dynamics resemble the material reality that students encounter in many areas of their lives, acknowledging these pedagogical power dynamics in class and learning how to negotiate both the dynamics and the resistance to these dynamics can actually be a practical benefit for students.

Move #2: Articulate one's own pedagogical assumptions. Before teaching a course, I reflect upon my assumptions about the course, the subject matter, the readings, the assignments, the students, the processes of learning that will be taught, and my relation to all of the above. Such reflection is important when teaching any topic, but it is especially important when teaching resistance-prone issues, such as the intersections of gender and whiteness, because it may help predict and explain what may happen in the classroom. When such reflection does not help explain and predict classroom interactions, then I reexamine my assumptions—and tell myself to be grateful for the learning opportunity. (Admittedly, this gratitude is sometimes hard won.)

When teaching about gender and whiteness, I start with several assumptions, which are grounded in my previous experiences with Marquette University students. First, I assume that most students will come to class with "a tendency to equate [sexism and] racism with an internal condition that shows up as individual acts of prejudice" and will not possess the knowledge or lexicon for discussing sexism and racism as structural problems (Elias and Jones 9). Second, I assume that many but not all students will be white and that whatever topic comes up will run the risk of mimicking U.S. culture and "[play] out against the backdrop of the assumptions that *everyone* [is] white" (Maher and Tetreault 159).[12] Third, I assume that most students will have had little exposure to an academic study of whiteness. Fourth, I assume that some student/teacher resistance will exist, based upon our feelings of discomfort with the topic and upon U.S. culture's lack of a lexicon for talking about it. But, fifth, I also assume that Marquette University students' lived engagement with service and social justice will help counter their and my resistance.

Move #3: Identify teacher goals and student learning outcomes. Distinguishing between these two concepts is important. As a teacher, I may have goals for students that I cannot assess; however, I should still recognize how these goals drive my pedagogy. For instance, when teaching a writing course, such as the one described in the appendix, I may have three teacher goals: (1) to help students understand how the rhetorical tactics we study may help them think more critically in future classes and in life after college, (2) to help students learn to use the rhetorical tactics effectively in subsequent classes and in life after college and (3) to encourage students to incorporate a consideration of gender and whiteness into all aspects of their lives, not simply one course paper. These goals may not be realized within a fifteen-week course. Sometimes they are realized a few years later, but I can know this for certain only if a student later e-mails me, sends me a card, or visits me.

Once my teacher goals are articulated, I identify measurable outcomes for student learning. When teaching an advanced writing course, such as the one described in the appendix, I may determine that by the end of the course, students should be able to: (1) define *analysis* as breaking an issue/idea into parts so as to better understand it, (2) define *style* as (un)conscious sentence-level choices with both personal and cultural functions, (3) recognize and employ elements of style, (4) recognize and analyze the tropological function of language, (5) recognize and analyze the way *whiteness* functions as a trope in culture and in daily life, and (6) employ conventions of creative nonfiction in their essays. In terms of the inquiry theme of whiteness, the unstated assumption of these objectives is that the class will resist the dominant culture's tendency to remain silent on this subject.

Move #4: Construct a course calendar that enables students to learn the outcomes and complete the assignment. In writing courses, my unit calendars usually focus on rhetorical concepts, such as invention and style, which are then coupled with inquiry themes for illustrating the concept. In an advanced writing course, such as the one described in the appendix, I may design a unit around analysis and style with an inquiry theme of whiteness. In addition to reading textbook information on analysis and style, students may read Lillian Smith, James Baldwin, Adrienne Rich, Nikki Giovanni, Peggy McIntosh, Dalton Conley, Jeanne Wakatsuki Houston, and Cherríe Moraga as well as the whiteness Web site constructed by Greg Jay, which is a wonderful pedagogical resource. Students especially enjoy Jay's link to the University of Northern Colorado's intramural basketball team, the Fighting Whites.

Focusing on rhetorical concepts and inquiry themes helps reduce resistance. When a student or anyone else asks, "What does whiteness have to do with this class?" I simply respond, "It is a matter of analyzing language and style." Students understand that our class focuses on rhetorical concepts and composition praxes and that the inquiry theme of whiteness serves as a vehicle for understanding these concepts and, thus, for improving their critical thinking, reading, and writing. Students also understand that the readings, which posit varying intersections of gender and whiteness, may serve as models of stylistic choices as well as points of invention for students' own papers.

Move #5: Design assignments to help students achieve these learning outcomes. To help students achieve the stated outcomes, I design short writings and longer writings that invite students to engage the ideas and processes to be learned in a course. In an advanced writing course, such as the one described in the appendix, I may ask students to write a creative nonfiction essay that takes whiteness as its starting point. Creative nonfiction works well here because it asks students to weave the personal and the cultural—that is, to tell a story that they have experienced and/or observed and then to reflect on the story's import, both personally and culturally. As Phillip Gerard notes in *Creative Nonfiction,* this genre possesses an apparent topic (usually a personal one, e.g., Richard Rodriguez's search for a sense of place in "Late Victorians") plus a deeper topic (usually a cultural issue, e.g., Rodriguez's reflections on the early AIDS epidemic in San Francisco). This genre prevents students from simply telling personal stories as if the stories occurred ahistorically or as if they were fiction; by intermingling narrative and reflection, this genre invites students to consider the stories of self and others. And because the final project for such a class is usually a student magazine (either print or online), students know that their essays will be read by, at least, an audience of their peers.

From a rhetorical listening perspective, creative nonfiction effectively helps students see how the personal is always implicated in the cultural—and vice versa. From a composition perspective, creative nonfiction effectively helps advanced students make visible the writerly choices (such as, topic selection, focus, arrangement, tone, audience needs, style) that have become "second nature" to them in standard thesis-support academic essays. When discussing creative nonfiction in terms of writing about whiteness, I inform students that I am not asking for personal guilt/blame papers, nor am I asking for what David Bartholomae once called road-to-Damascus papers. Rather, I challenge students to think about how language functions, specifically how *whiteness* as a trope plays out in U.S. culture, including in their lives. In this way, students reflect on their identifications with whiteness and on their accountability for these identifications . . . within the context of larger cultural structures, such as families, peer groups, schools, jobs, volunteer organizations.

Stipulating whiteness as a starting point for the writing assignment provides students the choice of whether or not to engage the issue of whiteness for a grade. By imagining whiteness as a starting point, students may find themselves turning in a paper far afield from the issue of whiteness, especially given that we discuss how whiteness intersects with other cultural categories, particularly gender and class. But students begin with whiteness and engage it via in-class writings and discussions. Even if they choose not to write about it, they have thought about it and traced their final paper from it. Interestingly, in all the times that I have taught this unit in its various guises, only one student has ever opted not to foreground whiteness in a paper. Yet, it haunted her paper as she recounted and reflected upon her spring-break service trip to Appalachia, a trip that opened her eyes to ways of life very different from her own upper-middle class one.[13]

Move #6: Decide upon a teaching ethos. Teaching is a performance of identity. Because all teachers' identities are multifaceted, teachers have multiple options from which to select a teaching *ethos*. For each teacher, the principle of selection ought to be: What teaching *ethos* can I perform that best promotes students learning? This principle breaks down into two important components: What can I perform, and what helps students learn? In terms of performance, teachers all have different identities and gifts, so one teacher cannot simply clone another teacher's pedagogy. In terms of student learning, students respond differently to different types of teaching, so a teacher must select an *ethos* based not just on his/her style but also on individual students' needs as well as on the historical moment, the institution, the assigned course, and even the events in the teacher's life at that particular moment.

Teachers' reflecting on multiple types of teaching *ethos* is especially important when teaching resistance-prone issues. As mentioned earlier, teachers may choose to perform the stances of gender-blindness and/or color-blindness, ignoring differences. Or as Shor, Jarratt, and others have argued, teachers may choose to perform the stances of critical pedagogy and feminist pedagogy (in all the multiplicity that these two terms imply), openly engaging differences. Or as Karen Kopelson has argued, teachers (especially "marginalized teachers") may chose to perform the stance of neutrality ("the very neutrality that students expect of teachers") as a "cunning" means of getting students to engage difference, a performance she posits as a corrective to what she considers the failures of critical pedagogy (118). Or teachers may perform a stance of listening pedagogically.

Listening pedagogically fosters a teacher *ethos* of openness, not neutrality. It asks students and teachers to recognize our resistance to differences, to analyze it, and, based on that analysis, to choose to reinforce, revise, and/or resist it. For example, in the Cornel West discussion mentioned earlier, I wish that, in addition to sharing my stance, I had asked the class to make two moves: (1) to associate the young white man's comment with a color-blind cultural logic, analyze that logic, and evaluate the assumptions and resistances undergirding that logic and (2) to associate West's text with a competing critical-race-studies cultural logic, analyze that logic, and evaluate the assumptions and resistances undergirding that logic. In this way, the student's claim would have been both acknowledged and challenged, as would have West's. I could have still articulated my stance but also simultaneously demonstrated via competing cultural logics how reasonable people of good will may disagree. In response, students would have been invited to reflect on these ideas and situate themselves according to their own reflections on our discussion, including their reflections on my stance and the power dynamics inherent in the classroom. In the process, we might have better heard and understood what one another was saying.

As the saying goes, hindsight is 20/20. Still, reflecting on what I wish I had done reminds me that teaching (like writing) is recursive and that teaching (like writing) is a life-long process of learning. Reflecting on what I wish I had done helps me plan what I may do in the future to set the scene for listening pedagogically.

Defining Listening Pedagogically

As a tactic of rhetorical listening, listening pedagogically has emerged from my pedagogical trials and mistrials. One such mistrial—the West discussion—challenged me to restructure my pedagogy,[14] with a particular emphasis on developing tactics for discussing how gender and whiteness intersect in classroom discourses and in daily life.[15] Such an emphasis, of course, invites (indeed encourages) conversations about how gender and whiteness intersect with other cultural categories that are used to classify people, such as class, ethnicity, age, region, nationality, sexual orientation, education, profession, political affiliation, religion, appearance, health, and family status.[16] This section demonstrates how I perform listening pedagogically in order to recognize, analyze, and resist post-Freudian resistance.[17]

When first thinking about listening pedagogically, I kept returning to Mary Daly's closing words from *Gyn/Ecology*: "In the beginning was not the word. In the beginning is the hearing . . . . We can weave and unweave, knot and unknot, only because we hear, what we hear, and as well as we hear" (424). Daly's words suggest that student/teacher resistance is not always based on an unwillingness to hear but sometimes on an incapacity to hear, an incapacity grounded in a lack of reflective lived experience or in a lack of the work necessary to understand commonalities and differences. Given this unwillingness and/or incapacity, an important question driving a rhetorical listening pedagogy is: How may students and teachers increase both their willingness and their capacity for hearing? The answer, in many ways, depends upon the identifications and identity of each student and teacher. But instead of retreating into a postmodern paralysis that precludes any generalizations about teaching, I want to recommend general moves for performing listening pedagogically, particularly in terms of teaching gender and whiteness. If employed by other teachers, these moves must, of course, be adapted to local conditions in ways that construct pedagogical moments that enable both students and teachers to hear as well as they possibly can.

Move #1: Study how language functions via tropes. The term *trope* is useful for helping students understand how people are born into an already existing language system wherein words (such as *gender* and *whiteness*) function as culturally coded tropes that, in turn, function as cultural categories that, in turn, inform how we see, order, analyze, and make meaning in the world. My decision to supplement the terms *word* and *meaning* with *trope* echoes Pamela Caughie's reasoning:

> [O]ne cannot understand Ferdinand de Saussure's concept of the sign if one translates "signifier" and "signified" for "word" and "meaning" as beginning theory students inevitably do. And yet the inevitability of that mistake can itself help students to understand why Saussure needs the concept of sign to challenge precisely the concept of language bound up with word-meaning and thereby to grasp the importance and the long-term effects of the structuralist revolution. The initial slip in translating the theoretical concept into familiar terms is a necessary one in order to conceptualize the difference a theory of sign makes to thinking about language. (5)

Shifting from *word* to *trope* helps students hear how language changes over time and place, how it carries historical and cultural baggage, how it signifies multiple meanings, and how it figures relationships between material things and their associated meanings.

To teach the tropological function of language, I sometimes use myself as an example and list on the board ways that my body[18] (a material thing) is troped (associated with historically and culturally coded words and their meanings that, in turn, function as tropes):

Thing	Trope	Associated Meanings (also tropes)
my body	*Kris*	shy, (not) funny, daughter, wife, Mama
my body	*Mama*	security/love, anger/exasperation
my body	*Dr. Ratcliffe*	(in)competent, professor, administrator
my body	*woman*	middle-aged
my body	*middle-aged*	(past) prime
my body	*white*	race privilege
my body	*feminist*	women's rights

Students and I discuss the following questions. How does each trope offer me a range of context-specific roles, that is, roles that afford me both opportunities and constraints for performing my identity? Which roles are culturally approved and, hence, deemed "normal"? Which are not? In what contexts? *Mama* and *feminist* are good terms for conducting such discussions as well as for exposing how tropes are culturally and historically grounded. Then we discuss how each term is a synecdoche, or one thread, of my ever-evolving identity.

Using these threads to demonstrate how language play via tropes is a culturally grounded yet never-ending process, I discuss how my being troped as *woman* in the U.S. in 2005 signifies that I may wear pants or a skirt; that I may wear makeup or not; that my insurance forms, tax forms, and daughter will probably be filed under my husband's last name, not mine; that students may expect me to be more understanding of their issues than some of my male colleagues are; and that I may be invited to serve on committees, in part, to represent gender equity. In addition, my being troped as *woman* may suggest *middle-aged*, which, in turn, signifies that my health needs will shift and that, while my career may be in its prime, my looks are past their prime in terms of the U.S. youth culture. And, finally, my being troped as *middle-aged woman* may also suggest *white*, which, in turn, signifies that on a daily basis I probably will not have to notice how race informs my life unless I choose to do so. But given a different context, all that could change. And so it goes.

Understanding the function of tropes (not simply as a matter of style but as the very "nature" of language itself) helps students and teachers understand how competing discourses can lie before us, reverberating with the potential to be negotiated and renegotiated via rhetorical listening.

Move #2: Define how gender *and* race *(including* whiteness*) function as tropes.* Once *trope* is defined, the particular functions of *gender* and *race* may be addressed. Like all tropes, they function as historically and culturally grounded terms associated with already existing attitudes and actions although that coding is constantly in flux.

As discussed in the introduction, *gender* and *whiteness* may signify biological or cultural differences or some combination thereof; more specifically, these tropes signify differently within different cultural logics. Consider what happens when *gender* and *whiteness* are defined as biological difference. The logic of patriarchy takes gender-as-biological-difference as a major premise for its existence just as the logic of white supremacy takes whiteness-as-biological-difference as a major premise. On the other hand, the logic of postmodern feminism argues that gender-as-biological-difference is grounded in the philosophical fallacy of essentialism, and the logic of critical race studies argues that whiteness-as-biological-difference is grounded in the scientific fallacy of categorizing humans by race. As a result of these multiple significations, students and teachers often "talk past" each other (Duncan 44), employing the same terms (*gender* and *race*) but invoking different definitions and cultural logics and never hearing the differences; thus, they remain oblivious to differences in intent and effect, becoming at best frustrated and at worst enraged.

To address such confusions in the classroom, I have learned to discuss the definitions and cultural logics outlined in the introduction. To study how *gender* and *whiteness* function as tropes, students and I may refer to the list of how my body is troped and discuss: (1) how all our bodies are born into an already existing language system that marks us via gender and race before we are even aware of it; (2) how that already existing language system has already existing definitions of terms, such as *woman, white, middle-class*; (3) how these definitions are coded to imply "acceptable" attitudes and behaviors for people associated with the terms; (4) how these codings socialize us all whether they are directly associated with us or only associated with us via the negative; and (5) whether we have an ethical imperative to make our socialization audible and then visible to ourselves (as much as possible, anyway, given the function of the unconscious) in order to negotiate our troubled identifications.

Listening pedagogically to such considerations offers students and teachers a degree of choice in terms of embracing, revising, and/or resisting our socialization and troubled identifications. Listening pedagogically to such considerations encourages us to think more critically about our own resistance, especially to gender and whiteness, and about how these tropes inflect all aspects of our lives, in the classroom and beyond.

Move #3: Reflect on how local conditions inform our definitions of gender and whiteness. Given that historical and cultural context determines the type of socialization that a person experiences, students and teachers need to recognize how their socialization informs their identifications with gender and whiteness.

To make identifications with whiteness visible to students in class, I often begin by asking in my most academic voice, "What does *whiteness* mean?" I may be rewarded with blank stares. A brave soul may lift her or his hand and say something like, "It's a color" or "It symbolizes purity." I nod and commend the class on a good start and toss a paperback dictionary to a student and ask him or her to look up *white* and *whiteness*. If no one answers my initial question, I begin by tossing the dictionary. After a student reads the definitions aloud, I say, "For fun, let's look up *black*." After a student reads that definition aloud, I ask for their responses. At that point, I may share OED definitions, demonstrating how *blood* and *color* haunt many of them; then I refer to the definitions and cultural logics outlined in the introduction to this book.

In the course of this discussion (sometimes lively, sometimes not), I make sure to cite three things: (1) Toni Morrison's *Playing in the Dark*, where she discusses how a Western symbol system (wherein *white* signifies purity and goodness while *black* signifies mysteriousness and danger) got laid onto the backs of real people early in U.S. history; (2) the Japanese symbol system, wherein *white* signifies death; and (3) Malcolm X's *Autobiography*, where he talks about looking up *black* and *white* in the dictionary while in prison and having an epiphany about how all language is culturally coded (I also tell students that this passage inspired this lesson plan). Then I ask about other "colors" associated with race, such as red, brown, and yellow.

To continue helping students recognize their cultural socialization on this topic, I next ask them in a much more let's-talk-turkey tone of voice, "OK, you all, what gets coded *white* in U.S. culture. Come on, you know this. Mind you, I'm not endorsing this coding, I'm just trying to get it on the board so that we can discuss it." At this point, they are off and running. I fill the board with responses, such as golf, suburbs, culture, classical music, not being able to dance, food, preppie clothes, doing well in school (i.e., acting white),[19] tables in their high school lunchrooms, magazines, Hollywood, models, the U.S. presidency. Then I ask them questions, based on their list: Does this list mean that only white people play golf? No, they tell me, it just means that a media circus erupts when someone like Tiger Woods enters the PGA. Does this list mean that all Latinos refuse to listen to classical music? No. Does it mean that all African Americans refuse to wear polo shirts? No. Does it mean that all white people really can't dance? No. Does it mean that white men and white women are given the same kinds of unearned race privilege? Well, not exactly. Then, I ask, what is the function and "origin" of this list: In other words, why are we able to make it, and where do these ideas come from?

By listening pedagogically to how definitions of *gender* and *whiteness* play out in our daily lives, students and teachers may recognize how the terms that we are born into influence what we see and what we cannot see as well as what we hear and what we cannot hear. In turn, students and teachers may understand not only how these terms provide the scaffolding for our world views but also how the gaps in such scaffolding provide spaces for personal agency. The end result is not a totalizing world view that explains and predicts all human actions and attitudes in terms of a static identity politics. Rather, the end result is simply another recognition: the terms that define us are fluid in ways that enable them to be redefined and enable us to redefine ourselves in our own eyes and in the eyes of others. But first we must hear the differences. Such recognition and hearing echo what Emmanuel Levinas might call the self's continuous ethical engagement with others and what Pamela Caughie might call passing.[20]

Move #4: Investigate how gender *and* whiteness *continuously intersect with each other as well as with other cultural categories, such as class, age, region, nationality, and so forth.* In "After Words" to *Feminism and Composition Studies*, Lynn Worsham argues that whiteness may be lonely but that it never exists alone (336–46). Beautifully relating her childhood story of Blue Betty, Worsham exposes how whiteness continuously intersects with gender, race, class, and region.

To study such intersections, I may ask students to revisit the list of white coding and consider *not* how gender can be "added on" but rather how gender has silently informed what we have been talking about all along. We may talk, for example, about how the U.S. presidency has been coded not just white but male (i.e., if you close your eyes and say the word *president*, the first image that comes to mind is probably a white male in a power suit even though women and non-white males are legally able to be president). We may talk about how in 1803 being white did not guarantee white women born in the U.S. equal rights of citizenship, such as voting rights, property rights, or parental rights; we also talk how about how being non-white in 1803 did guarantee an absence of all of these rights for non-white women, especially for those who were slaves. We may even talk about how the media fuss over golfer Annika Sorenstam was similar yet different than the fuss over Tiger Woods. In this way, students may understand Worsham's claim that whiteness and gender are cultural codes that never function alone; students may also recognize that they already know a lot about how these codes function, including that talking about them is uncomfortable.

The challenge of focusing on intersections of cultural categories is combating students' (and teachers') desire for a master narrative that explains and predicts everything related to gender and whiteness. Rich describes this desire for a master narrative as follows:

> Sometimes I feel I have seen too long from too many disconnected angles: white, Jewish, anti-Semite, racist, anti-racist, once-married, lesbian, middle-class, feminist, exmatriate southerner, *split at the root*— that I will never bring them whole. ("Split" 122)

Yet, as Rich teaches us, the trick is to release the desire for an impossible wholeness while committing to the practice of continually negotiating intersections:

> It's a moving into accountability, enlarging the range of accountability. I know that in the rest of my life, the next half century or so, every aspect of my identity will have to be engaged. The middle-class white girl taught to trade obedience for privilege. The Jewish lesbian raised to be a heterosexual gentile. The woman who first heard oppression named and analyzed in the Black Civil Rights struggle. The woman with three sons, the feminist who hates male violence. The woman limping with a cane, the woman who has stopped bleeding are also accountable. The poet who knows that beautiful language can lie, that the oppressor's language sometimes sounds beautiful. The woman trying, as part of her resistance, to clean up her act. (123)

Such moves are the grounds for listening pedagogically and, as Rich argues, for living an ethical life.

Move #5: Expose the perceived "universality" of tropes, such as gender *and* whiteness, *by culturally grounding them.* Students and teachers sometimes proceed as if terms, such as *gender* and *whiteness*, mean the same thing to all people in all cultures. As common sense tells us, a person is either a man or a woman, either white or non-white. But common sense can be myopic.

I first learned to expose the gender coding of *universality* by reading Rich's "When We Dead Awaken," where she discusses her training as a poet in the late 1940s and early 1950s: "I had been taught that poetry should be 'universal,' which meant, of course, nonfemale" (44). The modernist cultural logic in she was immersed dictated the universality of poetry while coding that universality mostly in terms of men's issues and experiences. By laying her feminist poetic impulses in the late 1950s alongside her earlier modernist training, Rich recognized how the term *universal* resonated differently within the cultural logics of modernism and feminism. Hence, *universality* is exposed as a situated term.

This method works well in the classroom when discussing the terms *gender-blind* and *color-blind*. Within a cultural logic that celebrates blindness as a means to equality, gender-blindness and color-blindness resonate as positive stances that signify equal treatment for all. But within a cultural logic that acknowledges differences, gender-blindness and color-blindness resonate as negative stances that deny already existing inequalities and prevent celebrations of differences. To be honest, after such class discussions, many students still embrace gender- and color-blindness as an ideal, but this *ideal* is coupled with the recognition of *real* differences.

Studying how *universal* is haunted by the ideal and the real produces a side benefit: exposing the predominance and problems of binary (either/or) thinking within Western culture. Binaries abound: real/ideal, general/particular, global/local, "master" narratives/excess, black/white. Students and teachers may critique binary oppositions via their terms and via the terms' functions within cultural logics, much as Rich critiqued the term *universal* within modernist and feminist cultural logics. Students and teachers may also critique binary oppositions via their slash mark, which represents the always existing, often-unspoken excess.

To make the slash mark visible to students, I may ask them to listen pedagogically to a binary opposition haunting our culture and then critique that opposition in terms of our course. For example, in the advanced writing course described in the appendix, I may ask students to contemplate the binary opposition that has been purposely established in the first two weeks of the course calendar between white writers and African American writers, a binary that emulates dominant patterns of thinking about race in the U.S. in terms of white and black. I may ask students to listen to excerpts from Jeanne Wakatsuki Houston and James D. Houston's *Farewell to Manzanar* and Cherríe Moraga's "The Breakdown of the Bicultural Mind." These excerpts expose and resist the white/black binary opposition and provide sites for pursuing multicultural and multiethnic threads.

Move #6: Expose the perceived "naturalness" of tropes, such as gender and whiteness by historicizing them. For many students and teachers, the terms *gender* and *whiteness* have become naturalized; that is, the terms signify as if they are as natural as breathing, as if they have existed ever since humans first populated the Earth. Historicizing the usage of such terms exposes that they have changed over time and place, sometimes quickly, often slowly.

To study the naturalization of terms, students and I revisit the list of what gets coded *male* and *white* in the U.S. today and discuss how this list might change if we were talking about, say, the U.S. in 1800. If they are stumped, I throw out the phrase "all men" from the Declaration of Independence and ask: What did it mean in theory in 1800, and what did it mean in reality? At that point, we discuss how the phrase was initially coded as "free white male property-owners." That signification is why Frederick Douglass invokes the promise, not the reality, of the Declaration in his 1852 "The Meaning of the Fourth of July for the Negro," which argues that the holiday is a white man's holiday. It is why Elizabeth Cady Stanton and committee make the same move in their 1848 "Declaration of the Sentiments and Resolutions," which rewrites the Declaration using *men* and *women* instead of just *men*. And it is why Martin Luther King Jr. makes the same move in his 1963 "I Have a Dream" speech. From these examples, we may add to our 1800 list of what gets coded *male* and *white*: freedom, citizenship, the right to vote, the right to make decisions about one's own children. As a corollary (to emphasize gender), I ask students how this list of what gets coded *white* and *male* would change if we were talking about *white* and *female*. As a corollary (to emphasize place), I ask students how this list would change if we were talking about, say, 1990 South Africa, the year Nelson Mandela was released from prison.

Even with these examples, students often argue that gender and race issues are now fixed (pun intended), and students often draw a blank when asked about the origin of *whiteness*. They are often surprised to learn via Theodore W. Allen's *Invention of the White Race* that term *white* did not have legal or social currency in the U.S. until the seventeenth century. Before that, people tended to identify themselves according to ethnic traditions, that is, the Irish race or the British race. Students are also intrigued by Noel Ignatiev's thesis in *How the Irish Became White*, which asserts that early Irish immigrants in the U.S. were not coded white (because at that time whiteness intersected with religion and ethnicity a la WASP) and only became white over time. Using these ideas as springboards for thought, students may investigate why the term *white* gained legal and social currency in the U.S., how it evolved via a five-races-of-man theory in biology textbooks, and how it is performed by people of all ethnicities.

Listening pedagogically to such scholarly investigations invites students and teachers to resist the frequent invisibility and unspokenness of whiteness in U.S. public spheres and to reflect on how the trope of whiteness informs our own lives, regardless of our ethnicities. Such a focus on our identifications with whiteness radically departs from a consideration of people as essentially white or nonwhite; this focus also foregrounds the real-life effects of socially constructed categories, such as gender and whiteness.

Move #7: Distinguish between physical bodies and rhetorical tropes, such as gender *and* whiteness. One reason that language use in the U.S. is so confusing is that the distinction between bodies and tropes is often collapsed: such as, white man or non-white woman is commonly perceived as an essential identity, and that essentialism becomes the grounds for stereotyping of all kinds. Listening pedagogically to tropes, such as *gender* and *whiteness*, is one way to identify this collapse and distinguish body from trope.

To challenge this collapse of body and trope, I sometimes paraphrase a scene from *Dinah Was*. This play narrates the life of blues, jazz, and R and B singer Dinah Washington who gained crossover fame in 1959 for her "white" rendition of "What a Difference a Day Makes." In one 1959 scene, Dinah parks herself on her suitcase in the middle of the Las Vegas Sands's lobby to protest the management's letting her sing in the hotel but not sleep there. A kitchen worker, an African American woman, brings Dinah toast and coffee, and when Dinah starts asking questions, the worker hesitates, throwing glances at the white man standing off to the side. Dinah follows the young woman's gaze, and says something to the effect, "Don't worry about him. He works for me. And he's not as white as he looks."

This claim exemplifies the slippery relationship between bodies and tropes in three ways. First, in a culture's "common sense," bodies become identified in terms of tropes; for example, in the 1950s U.S., the man standing off to the side is coded as a "white" man and, as such, signifies potential danger to the kitchen worker who fears that he might report her to the hotel management for fraternizing with Washington. Second, bodies are not necessarily identical to a trope's current usage; for example, in 1959 the "white" man is actually sympathetic to Washington and even works for her as her manager. Third, regardless of their individual sympathies, troped bodies benefit from the privileges or lack of privileges associated with their cultural codings; for example, even though the white man works for Washington and is sympathetic to her cause, he can choose whether or not he wants to sleep at the Sands. She cannot.

Listening pedagogically to distinguish between bodies and tropes helps students and teachers understand how bodies are marked by gender and race/ethnicity in productive ways and how bodies are also stereotyped in nonproductive and dehumanizing ways. Such understanding, then, becomes grounds for accountability and action.

Move #8: Acknowledge the embodiment of tropes. Although distinguishing between bodies and tropes is important, it is equally important to understand how tropes, such as *gender* and *whiteness*, become embodied in people via socialization and also how people may (to some degree) resist this socialization.

One way to illustrate the embodiment of tropes is to discuss Morrison's *Playing in the Dark*. She argues that early in its history, the U.S. embraced a Western symbol system in which *black* signifies mystery, dread, and evil, and *white* signifies clarity, safety, and purity. This symbol system reached its peak in Romanticism and became entangled with a color-coded slavery system. This entanglement got laid onto the backs of very real bodies: The Western symbol system was associated with bodies that were legally and socially coded black or white within the slave system, even though the bodies themselves were not, in actuality, black or white in color (36–39). As such, bodies and groups of bodies were coded according to these entangled symbol systems. This entanglement became an obsession in U.S. culture that haunts us to the present day. This entanglement is a mind-numbing, heartbreaking example of how a socially constructed category, in this case race, becomes embodied in people and influences how they perceive the world, themselves, and each other. Moreover, this embodiment is intersectional: Raced bodies are also gendered in terms of actions and attitudes that are coded for white men and non-white men as well as for white women and non-white women.

Listening pedagogically to texts, such as Morrison's, helps students and teachers recognize and analyze the embodiment of tropes as well as their entanglements and intersections. Once such embodiments are recognized and analyzed, students and teachers have choices: to continue performing the embodied socialization and/or to try to resist the naming, thinking, and valuing that accompany such socialization. Renaming, rethinking, and revaluing does not rid U.S. culture of tropes; these moves simply afford us a means for employing tropes more equitably, both culturally and personally.

Move #9: Develop and share pedagogical theory, research, and tactics for linking a gendered and raced rhetoric to writing instruction. This chapter and the teaching materials in the appendix attempt to enact this recommendation, joining a vigorous scholarly conversation about gendered and raced writing instructions, as well as the resistance to it.[21]

What is important to remember is that all pedagogy is local. Consequently, this chapter is offered not as the defining word on teaching intersections of gender and whiteness; it simply contributes my experiences with listening pedagogically to a scholarly conversation that invites students and teachers to engage these intersections—and others—in their own ways. Listening pedagogically may encourage students and teachers to recognize their resistances and to give a person, a text, or an idea that they might have initially rejected another hearing, one that results in a fuller understanding even if it reaffirms the conclusions associated with their initial resistance.

Move #10: Keep listening for cultural privilege and its lack within an accountability logic as a way to critique the power differentials of sexism, racism, and their intersections. Despite the U.S. grand narratives of individualism and equality, power differentials haunt all interactions among people. This is the structure of human communication, whether the issue is gender, race, class, or anything else; the only variance in this structure is the degree to which the power differential influences the communication. Those with power often deny or downplay this differential; those with less power often feel it acutely.

This power differential triggers different kinds of resistance in the classroom. When trying to write and talk about issues of sexism and/or racism, students and teachers often find it easy to resist such conversations via the following claims: (1) the problems have been solved; (2) the problems are not the students' and teachers' problems; (3) the problems are too large for individual people to address; and (4) the classroom is no place to hold such discussions.

To resist such resistance in my classes, I have learned from Peggy McIntosh's "White Privilege: Unpacking the Invisible Knapsack" that, for me, the most effective means of discussing sexism and racism in the classroom is to introduce the idea of earned and unearned cultural privilege. Earned privilege is a privilege that someone has done something to deserve, such as working hard in school in order to get a good job; unearned privilege is a privilege that someone is born into and has done nothing to deserve, such as being born white in the U.S. and not usually having to think about race on a daily basis. Once this distinction is introduced, students and I may discuss how unearned privilege haunts sexism and racism in U.S. culture at different points in history. Finally, we reflect on the accountability and choices implied by such unearned cultural privilege and its lack.

In order to recognize unearned cultural privilege and its lack, I ask students to *listen* to the discourses that surround them—assigned readings, classroom discussions, dorm conversations, TV shows, movies, workplace exchanges, family stories. For like Ruth Salvaggio, I believe that students and teachers

> need to fine-tune our own audible senses as we read and write, listening carefully to *what can be heard*. I say this not to turn away from vision and embrace sound as an alternative mode of communication (another false dichotomy), but to begin to discern the effects of sound. (4)

Such listening is a first step in laying our stories alongside one another and challenging the *logos* as we know it.

Listening pedagogically for earned and unearned cultural privilege and its lack reinforces several lessons. First, all cultural privilege is context-dependent. Second, all people circle in—and out—of privileged positions every day. Third, there is no essential privilege or essential lack of privilege—just culturally constructed ones that may be (pardon the term) deconstructed and reconfigured more equitably, which, of course, is easier said than done. When focusing on privilege—whether gender privilege, white privilege, class privilege, age privilege or other privilege—students and teachers are invited to determine whether the privilege is earned or unearned and whether we are accountable or not for the opportunities that such privilege affords and denies us—and others.

This focus on earned and unearned cultural privilege and its lack inculcates the performance of pedagogical listening in students and teachers; as such, it provides a means of discussing resistance-prone topics, such as gender and whiteness. This focus also potentially extends such performances beyond the classroom. But whether students and teachers are located in or out of the classroom, my hope is that we (all of us) learn to listen pedagogically—learn, when necessary, to resist our own resistance.

Sometimes we will.

Sometimes we will not.

Despite the strategic idealism of this study, I am pragmatic.

Students' Listening Pedagogically

To add students' voices to academic discussions of gender and whiteness, I asked four former students for permission to publish and discuss their writings, and they kindly conferred it. To historicize this discussion, I want to describe the context within which they wrote. Although many different Marquette University classes have informed my thinking about listening since I began teaching there in 1993, this section focuses on a particularly vigorous 2000 advanced writing class of mainly junior and seniors. In this class, four portfolios were assigned, each containing one creative nonfiction essay and one short piece modeled after a *New Yorker* column, the point being that students had to read these genres, extrapolate the writing conventions, and then employ these conventions in ways that negotiated the conventions with the students' own interests and voices. Each portfolio was framed around a rhetorical concept, with an inquiry theme that illustrated the concept. As the teaching materials in the appendix indicate, unit three of this course focused on the rhetorical concepts of analysis and style with an inquiry theme of whiteness.

So what did students do with the assignment to write a creative nonfiction piece on how the trope of *whiteness* functions in the U.S. and in their own lives? By engaging this assignment, students resisted the dominant impulse in U.S. culture to render *whiteness* invisible and inaudible; in the process, each student struggled with the particular ways that this dominant impulse had become embodied. What follows are examples of how four students listened pedagogically to assigned readings, class discussions, and discourses in their own lives in order to write their essays. What also follows are examples of how I listened pedagogically to each student's essay, learning lessons that continue to inform my pedagogy.

The first paper was written by a young white man, Ben Weiler, who identifies race as a problem in the U.S. and offers this solution: "America needs to drop the racial tags." What follows is his reasoning.

When I was growing up, my mother taught me that I should respect all people as equals. My grade school teachers taught the same thing to their 30 or so all-white classes. I listened to my mother and I paid heed to my teachers, but it wasn't enough. I'm a racist. I look at a white person and I make a totally different set of assumptions that I would if that person were of a different race. I get uneasy when an African American pulls up next to me at a stoplight; I try not to make eye contact with the Hispanic. Maybe my parents and teachers were putting thoughts in my head that they didn't even know about, maybe they are racist too. In fact, I'm sure of it—it comes along with being white in society today. Did I mention that it comes with being Indian, or Puerto Rican, or any other race too? Society breeds racists, only this century, we'll be quieter. We say that we won't judge others, that we won't make broad assumptions about them, but I find myself making quick judgments about race all the time. I can't be the only one who does this, and I know I'm not the only one who works to suppress these judgments. . . .

Race relations in this country need to be improved. But America is going about it in the wrong way. If we see each other in terms of difference, we'll never come to stand on equal ground. Parents need to teach their children true equality. When my mother took me in her arms and told me that people of all races are equal, she also told me two other things. First, she told me that people with different skin color are often seen as quite different, and second, she told me that people with different skin color are not given equal opportunity. Even as a kid, these unspoken messages seep through. Humans are not naturally racist. We are taught to look at differences, and we see them. We see them all over the place.

America needs to drop the racial tags. We need to take the terms Black, African American, Hispanic, Asian, Eastern European, Indian and all the rest and forget them. Why do we need to classify everyone? How does it help? Instead, let's call people what they really are. It will make things less confusing. Let's try it:

That person is . . . "Black."

No, no. That person is . . . "African American,"

No, try again. That person is . . . "I don't know."

That person is Joe. And that person is Ricardo. And that person is Eileen.

Perhaps I am being unrealistic when I propose that we simply drop all racial tags, but years of working to make the races equal by recognizing the differences has left us far short of our goals. Something different needs to be done. New breath needs to be blown into the staleness of racial issues. If we raise our children to forget about race as an issue altogether, they might have a small chance of moving forward.

Ben is articulate and cognizant of problems haunting his identifications with whiteness, his paper, and U.S. society. To address these problems, he invokes two competing logics of race in the U.S. First, he names and rejects a logic of race supremacy (as opposed to white supremacy), which enables anyone of any race to believe that his/her race is superior to all others simply because he/she feels more comfortable around similar people. As a corrective to this logic, Ben offers the logic of color-blindness, which denies racial differences and focuses on human commonalities.

Although I applaud Ben's motives, I find myself resisting the logic of color-blindness because it too often functions as an ideal that masks very real discriminations, but I purposely make spaces for students to articulate this logic (which is very popular at my school) so that it may be critiqued. If units on resistance-prone issues are to be productive—if they are to echo in students' ears long after the class is over—then a teacher may want to find ways to assert her or his own beliefs as a means of giving students something with which to agree and/or disagree. In this way, the classroom may be imagined as a space wherein students are not ridiculed or objectified, and their grades are not penalized if the students disagree with the teacher. To construct such a space, students and teachers need to embrace two premises: (1) show respect for one another, and (2) agree that reasonable people may disagree. Students and teachers also need to be prepared to negotiate additional rules of engagement throughout the semester, beginning on day one.[22]

I include one addendum to this discussion of Ben's paper. A couple semesters later, Ben enrolled in an English methods course that I was teaching while the professor who usually taught it was on sabbatical. One day, when another student brought up color-blindness, Ben responded that he, too, used to think that way but that his teaching clinical in the Milwaukee Public School system the previous semester had taught him differently. He found that his Latino, African American, and white students assumed certain things about him simply because he was a *white man*. So although he had not given up his ideal of a color-blind society, he had learned that he had to deal with students' very real assumptions about white men. That is, he had begun to address the assumptions head on, not pretend to be blind to them. In this way, it seems to me, he began to hear the intersections of gender and whiteness as well as his identifications, disidentifications, and non-identifications with them.

Ben and his essay taught me several lessons about pedagogy. First, students and teachers need to discuss color-blindness, given its pervasive influence in U.S. culture; thanks to Ben, I am much more tolerant of the need for such discussions. Second, students and teachers need to reflect on resistance-prone issues long after the class is over, much as Ben did during his subsequent student teaching in the Milwaukee Public School system. Third, students and teachers need to contemplate how identifications with whiteness are complicated by gender, not as an add-on category but as an already existing presence. That is, how do intersections of gender and whiteness code the term *teacher* differently for whites and non-whites, men and women, students and teachers within different contexts? And how are these intersections complicated by other cultural categories, such as class?

The second paper was written by a young woman, Carol Sales, a U.S. citizen whose parents had emigrated from the Philippines prior to her birth. Echoing Rich's opening to "Split at the Root," Carol writes about her writing block that results from the lack of a lexicon in the U.S. for discussing whiteness:

> I sit here at my desk, tired and sleepy. I have put off writing this essay until the last minute, which is not unusual for me. However, I have never procrastinated until this late at night. I don't know why it's difficult for me to write an essay on whiteness. After all, I did grow up in a white neighborhood and I have only white friends. This should have given me more than enough to write about, but it didn't.

With no ready lexicon, Carol turns to a concrete task (filling out college forms) as a way of helping her think about whiteness:

> I was filling out an application in hopes of being accepted at a school or job, (I don't really remember), when I came across a checklist. This was all too common; so common that I usually never think about it. Most Americans have seen this mini-survey. It is a list of various ethnic descriptions, such as white, African American, Hispanic. The classification system separates people and makes distinctions between

them according to color and heritage. However, these simple categories disguise a messy, complicated series of racial issues. Although the information that the person provides on these inventories is not always required and does not affect admission status, its significance is hidden in the agenda of those who record such data. Is there a quota that must be met? Will this data be transformed into a color pie chart for future reference? Who wants to know this and why do they want to know? We never ask these questions out loud; we don't even know whom to ask. Rather we just put a check in the box and forget about it.

When I encounter these checklists, I automatically mark the box that says "Asian/Pacific Islander." How strange it is for a person born in Evanston, Illinois, and raised in the Midwest to claim that she is an "islander.

But identifying the issue is not enough for Carol. She offers tactics for acting on it:

Doing way with racial checklist questionnaires would help us to unify the country. We would be taking the first step to create the rich American culture that so many people ache for. Never again would we have Japanese concentrations camps in America during wartime, because all Americans will actually be considered full-fledged Americans. Even so, this would only be a first step in solving the problem of racism. . . . As Martin Luther King said in his "Letter from Birmingham Jail," "Time is neutral." He meant that problems do not get better over time. Rather, people have to exert their influence to stop injustice. My checklist suggestion fails in this aspect: it does not directly affect people's perceptions. It is just too unobtrusive and weak. Therefore, we need to take action and fight injustice when we find it among us. Most often this occurs in verbal form, when people make generalizations or shout racial slurs. The worst thing we can do is remain silent and wait for time's magic hands to fix these dilemmas. After all, time's hands are just like ours—they must be moved by human will.

Carol, too, is articulate and cognizant of contradictions haunting her piece as well as U.S. culture. In addition to identifying her lack of lexicon, Carol makes another important point: Changes in language without changes in attitude (i.e., nominalism) will not eradicate injustice in the world of our daily lives.

While contemplating her identifications with whiteness, Carol invokes several cultural logics of race in her essay. First, she names and rejects the logic of white supremacy that enabled the U.S. government to intern Japanese Americans but not German or Italian Americans. Second, she flirts with the logic of color-blindness when she states her desire for "all Americans to be considered full-fledged Americans." But her lived experiences expose the difficulties inherent in this logic, so, ultimately, she does not find it satisfactory. Third, she acknowledges the logic of multiculturalism when she discusses distinctions among people's ethnic heritage, but again, this logic is not totally satisfactory. So fourth, she invokes the logic of critical race studies, claiming that issues of ethnic heritage actually "disguise a messy, complicated series of racial issues" that need to be acted upon.

In terms of the intersections of gender and whiteness, Carol's text offers an interesting sentence: "How strange it is for a person born in Evanston, Illinois, and raised in the Midwest to claim that *she* is an '*islander*'" (emphasis added). Note that when discussing gender, Carol refers to herself in the third person, a kind of discursive distancing from the categories that society places upon her; at the same time, gendering the term *islander* suggests actions and attitudes associated with a gendered body, in her case a woman's body. Yet, by asserting that her socialization consisted of "a white neighborhood and . . . only white friends," Carol demonstrates how whiteness may be embodied within bodies otherwise designated on census forms.

Carol and her essay taught me several lessons about pedagogy. First, when discussing resistance-prone topics such as gender and race, students and teachers need to develop a lexicon for discussing them, an example being the definitions and cultural logics outlined in the introduction. Second, we need to evaluate language function in terms of tropes and in terms of nominalism, that is, how language may socially construct our realities yet how simply changing a word does not necessarily change a person's actions or attitudes. Third, we need to study how competing cultural logics may intersect within one person's thinking, much as Carol demonstrates when she invokes color-blindness, multiculturalism, and critical race studies. Fourth, we need to contemplate differences between *race* and *ethnicity* when investigating intersections with gender. For example, how do identifications with whiteness (as a racial category that codes dominant cultural practices in the U.S.) intersect with a census term like *Pacific islander* (as an ethnic category that marks a person)? How is a person's identify affected when the dominant culture's trope for that person feels to her like a dead metaphor—in

Carol's case, the Illinois native being called an islander. And how does the catch-all ethnic category of *Pacific islander* resonate differently for men and women who belong to different "Pacific island" cultures?

The third paper was written by a young African American woman, Kamenka Robbins, who told me that she also had trouble finding a lexicon for writing about whiteness but not because she could not recognize and define it in her own life. She could.

> As a young adolescent with a frail self-image, I was abruptly thrust into a predominantly white intermediate school from my black neighborhood school, an unwelcome transition. Even now, to find the word to articulate the feeling of being a brown pebble in a sea of salt proves to be a difficult task. As unwelcome as the transition was, my lessons in whiteness began immediately. Whiteness became Abercrombie and Fitch; spring break at Myrtle Beach; blank stares; not saying excuse me in the hall and barely audible "hellos" that made me feel like I was shouting when I actually said "hello" back. Whiteness became snappy answers and insulting poems about freedom on one of the 28 days of black history month. What did people who had never been oppressed physically, socially, and economically know about freedom?
>
> James Baldwin pondered what white people talk about when they are together. I too wonder. I wonder if they talk about why their throats close when it comes to greeting me as we pass one another? Do they discuss the advantages of being white? Have they ever examined the inherited perks of white skin available to them for the seizing from day to day, month to month, year to year, century to century? . . .
>
> My experiences dictate that my white friends in high school were great people, but would never come to my house for a pre-basketball game spaghetti dinner. [These experiences] lead to my assumption that surface interaction is only good enough for social arenas.

Kamenka is articulate and cognizant not only of how she sees whiteness playing out in her personal life but also of how she sees it working throughout history.

In the process of naming her identifications with whiteness, Kamenka refers to several cultural logics of race in her essay. First, she names the logic of white supremacy or, rather, its contemporary legacy. She grounds her identifications in concrete experiences with people (her white classmates), behaviors (saying hello), and things (clothes). She assumes that her white classmates "have never been oppressed physically, socially, and economically." Kamenka's assumption may be faulty because whatever unmarked abuses and/or oppressions her classmates may have suffered remain unmarked and, thus, unknown. Yet Kamenka's assumption is true in that her classmates have never been slaves or lived under Jim Crow. Of course, neither has she. But the difference between Kamenka and her white peers lies in the then-that-is-now legacy of slavery in the U.S. and in the privileges—"the inherited perks of white skin"—that this legacy affords her white peers.

Second, Kamenka invokes the logic of critical race studies, which argues that race issues must be addressed instead of swept under the rug of feel-good commonalities and differences. To address these differences, Kamenka (echoing James Baldwin) expresses a desire to eavesdrop . . . to discover what whites talk about when they are with one another, particularly what they say (if anything) about being white. This desire signifies more than two people's curiosity; it signifies a cultural need in the U.S. for more cross-cultural communication about whiteness and a host of other topics.

In terms of how gender intersects with whiteness, Kamenka notes:

> I used to joke about the top three questions white people would ask me when we'd meet. When telling them my name, their typical responses would be: Where are you from? Is your name African? What does your name mean? . . . It seems as if their inquiries were meant to . . . establish what "kind" of black person I am.

And, it seems, a fourth question is implied here, too: What "kind" of black *woman* is she?

Kamenka and her essay taught me several lessons about pedagogy. First, students and teachers need not just a lexicon for discussing race but a lexicon that enables *public* discussions about race and its competing cultural logics. Second, we need to contemplate the gendering of racial claims in terms of fashion, friends, and conversation topics. And third, we need to study the effects of history on the present, that is, the *then-that-is-now*, when discussing the intersections of gender and whiteness in people and in cultural structures. For example, how are the halls of today's high schools affected by the historical legacy of gender and racial oppression and privilege in the U.S.? How are *all* students affected by our country's hesitancy to entertain such questions? Is this hesitancy productive or not? If so, why? If not, what are the best strategies for encouraging such conversations, and what might be the desired objectives of the conversation?

The fourth paper was written by a young white man, Paul Doro, who reflects on how his small-town socialization informs his identifications and disidentifications with whiteness:

> I am a racist. That is easy to write and no easier to think about. . . .
>
> When you are raised in a town straight out of a John Cougar Mellencamp song, there is no outside world. There is your backyard and the park and your school. The list for what there is not is much bigger. There is no crime and there is no punishment, there is no hunger and there are no homeless, there is no fear and there are no hardships. You have no concept of these things and they do not exist. . . .
>
> All it took was moving to a city where colored people roamed the streets just like everybody else. Now these people who were either athletes or criminals on TV were walking around my neighborhood or going to the malls I shopped at. Out of the box I came.
>
> I moved to Milwaukee for school in August of 1997, and I became a racist. Not because of my beliefs or words, but because of my actions. It doesn't matter what did or did not come out of my mouth. It doesn't matter what I did or did not believe. Good intentions do not apply here. It was the things I did that mattered, and to this day I fight them.
>
> If I saw a young Black or Hispanic man walking my way, my instinct was to walk faster and grab my wallet. My heart beat faster and I wondered if he was a drug dealer or a gangster. These are things I never said, yet they instantly leapt into my thoughts. Anytime I saw a young man of color, I thought bad things without even thinking about it.
>
> My life has never been threatened. My car has never been broken into. I have never been mugged. Nobody has ever beaten me up. Yet I would be lying if I said that to this day I did not struggle with stereotypes and racism inside my own head. Does this make me a bad person? Am I the only one with these thoughts? Will I ever be able to win the war within myself?
>
> I have known plenty of colored people in my life, all in the last couple years. I have lived with them, and traveled with them, been friends with them, and even dated them. They have been a part of my life and my heart. They are some of the best people I have ever known. I wonder what they think of me. Not my looks or my personality or

my intelligence, but my obstacle? Did they see it? Have they helped me see it? I believe the questions have the same answer.

I hope the war isn't over. I still have plenty of fight left in me and I refuse to give up or give in. The goal is defined. I want to have the same thoughts every time I see a person walking down the street or sitting in a movie theater. I do not want to see color or race. I want to see only a person.

Paul, too, is articulate and cognizant of how whiteness plays out in his life.

In the process of articulating his identifications and disidentifications with whiteness, Paul invokes several cultural logics. The logic of white supremacy has a lingering effect on his writing and world view. He, too, claims that white America lacks a lexicon and a dialogue about whiteness, and he attempts to explain why: "When you are raised in a town straight out of a John Cougar Mellencamp song, . . . [y]ou have no concept of these things and they do not exist." He succinctly describes the effects of this cultural logic on his unconscious when he narrates the internal dialogue that accompanies him as he walks down the street: "If I saw a young Black or Hispanic man walking my way, my instinct was to walk faster and grab my wallet. My heart beat faster and I wondered if he was a drug dealer or a gangster. These are things I never said, yet they instantly leapt into my thoughts."

To counter this logic of white supremacy, Paul calls on the logic of critical race studies to demonstrate his own willingness to critique whiteness as a socializing racial category, not as an innate part of his nature. But he cannot do it in a vacuum. He situates himself in relation to his town, his entertainment via TV, and especially his African American friends: "I wonder what they think of me. Not my looks or my personality or my intelligence, but my obstacle? Did they see it? Have they helped me see it? I believe the questions have the same answer." Such situating may be read as reinforcing old patterns of appropriation, which bell hooks describes:

> Such appropriation happens again and again. It takes the form of constructing African-American culture as though it exists solely to suggest new aesthetic directions white folks might move in. Michelle Wallace calls it seeing African-American culture as "the starting point for white self-criticism." ("Politics" 21)

While the danger of such appropriation is very real and very pervasive in U.S. culture, it is not the only possible reading of Paul's situation nor even the best reading. By situating himself in relation to his friends, Paul may be read as exposing his always already existing self-other relations within different cultural contexts. Such relations, whether easy or complicated, drive his (and all human) identifications. When Paul lays his own story alongside the stories of his friends (people he knows and cares about) as opposed to the images provided by the television shows of his childhood, the identifications with whiteness haunting his own story are thrown into sharp relief, exposing gaps in his world view. Within those gaps, Paul finds sites for agency, filling in his "no concept of these things" with content based on the lived experiences and reflections of himself, his friends, and their interactions.

Interestingly, the logic of white supremacy and the logic of critical race studies converge when Paul uses the term *colored people*. This convergence exposes the complexity of the trope *race* and the slipperiness of language coding. Paul's occasional use of the outdated term *colored people* coupled with his willingness to critique his identifications with whiteness create an interesting tension in his paper. While Paul's usage may signify his level of (un)awareness of language politics at the time he wrote the paper, it does not seemingly signify for him the baggage often associated with the white-supremacy logic that was dominant in the U.S. when the term *colored people* was in vogue; however, readers (especially older readers) may find it difficult to read this term without flashing to its historical baggage. Yet it is precisely the slipperiness of language coding that enabled Paul to think beyond the historical baggage and fill the term with his own meanings. What emerges from his usage of the term is the tension between intent and effect (or even between intent and affect) as well as the rhetorical and pedagogical need to be aware of that tension.

Paul concludes by invoking the logic of color-blindness as an ideal to work toward even as he critiques the problems inherent in the race blindness of his own childhood. This desire for color-blindness is popular with many students, and instead of dismissing it out of hand, teachers may find it prudent to discuss the reasons for its popularity in the U.S. Some reasons include: our country's obsession with an egalitarian present, our obsession with the bootstraps of individualism, and our obsession with silencing discussions of race—and its intersections with other cultural categories. Moreover, teachers may find it prudent to discuss how a person's ability to embrace and/or reject this logic may be driven by privilege and/or by its lack.

Yet even as Paul embraces the ideal of a color-blind logic, he hints at his very real identifications with the intersections of gender and whiteness.

He specifies that "young *man* of color" [emphasis added] initially signifies danger to him, which reflects hooks's claim that "white people fear that our presence will cause violence" ("Counterhegemonic" 175), but he also specifies that "young *man* of color" later signifies friend. As for specific references to young *women* of color, he is more vague. If Paul's readers, however, place young women of color within the category of people of color (and, of course, readers should), then *young women of color* may also signify friend.

Paul and his essay taught me several lessons about pedagogy. First, students and teachers need to reflect on their lexicon for discussing race and gender, contemplating distances between writerly intent and possible readerly effects. Second, we need to study slippages in terms, such a *people of color* and *colored people*, which resonate differently in different cultural logics in the twenty-first century. Third, we need to contemplate the connections between tropes and their ever-changing meanings, especially in terms of intersecting gender and racial coding. For example, given the line in Paul's introductory paragraph—"When you are raised in a town straight out of a John Cougar Mellencamp song"—how is that small-town *you* gendered differently for Jack and for Diane? (And for students to understand that question, I may need to play Mellencamp's song.) How does *friend* resonate differently in terms of women and men . . . for women and men, and how are these resonances complicated by intersections with race and/or ethnicity?

The essays written by Ben, Carol, Kamenka, and Paul represent what Marquette students are capable of writing when they focus on rhetorical concepts, genre conventions, and inquiry themes. These essays also represent what students are capable of producing when they listen to how discourses of whiteness are performed by themselves and/or others. These essays do not provide a "solution" to the "problem" of whiteness as it functions in the U.S.; rather, they articulate honest statements by students who are located at a particular place and time. Such statements may lead students to greater understanding and, perhaps, to productive action in their own lives. Such statements may provide teachers opportunities to learn from students—not only about students' personal identifications with whiteness, not only about students' opinions of how whiteness functions in U.S. culture at large but also about teachers' own thinking and pedagogy. Personally, I owe thanks to these four students and their essays—and to many, many other students and their essays—for helping me in my never-ending but ever-evolving struggle to learn how to become a better pedagogue when teaching about rhetoric, writing, gender, and whiteness.

Rhetorical listening and its attendant tactics of eavesdropping, listening metonymically, and listening pedagogically will not solve all the world's problems, nor will they work well in all classroom situations. No rhetorical tactic could meet such a test. But rhetorical listening and its tactics may supplement agonistic rhetorical strategies by providing listeners (whether students or teachers or anyone else) possibilities for greater understanding and, at times, more effective and perhaps more ethical rhetorical conduct.

For example, if students and teachers study how pronouns function as tropes, then we may understand the slipperiness of *we*; that is, students and teachers may realize not just that *we* changes over time and place but that the very real material actions of our daily lives can work to make the circumstances of *we* more inclusive, or not. With such understanding, we (all of us) have a better chance of tackling the pronoun problem that haunts all our identifications: how to see *we* in *they* and *they* in *we*.

In such moments of listening to each other, to our institutions, to our cultures, and to ourselves, we may hear and then see how our identities are always already grounded in our identifications, disidentifications, and nonidentifications with others. In such moments, students and teachers of rhetoric will have circled back to Aristotle, Kenneth Burke, and Jacqueline Jones Royster . . . to hear them anew . . . when they enjoin us, as *listeners*, to know our audiences.

Appendix
Notes
Works Cited
Index

Appendix
Teaching Materials for Writing about Gender and Whiteness

These teaching materials are designed for a Marquette University advanced writing course, consisting mostly of junior and seniors. This third unit focuses on the rhetorical concepts of analysis and style with an inquiry theme of whiteness; this unit is third because students engage resistance-prone issues better in class if they have already developed a sense of community. Although I first began teaching such a unit in the mid-1990s, these materials represent a recent manifestation. I offer them here simply as ideas for teachers who are interested in designing their own pedagogical materials about gender and whiteness.

UNIT 3 CALENDAR: Profile and Essay #3
Analysis and Style with an Inquiry Theme of Whiteness

Unit Objectives: *Students will learn to*
(1) Define *analysis* as breaking an issue/idea into parts so as to better understand it
(2) Define *style* as sentence-level choices with both personal and cultural functions
(3) Recognize and employ elements of style
(4) Recognize and analyze the tropological function of language
(5) Recognize and analyze the way *whiteness* functions as a trope in culture and daily life
(6) Employ the conventions of profile in short writings and of creative nonfiction in essays

---

Week 7—Analysis and Style: The Politics of Language
M   Define analysis and style; discuss assignment #3; extrapolate profile conventions; brainstorm profile topics
    Read: *NY*   "Profile" (from two most recent issues)
W   Discuss definition; extrapolate creative nonfiction conventions
    Read: HO   Lillian Smith, Excerpt from *Killers of the Dream* (1949)
                WA   "Strategies for Using Definitions Analytically" (214–16; 208–9)
F   Discuss comparison; extrapolate creative nonfiction conventions
    Read: HO   James Baldwin, "White Man's Guilt" (1965)
                WA   "Comparison/Contrast" (209–12)

NY = *The New Yorker* magazine; WA = David Rosenwasser and Jill Stephen's *Writing Analytically*; HO = handout. Sources for all rhetorical concepts are Joseph Trimmer and Maxine Hairston's *Riverside Reader* and Rosenwasser and Stephen's *Writing Analytically*.

Week 8—Analysis and Style: Parallel Structure and Point-of-View

M   Discuss parallel structure; brainstorm topics for Essay #3; extrapolate creative nonfiction conventions

    Read: HO   Adrienne Rich, "The Distance Between Language and Violence" (1993)

              WA   "Parallel Structure" (328–30)

W   Writing Workshop

    Write: **Profile due** (bring author sheet, peer-review sheet, and profile draft)

F   Discuss point-of-view and binary thinking; extrapolate creative nonfiction conventions; brainstorm essay topics

    Read: HO   Nikki Giovanni, "Annual Conventions of Everyday Subjects" (1994)

              WA   "Binaries" (91–95)

    In-Class: HO   Excerpts from Cherríe Moraga and Jeanne Wakatsuki Houston

              HO   Peggy McIntosh, "White Privilege"

Week 9—Analysis and Style: Clarity/Conciseness and Emphasis

M   Discuss clarity/conciseness; in-class writing; extrapolate creative nonfiction conventions

    Read: HO   Dalton Conley, excerpt from *Honky* (2001)

              WA   "Getting the Right Word . . ." (305–11)

              Web   Greg Jay's Whiteness Web site: http://www.uwm.edu/~gjay/Whiteness/

W   Writing Workshop

    Write: **Essay #3 due** (bring author sheet, peer review sheet, and essay draft)

F   Discuss emphasis

    Read: Web   Continue discussion of Whiteness Website

              NY   Feature (to be decided, depending on the week's issue)

              WA   "The Periodic Sentence" (330–32); "The Cumulative Sentence" (332–33)

    Write: Bring your essay draft for in-class work on sentence style

Week 10—Analysis and Style Wrap-Up

M   **PORTFOLIO 3 DUE: Profile and essay, plus author sheets and peer-review sheets for each**

LESSON PLANS: Definition and Lillian Smith

Week 7—Analysis and Style: The Politics of Language

W Analysis via definition; extrapolate creative nonfiction conventions

Read: HO Lillian Smith, Excerpt from *Killers of the Dream* (1949)

WA "Strategies for Using Definitions Analytically" (214–16; 208–9)

1. Discuss definition [put on board].
   a) Types of definition: 1) lexical; 2) stipulative; 3) extended
   b) Strategies of definition:

1) Give examples	6) Define negatively
2) Analyze qualities	7) Test definition against evidence
3) Attribute features	8) Explore competing parts of a definition
4) Give functions	9) Use one definition to critique another
5) Draw analogies	10) Shift from questions of *what* to questions of *how* and *why*

2. Define *whiteness*. [Any of the following questions may be a freewrite prompt.]
   a) Define *race* and *ethnicity* (cf. introduction to *Rhetorical Listening*)
   b) Ask class: When do you have to think about being white or non-white? [**Hint**: Be prepared for silence . . . And let it fill the room. Then . . . I talk, or white students often talk about filling out college applications and census forms or walking around MU's campus, which abuts an African American section of Milwaukee. Non-white students may talk about being "the only one" in some MU classes. Then I share anonymous stories from former students, stories that they have privately shared with me but would not mention in class; I ask students what is significant about this private sharing and public silence.]
   c) Ask class: Do you think being white or non-white should matter? [**Hint**: Of course, most students will say "no." Students often argue for a color-blind society. This question is good for putting that discussion on the table. I have found that the best way to respond to the color-blind argument is to (1) agree that *ideally* we should all be color blind but (2) assert (and use their comments from the previous question as evidence) that *in reality* we are not color blind; thus, we need to find ways to negotiate our reality in more equitable ways.]

3. Discuss the connections between whiteness as a cultural category and people designated white and non-white.
   a) Ask students:
   1) What does *whiteness* signify? [**Hint**: Often, this question is met with silence. I use this silence, asking why this topic is so hard to talk about—e.g., because discussing white-

ness is popularly associated with the KKK et al., because U.S. culture does not have a ready lexicon for this topic.]

b) Ask the students:

1) What gets coded *white* in U.S. culture?
[**Hint:** Answers may include suburbs, golf, preppie clothing, food, money, people]

2) What attitudes and actions are (rightly or wrongly) associated with white people?
[**Hint:** Answers may include dancing the polka, not being able to dance, not getting race questions]

3) Can these attitudes and actions be performed by anyone?
[**Hint**: Eddie Murphy, Paul Rodriguez, and Chris Rock routines are useful here: They not only identify attitudes and actions associated with white people (in U.S. culture) but also demonstrate that one does not need a white body to perform these actions and attitudes. Also talk about "acting white." Discuss how identifications with whiteness work. Discuss connections between bodies and tropes.]

c) Offer them definitions of whiteness studies (cf. the handout at the end of this appendix)
[**Hint**: I briefly define whiteness studies and discuss its pros and cons as well as whether *whiteness* is even a term to continue using; I suggest they research via the Web, taking care to avoid the militia pages.]

4. Discuss the strategies (refer to the list on the board in #1) that Lillian Smith uses to define *whiteness* in 1949.
a) Put students into pairs to find these strategies
b) Pull the group together and discuss, making a list on the board
c) Ask students: Are these definitions still in play today? How? How not? Why? Why not?

5. Ask students how gender informs Smith's concept of *whiteness*.

LESSON PLANS: Comparison/Contrast and James Baldwin

Week 7—Analysis and Style: The Politics of Language

F   Analysis via comparison; extrapolate creative nonfiction conventions

Read: HO   James Baldwin, "White Man's Guilt" (1965)

          WA   "Comparison/Contrast" (209–12)

1. Discuss comparison/contrast [put on board].
   a) Types: [in terms of genre, paragraph, and critical thinking strategies]
      1) Divided
      2) Alternating
   b) Strategies:
      1) Discuss revealing similarities and differences
      2) Argue for significant key points
      3) Use one side to illuminate another
      4) Imagine how one side might respond to the other
      5) Focus on unexpected similarities and differences

2. Articulate Baldwin's definition of *whiteness*.
   a) Have students freewrite on how they think Baldwin defines *whiteness* in 1965
   b) Put list of students' ideas on the board
   c) Have them search for textual evidence to support (or refute) these claims

3. Compare/contrast Smith's and Baldwin's definitions of *whiteness*.
   a) Put students into pairs
   b) Have them compare/contrast the two readings, using the strategies listed on the board
   c) Then pull the group back together and make a compare/contrast list of definitions on the board
   d) Ask students which reading most appeals to them—and why.
      [**Hint:** If there is time, I have them freewrite on this last question before discussing it.]
   e) Ask students: How does gender inform Smith's and Baldwin's concepts of whiteness? How does class?

Week 8—Analysis and Style: Parallel Structure

M   Parallel structure; brainstorm topics for Essay #3; extrapolate creative nonfiction conventions

        Read: HO   Adrienne Rich, "The Distance Between Language and Violence" (1993)

                     WA   "Parallel Structure" (328–30)

1. Discuss parallel structure [put on board].
   a) Types/strategies of parallel structure
      1) Grammatical positions
      2) Logical points
   b) Show 2–3 examples of parallel structure on overhead or document camera, culled from readings or student papers.
   c) Show 3–4 sentences, culled from students' former drafts, that would benefit from parallelism. As a class, revise the sentences.

2. Articulate Rich's definition of *whiteness* from 1993.
   a) Put students in pairs to develop Rich's definition of *whiteness*
   b) Put list of students' ideas on the board

3. Compare/contrast Smith's, Baldwin's, and Rich's definitions of *whiteness*. Using the Rich list, develop comparisons/contrasts, focusing on how the definitions have (not) changed over time.

4. Study use of parallelism in Rich. Have pairs find samples of grammatical/logical parallelism in Rich and discuss the rhetorical effect (especially but not only as they inform her definition of whiteness).

LESSON PLANS:
Giovanni and Point-of-View/Binary Thinking with Moraga, Wakatsuki Houston, and McIntosh

---

Week 8—Analysis and Style: Point-of-View/Binary Thinking

F   Analysis via POV and binary thinking; extrapolate creative nonfiction conventions; Brainstorm essay topics

Read: HO   Nikki Giovanni, "Annual Conventions of Everyday Subjects" (1994)

WA   "Binaries" (91–95)

1. Discuss point-of-view and its connection to binary thinking in Western cultures.
    a) Define *point of view* and *binary thinking*
    b) Ask students for examples of binaries (good/bad, man/woman, heaven/hell, right/wrong, in/out, white/black)
    c) Strategies: Write on board strategies for using binaries analytically
       1) Locate a range of opposing categories within the binary and without
       2) Analyze and define the opposing terms
       3) Question the accuracy of the binary
       4) Change "either/or" to "the extent which" or to "both/and"

2. Articulate Giovanni's definition of *whiteness* from 1994.
    a) Put students in pairs to develop this definition
    b) Put list of students' ideas on the board

3. Compare/contrast Smith's, Baldwin's, Rich's, and Giovanni's definitions of *whiteness*. Using the Giovanni list, develop comparisons/contrasts.

4. Study rhetorical use of binary thinking in Giovanni.
    a) Ask students to call out the binaries they find; make a list on the board
    b) Analyze Giovanni's use of binary thinking (i.e., in what ways is she embracing binary thinking, and in what ways is she signifying on readers by using binaries?)

5. Reflect on the binary thinking presented by all the assigned readings and discuss ways to negotiate these binaries.
    a) then/now . . . the-then-that-is-now
    b) white/black . . . What does the slash signify? Who is left out?

6. Put the following quotes overhead to exemplify what the slash mark in the black/white binary may signify—and again, how gender informs it.

a) Jeanne Wakatsuki Houston, *Farewell to Manzanar*
In the Japanese-American internment camp during WWII, "my oldest brother, Bill, led a dance band called The Jive Bombers. . . . He didn't sing "Don't Fence Me In" out of protest, as if trying quietly to mock the authorities. It just happened to be a hit song one year, and they all wanted to be an up-to-date American swing band. [List lyrics to "Don't Fence Me In."] (73–4).
[Ask students: How do you hear this song differently here than during Embassy Suite commercials on TV? Why?]

b) Cherríe Moraga, "The Breakdown of the Bicultural Mind," *Names We Call Home*
"With a Black lover in apartheid Boston I was seen as a whitegirl. When we moved to Brooklyn, we were both Ricans. In Harlem I became 'Spanish.' In México, we were both Cubans. With my brown girlfriends we be brown girls sitting on brownstones. We be family. Among Indians in the States I'm a half-breed who looks like every other breed, colored mixed with cowboy. Among Chicanas, I am everybody's cousin Carmen. Whitegirls change my shade to a paler version. People think I'm Italian, Jewish" (233).
[Ask students: What is this paragraph saying about ethnicity? What is the significance for defining *whiteness*?]

7. Put on overhead and discuss privileges listed in Peggy McIntosh's "White Privilege: Unpacking the Invisible Knapsack."

8. Ask students to identify conventions of creative nonfiction. Put list on board.

9. Ask students to talk (first in pairs and then as a class) about how they are developing their paper topics.

WHITENESS STUDIES

Whiteness studies is an interdisciplinary field—literary studies, sociology, history, art, film studies, anthropology, and others—that analyzes the meanings of *whiteness* in a race-conscious society.

Debates about Whiteness Studies

Arguments against studying whiteness

1. It may be a politically conservative move that returns discussions once again to white people, especially white men (Hill).
2. It may be "a sneaky form of narcissism . . . [that shifts] the focus and maybe even the resources back to white people and their perspectives" (Michael Eric Dyson qtd. in Talbot 118).
3. It risks reifying and perpetuating false categories of race (Keating 913).
4. It risks inciting even more discord than already exists in our culture.

Arguments for studying whiteness

1. To understand racism, people need to "see" whiteness and "listen" to its resonances so as to articulate how whiteness (especially its dysfunctions) informs *everyone*'s culture and identity.
2. To promote antiracist work, whiteness studies tries to put all the racial cards on the table with hopes for more honest and effective negotiations.

Definitions of Whiteness

1. *Whiteness* is trope, a rhetorical figure (all words are tropes because words always refer to something other than the word itself).

2. As a trope, *whiteness* functions as a cultural category that signifies both people and practices (practices being, in Kenneth Burke's terms, attitudes and actions). Yet, as AnnLouise Keating reminds us, a "conditional" relationship exists between white people and white practices: Not everyone can be classified as a white person, but everyone can perform white practices (907).

3. Performing whiteness is a very visible practice for non-white people. "Acting white" on the job or in school may garner promotions or good grades (or in the case of a comedy routine by Eddie Murphy, Paul Rodriguez, or Chris Rock, lots of lucrative laughter), but "acting white" may also garner charges of betraying one's community.

4. Conversely, performing whiteness is often an invisible practice for white people who assume their own attitudes and actions to be the norm. When asked what it means to be white, white people today are often stumped for an answer (maybe because they have never thought about it; maybe because they

have been told it is not a subject for polite discussion; maybe because they fear association with KKK–like groups).

5. Like any trope, whiteness is historically and locally grounded (taking meaning from its context), is already evolving, and is open to multiple interpretations. But as American Studies professor Ruth Frankenberg reminds us, for the past five hundred years, whiteness has consistently signified privilege—a privilege that fosters stasis by resisting and denying differences (236–37).

6. According to historian David Roediger, whiteness often defines itself via the negative: "Whiteness describes, from Little Bighorn to Simi Valley, not a culture but precisely the absence of culture. It is the empty and therefore terrifying attempt to build an identity based on what one isn't [whiteness is often defined in terms of what it is not—*not* African American, *not* Latina, *not* Chippewa, etc.] and on whom one can hold back" (qtd. in Talbot 118).

7. Whiteness is a cultural category that cannot be considered apart from its intersections with other cultural categories, such as gender, class, sexual orientation, age, region, religion, political affiliation, nationality (Thompson 94). In other words, because these cultural categories converge differently in different people, depending on each person's particular socialization and identifications, we cannot make sweeping claims such as "All white people (x)." We can, however, discuss whiteness as one of many factors influencing a person, an event, a text, as well as the degree of influence.

8. Whiteness"–*whatever* it is, and I would argue that at this point no one really knows–"is slippery (Keating 916).

9. Slippery or not, *whiteness* signifies many different things to many different people. Some dysfunctions of whiteness include: acting white in school or at work; the terror of white violence; the drive to consume others' lands and cultures; hypocrisy, especially religious hypocrisy; denial of race issues, stemming from fear and guilt and hiding behind middle-class manners; an ignorance of other cultures; and an often unrecognized privilege (Ratcliffe, "Eavesdropping").

ASSIGNMENT SHEET

ESSAY #3: Writing about Whiteness

TASK   Write a creative nonfiction essay that takes the topic of whiteness as a *starting point* for your reflections. If appropriate, you may revise the profile into a longer essay, or you may write an essay that is totally unrelated to this shorter piece. Your essay may respond to our readings or go in an entirely different direction, even away from the topic of whiteness.

PURPOSE   To improve your critical reading skills through class readings and peer review
To improve your critical listening and thinking skills as well as writing skills
To practice negotiating your intentions as a writer with your audience and your available textual conventions (in this case, the conventions of creative nonfiction)

AUDIENCE   Our class and readers of the class magazine

FORMAT   5–6 pp. (1,250–1,500 words) typed, double-spaced
The format you select should reinforce your purpose, audience, and intentions.
Use the following heading in the upper left-hand corner of your paper:

> Your name
> Advanced Composition
> Ratcliffe
> Date
> Essay #3

GRADES   To be included in Portfolio 3

GRADING CRITERIA   Personal voice
> 1. How well do readers get a sense of the writer talking to them throughout?

Personal/cultural intertwining
> 2. How effectively does the personal story speak to a larger cultural issue that would interest readers?

Organization
> 3. How well does the organization construct a logic that is rhetorically effective?

4. Is there a connecting thread (e.g., an image, idea, word, metaphor) throughout the essay?

Development

5. Is there an effective balance between story and reflection?
6. How well do specific details provide readers with knowledge about the writer's main points?

Purpose/audience negotiation

7. How clear is the essay's purpose?
8. How effective is this purpose for readers?

Readability

9. How well do the shape and content of the sentences reinforce one another?
10. Are there any spots where sentence shape (length, punctuation, wording) interferes with a reader's reading? (Think about parallel structure, clarity/conciseness, and emphasis)

DUE DATE	W, Week 8	Draft of Essay #3. Hand in author sheet, essay draft, and peer-review sheets.
	M, Week 10	Portfolio 3. Hand in author sheets, profile, and creative nonfiction essay

Notes

Introduction: Translating Listening into Language and Action

1. Royster is not alone in calling for "codes of cross-cultural conduct." Michael Eric Dyson argues that articulating such codes is necessary because "[w]e still don't know the rules of race" (8). By "rules of race" Dyson refers not just to codes of cross-cultural conduct but also to "the unwritten codes of conduct within black communities" (8). I agree with Dyson; however, I would extend his argument and claim that we need to explore the written and unwritten codes of gender and race within other communities as well and that we need to explore the functions of whiteness in every community. For too often, the functions of whiteness are invisible (e.g., in U.S. culture today, we rarely think of white as a "color" as evidenced by common usage of terms such as *women of color* and *people of color*), and too often the functions of whiteness create a double-bind (e.g., in certain circles succeeding in school can be perceived as "acting white").

2. *Anglo-American* is a term used by Toril Moi in *Sexual/Textual Politics* to refer to British and U.S. feminists (e.g., Kate Millet and Ellen Moers) whom Moi associates with a liberal-humanist realism and whom she positions herself against as she champions French feminists (especially Julia Kristeva). My book attempts to break this binary by demonstrating that feminists, whom Moi would probably label *Anglo-American,* are not necessarily naïve and may productively contribute to rhetorical traditions.

3. My assumption here is that because sexism and racism are structurally embedded in our culture and, hence, our bodies, they affect everyone's daily lives, just in different ways. Consequently, everyone has gender and race work to do in order to avoid replicating old patterns of thinking, being, doing, and becoming.

4. As Devon W. Carbado argues when addressing other men, "[m]en's realization of gender difference and gender hierarchy can provide us with the opportunity to theorize about gender from the gender-privileged positions we occupy as men. . . . Manhood is a performance. A script. It is accomplished and re-enacted in everyday relationships" (525–26). Thus, the question of how gender marks people is an important site of reflection not just for women but also for men.

5. For a history of *gender* as an analytical category within academic scholarship and for a discussion of whether gender studies should replace or supplement feminist studies, see Elaine Showalter (1–13). She traces a history of *gender* as follows: First, "all speech is necessarily talk about gender, since in every language gender is a grammatical category, and the masculine is the grammatical norm" (1); second, "'gender' has been used . . . to stand for the social, cultural, and psychological meaning imposed upon biological identity" (1–2); third, "talking about gender means talking about both women and men" (2).

6. For a history of the term *race* in the U.S. and for excellent discussions of current thinking about alternatives to its usage, see Gerda Lerner (184–98) and Dyson (36–42).

7. Few people realize that the full title of Charles Darwin's ground-breaking 1859 text is: *On the Origin of the Species: By Means of Natural Selection or the Preservation of Favored Races in the Struggle for Life*. In chapter 7 of his subsequent book *The Descent of Man* (1871), Darwin explores scientific debates about the existence of different races, ultimately using the idea of multiple races to justify his belief in evolution:

> As it is improbable that the numerous and unimportant points of resemblance between the several races of man in bodily structure and mental faculties (I do not here refer to similar customs) should all have been independently acquired, they must have been inherited from progenitors who had these same characters.

Even though he posits differences among races as "unimportant," he nevertheless employs the category and posits these differences in terms of body and intelligence, thus reinforcing racial stereotypes.

8. For explanations of how DNA variation differs from racial classifications, see University of Arizona professor Joseph Graves scholarship ("Between" 300–2; *The Emperor's New Clothes: Biological Theories of Race at the New Millennium*).

9. For a discussion of how economics and whiteness intersect, see Derrick A. Bell Jr.'s "Property Rights in Whiteness." It is also worth noting two examples of how economics drives definitions and values associated with *race*. When the dominant white culture in the pre–Civil War U.S. wanted to maintain slaves as property, a one-drop rule was instituted: People with only one drop of "slave blood" were considered slaves. Conversely, when the dominant white culture in the 1930s wanted to maintain its money and land as property, a 25% rule was instituted: In the 1930 U.S. census, people needed at least 25% "American Indian blood" to be eligible for tribal enrollment and, thus, for land allotments.

10. For a history of the eugenics movement in the U.S., see "Image Archive of the American Eugenics Movement," a Web site sponsored by contemporary academic societies, such as the National Human Genome Research Institute; this Web site delineates the eugenics movement's research practices, false assumptions, recommendations for laws, and so forth. For an analysis of the movement's social effects, see Graves (*Emperor's* 105–54).

11. The first principle of Black studies programs established in the 1960s and 1970s was that Africans had to come to the American colonies, later the U.S., in order to discover that they were "black." In other words, Africans had to be thrust into U.S. culture to "understand" slavery logic, which posited black people as an animalistic or childlike race, worthy only of slave status.

12. *Ethnicity* is a category that signifies the socially constructed common-sense" attitudes and behaviors associated with cultural groups (Irish American, Asian American, African American). Like definitions of *gender* and *race,* definitions of

ethnicity change over time and place. For example, Chicano/as (Mexican Americans) reject the term *Hispanic* because (1) it was created by the U.S. Census Bureau and imposed upon them, (2) it defines them only in terms of European-Spanish ancestry, erasing indigenous ancestry, and (3) it lumps together very different cultural ancestries, such as Cuban American, Puerto Rican, and Venezuelan American. Like *gender* and *race*, *ethnicity* never exists alone but always intersects with other cultural categories (age, nationality, race, gender, etc.). Moreover, as Showalter argues about gender, ethnicity is always a question not only of difference but also of privilege and power (4).

For other definitions of *ethnicity*, see Sandra Gilbert's sociological one and Homi Bhabha's psychoanalytical and cultural one. To study how the terms *race* and *ethnicity* have been historically employed in the U. S., see Ruth Frankenberg's *White Women/Race Matters: The Social Construction of Whiteness* (13).

13. For definitions of critical race studies, see the two collected editions by Kimberlé Williams Crenshaw et al. and by Richard Delgado and Jean Stefancic (*Critical Race Theory*). Also see an influential work by legal scholar Patricia Williams (*The Alchemy of Race and Rights*).

14. I use this list in my classes; it was inspired by Jayne Chong-Soon Lee's slightly different categorization of *race* as "simultaneously biological, social, cultural, essential, and political" (443).

15. My use of the term *tactics* is deliberate, both employing and revising Michel de Certeau's use. In *The Practice of Everyday Life*, he defines *strategies* as belonging to and operating within the dominant culture's discursive domain of power; he defines *tactics* as being momentary interruptions of or resistance to the dominant culture's discursive domain. Though he claims that tactics may be used intentionally, he does not believe they are capable of existing as a discourse (29–41). I am nevertheless interested in how *tactics* of rhetorical listening might be invited into the discourses of rhetorical theory and praxis. The danger of such a move, of course, is that once a tactic is invited into a dominant discourse, the tactic will be appropriated and co-opted, its potential for resistance greatly reduced. But potential benefits seem, to me, worth the risk. So in chapters 3, 4, and 5, I offer what I call tactics of rhetorical listening, identifying moves for each. The stated moves of these tactics are not intended to signify a lockstep, paint-by-number, systematic process but, rather, options that listeners may invoke to resist any troubled identifications that have been brought to consciousness.

1: Defining Rhetorical Listening

1. By using the term *interpretive invention*, I hope to demonstrate the necessary intersections between *interpretation*, which is the dominant term for making meaning in philosophical hermeneutics, and *invention*, which is the dominant term for making meaning in rhetorical studies. For a discussion of the intersections of rhetoric and hermeneutics, see Ratcliffe, "Listening to Cassandra."

2. Rhetorical listening may be used to listen to identifications with any cultural categories (e.g., age and class, nationality and history, religion and politics)

or with any cultural positions (e.g., parent and child, patient and doctor, clergy and parishioner, teacher and student) (Pradl 67–72). This project's particular focus is on the cultural categories of gender and whiteness.

3. In his foreword to Andrea Lunsford's collection *Reclaiming Rhetorica,* James Murphy claims that the authors in the collection "point to new places to *look*" for rhetorical history, theory, and practice (xi; emphasis added); his claim reflects the dominant trend in our field of employing a sight metaphor. Lunsford's use of an auditory metaphor, listening, supplements the sight trend.

4. Michelle Ballif argues that what is needed is a "transgendered" approach, and she cites the hermaphrodite as representative of this approach.

5. For more information on how *Imitation of Life* may inform pedagogical discussions of gender/ethnicity connections, see Pamela Caughie's *Passing and Pedagogy,* which analyzes the Fannie Hurst novel as well as the 1934 John Stahl film and the 1959 Douglas Sirk film, the latter being Giovanni's and my point of reference.

6. Martin Jay provides a definition, history, and critique of "ocularcentrism" in order to argue for a hermeneutic revival of hearing via Frederich Nietzsche, and Martin Heidegger: "[O]ur increasing interest in the truths of interpretation rather than the methods of observation bespeaks a renewed respect for the ear over the eye as the organ of greatest value" (57). Other philosophers have set the stage for Jay's claims. G. W. F. Hegel locates hearing as an ideal, arguing that hearing "does not belong to the sense of action [*sens pratiques*] but those of contemplation [*sens théoriques*]; and is, in fact, still more ideal than sight" (*Philosophy* 341; qtd. in Derrida, "Violence" 100). And Emmanuel Levinas, an anti-Hegelian who champions the ethical, not the ideal, also elevates sound over sight. Jacques Derrida explains: "[T]he glance by itself, contrary to what one may be led to believe, does not respect the other. . . . This is why Levinas places sound above sight" ("Violence" 99).

7. I am indebted to Doug Day of Allyn and Bacon Longman for calling this idea to my attention.

8. Gordon Pradl pointed out in his review of my *CCC* article "Rhetorical Listening," that Louise Rosenblatt introduced a method of reading that closely resembles what I am calling listening in that her method also works to preserve the ideas of others within one's interpretation.

9. Their cross-cultural listening may be further complicated by the animosity between their cultures. Scholars disagree about the date of the book of Ruth, a disagreement that has implications for the degree of animosity existing between the Judeans and the Moabites:

> Some scholars consider Ruth a postexilic literary creation, though perhaps based on an older tale; on this view, it was intended to counteract the harsh decrees of Ezra and Nehemiah against foreign wives (Ezra 10.1–5; Neh. 13.23–27). Other scholars, however, date it much earlier, during the reigns of the first kings of Judah, before bitter enmity toward Moab had developed. (*New English Bible* 277)

10. In the *CCC* article "Rhetorical Listening," I use the term *responsibility* instead of *accountability*. But after thinking about the resonances of *responsibility*, I decided to shift the term here because, in popular usage, *responsibility* resonates a little too closely to guilt and blame—as in the question "Who is responsible for the current situation of gender and race relations in the U.S.?" For more on *accountability*, see bell hooks ("Race and Feminism"); for an alternative view of *responsibility*, one that links *responsibility* and *response*, see Caughie (85–86).

11. Richard Delgado argues that charges of idealism or naïveté may work in congress with the status quo, reinforcing it: "[P]atterns of perception become habitual, tempting us to believe the ways things are is inevitable, or the best that can be in an imperfect world. Alternative visions of reality are not explored, or, if they are, rejected as extreme or implausible" (62).

12. For a brief history of the term *understanding* in narrative studies from Cleanth Brooks and Robert Penn Warren to the mid-1990s, see James Phelan and Peter Rabinowitz (5–11). For an accounting of the relationship between *understanding* and *interpretation* in classical hermeneutics, see Josef Bleicher (11–26) and Gerald Bruns (21–138).

13. My use of *standing under* does not reflect the foundational meanings that Kenneth Burke ascribes to John Locke's use of the Greek term *hypostasis*, which means

> literally, a standing under, hence anything set under, such as stand, base, bottom, prop, support, stay; hence metaphorically, that which lies at the bottom of a thing, as the groundwork, subject-matter, argument of a narrative, speech, poem; a starting point, a beginning. And then come the metaphysical meanings. . . : Subsistence, reality, real being (as applied to mere appearance, nature, essence. (*Grammar* 23)

Standing under implies a place, a location, a standpoint for listening. For a discussion of static versus dynamic theories of feminist standpoints, see Ratcliffe (*Anglo-American Feminist* 70–71).

14. In our current theoretical milieu, *other* is a loaded term. For example, in her feminist critique of Lacanian theory, Elizabeth Grosz describes the *other/Other* as follows: for Lacan, the "other is the object through whom desire is returned to the subject; the Other is the locus of signification which regulates the movement by which this return is made possible" (80). In other words, "the Other is not a person but a place, the locus of law, language, and the symbolic" (67). As such, it "is understood here in two senses: as a socio-symbolic network regulated according to language-like rules; and as a psychical structure, representative of this social Other, internalized in the form of the unconscious" (117). As I use the term *other*, I am invoking Lacan's small-*o* other, specifically as a person other than the listening subject or as the listening subject listening to itself. My goal for listening is an intersubjectivity, not a continued subject/object relationship.

15. For a specific tactic of how to listen to the discourses of self and other, see Ratcliffe, "Eavesdropping as Rhetorical Tactic" and "Eavesdropping on Others."

16. In terms of ethics, consideration of the other necessitates a respect for the other, or as Levinas puts it: "The only possible ethical imperative, the only incarnated nonviolence . . . is respect for the other" (qtd. in Derrida, "Violence" 96).

17. For a discussion of how autobiography and ethnography may merge to create a strategy of autoethnography, see Jay Watson, who argues that women may learn to articulate their own stories if they learn to read their bodies as culturally inscribed texts; also see Patricia Ticineto Clough and Alice A. Deck.

18. For other arguments on why whiteness needs to be articulated in our culture, see Kate Davy, Dyson, Shelley Fisher Fishkin, Mike Hill, hooks ("Representations"), Noel Ignatiev, and Toni Morrison (*Playing*).

19. For excellent discussions of how authorization and privilege (or lack thereof) function in academic discourse and how their consequences play out, see Judith Roof and Robyn Wiegman's collection, which explores the question that is also their title: *Who Can Speak?*

20. Marshall Gregory describes scholarly debate as warfare:

> So much critical discourse in the humanities—at least since the contemporary culture wars began about twenty years ago—is conducted in a scorched-earth, take-no-prisoners tone that at first irritates, then pains, and eventually numbs everyone's professional nerves, leaving the main combatants (and many of the rest of us as well) worn out with struggle and wondering if internecine warfare is really what we meant to sign up for when we enthusiastically and jauntily set out for graduate school years ago. (89)

21. What constitutes a "white" body and a "non-white" body changes over time and place as demonstrated in Ignatiev's *How the Irish Became White.*

22. Audre Lorde calls such a cultural norm a "mythical norm" and defines it as "white, thin, male, young, heterosexual, christian, and financially secure ("Age" 116).

23. Karen LeFevre cites four categories of invention: (1) a private apprehension of truth, based on Platonic theory; (2) an internal dialogue of selves, based on Freudian theory; (3) a group of people's collaborative construction of truth, based on George Herbert Mead's theory; and (4) a collective analysis of how cultural codes socialize people's behaviors and attitudes, based on Émile Durkeim's theory (48–50). Like LeFevre's categories of collaborative and collective invention, rhetorical listening is concerned with how people construct meanings as well as with how cultural codes socialize people and how people both employ and change these codes to negotiate with one another. Like classical and neoclassical invention, rhetorical listening asks questions of texts; it also asks questions of the cultural logics within which these texts exist. Like postmodern invention, rhetorical listening searches for the gaps, the omissions, the unknowns, the contradictions, the questions not in order to reconcile them but in order to imagine where they may lead. Like a cultural-studies invention, rhetorical listening also locates interpretation within particular moments and places to demonstrate how time and place affect interpretation. And given my particular interest, rhetorical listening may be employed

as a feminist invention process to expose how gender intertwines with race and other cultural categories.

2: Identifying Places of Rhetorical Listening: Identification, Disidentification, and Non-Identification

1. Theorists have imagined the modern/postmodern divide in multiple ways. For a discussion of why this divide is "incompatible," see Vincent Leitch's discussion of Frank Lentricchia and Paul de Man (48); for a discussion of how this divide is more complicated than a simple binary opposition, see Jonathan Culler (110).

2. Disidentification is inextricably entangled with identification. See Diana Fuss for how disidentification "may actually represent 'an identification that one fears to make only because one has already made it'" (*Identification* 7). Or see Judith Butler for how disidentification may emerge when we are unable to deal with an issue:

> It may be that certain identifications and affiliations are made, certain sympathetic connections amplified, precisely in order to institute a disidentification with a position that seems too saturated with injury or aggression, one that might, as a consequence, be occupiable only through imagining the loss of viable identity altogether. (100)

For a brief discussion of Gloria Anzaldúa's challenge to consubstantial identification, see Foss, Foss, and Griffin (123).

3. For discussions of Freudian identification, see *The Standard Edition of the Complete Psychological Works of Sigmund Freud*. [vol. 1, 248–50; vol. 13, 80–82, 142; vol. 18, 108–9, 113–14, 133–35; vol. 23, 193). Fuss summarizes Freud's thinking as follows: "To the extent that every social group is constituted for Freud through identification between its members, through social ties based upon a perception of similarity and shared interests, there can be no politics without identification" (*Identification* 10). For a witty and insightful history of Freud's concept, see Fuss (*Identification* 21–51); for in-depth analysis of the similarities and differences in Freud's and Burke's theories of identification, see Mark Wright (302–6).

4. The psychoanalytic tradition of identification is traced in Fuss's *Identification Papers* (1–19), which exposes the limitations of this tradition, particularly its heterosexual assumptions of having/being the other.

5. For a discussion of modern and postmodern theories as they apply to rhetoric and composition studies, see Ray Linn's *A Teacher's Introduction to Postmodernism*. Also see James Berlin (*Rhetorics* 41–176).

6. One exception to this trend is Daphne Desser's discussion of the relationship between *ethos*, identification, and identity. In her *Rhetoric Review* article, she employs Bakhtinian theory to supplement Burke's concept of identification with nonidentification and reidentification. Desser and I differ in our use of the term *nonidentification*: her use parallels what Butler and Fuss call *disidentification* (Desser 324); my use attempts to move non-identification beyond the place of disidentification. Although I do not employ the term *reidentification,* Desser and I agree that identifications may emerge again and again, differently, in different times and places.

7. For a discussion of how identification fits into the rhetorical tradition via Burke, read Frank Lentricchia (148–49) and Christine Oravec (180).

8. Oravec juxtaposes her argument against Frederic Jameson and Frank Lentricchia (174).

9. For more on Burke's ideas about *acting together,* see his *Grammar* (14–15).

10. For Burke's extended discussion of *substance,* see his *Grammar* (21–58). For his discussion of four main types of substance (geometric, familial, directional, and dialectical), see (29–35).

11. In contemporary theory, substance is often linked via a false dichotomy to a naïve biological essentialism, that is, identity is either *fixed* by an ineluctable essence (substance) or *constructed* by inescapable discursive socialization (Culler 117; Butler 93–95). The first option, often associated with modern theories of rhetoric, presumes an identity in stasis, a liberal humanist self. The second option, often associated with postmodern theories, presumes an identity always in flux, a postmodern subject. At their extremes, neither option provides much space for personal agency because the first gives agency to biology and the latter to cultural discourses.

In contemporary theory, metaphor is also often associated with essentialism via a false linkage: Metaphor is haunted by the presumption of a corresponding substance or essence, which may lead down the slippery slope to a naïve biological essentialism. Granted, this linkage occurs. According to Paul de Man, although metaphor deals with resemblances, it usually assumes the existence of a corresponding essence (Norris 102–3; Derrida, "White Mythology" 50), hence the specter of essentialism. But this linkage is not inevitable. According to David Williams, metaphor may be used to avoid a naïve essentialism—that is the "[i]nterpretation of metaphor . . . can occur without [this] gross error 'only if we know how to "discount" a metaphorical term'" (206). Burke's identification successfully discounts metaphorical terms. He defines *metaphor* as "*perspective*" or "a device for seeing something *in terms of* something else," which "involves the 'carrying-over' of a term from one realm into another, a process that necessarily involves varying degrees of incongruity in that the two realms are never identical" (*Grammar* 503–4; D. Williams 206–9). Burke's definition of *metaphor* does assume an associated concept of consubstantiality and, hence, substance. But because his definitions of first- and second-nature *substance* do not presume a naïve biological essentialism, his concept of metaphor-cum-substance successfully averts charges of a naïve biological essentialism.

12. Although I find Fuss's work on identification and disidentification compelling, bell hooks criticizes Fuss's text for discussing race while failing to cite African American feminist critics (*Teaching* 78–92); Margaret Homans makes a similar argument in "'Women of Color' Writers and Feminist Theory."

13. For an in-depth discussion of these three metaphors, see Fuss's first chapter (21–51).

14. Care must be taken to avoid appropriation or voyeurism when learning about one another's home places, for as hooks describes, in African American communities, *homeplace* signifies as "a safe place where black people could affirm one

another and by so doing heal many of the wounds inflicted by racist domination" ("Homeplace" 42).

15. This risk, its annihilating effects, and the potential for resistance are precisely what Royster articulates throughout "When the First Voice You Hear Is Not Your Own."

16. The dance of Fuss's and Burke's theories of identification establishes the following patterns. Both theories imagine identification as a psychical place a la Freud (although Fuss is further influenced by Derrida, Lacan, and Butler), and both imagine identification as a cultural place a la Marx. Both claim that identification is predicated upon division, that is, "upon the *unlikeness* of the self and the other it emulates" (Fuss, *Identification* 19.n 27). And both claim identification "works simultaneously to construct and to displace identity" (19.n 27). A key difference in Burke and Fuss is in how they define a rhetorical agent's identity. For Burke, an agent's identity is grounded in first-nature substances (material reality) and second-nature substances (cultural reality known via discourse); for Fuss, an agent's identity is grounded, a la Lacan, in the real, the symbolic, and the imaginary. Still, the functions and the ends of their agents are remarkably similar: Both Burke and Fuss posit agents who function at conscious and unconscious levels, with the conscious level allowing people agency to participate in some degree via language in the construction of their realities and identities. Going further in her theorizing of identification than does Burke, Fuss analyzes in more detail the influence of the unconscious on personal agency, and she gives more attention to differences, especially those of colonized peoples. In sum, Burke gives us a theory that more clearly articulates how identity (substance) cum identification is linked to rhetoric; Fuss gives us a theory that more clearly articulates how differences may serve as a ground for identification via disidentifications. So even given their differences, juxtaposing these two theorists' ideas on identification provides a productive place for locating rhetorical listening in places of identification, disidentification, and non-identification.

17. In shifting the imagery of identification, I am following in the footsteps of Burke who argues that shifting imagery "enables us to transcend the narrower implications of this imagery, even while keeping them clearly in view" (*Rhetoric* 20)

3: Listening Metonymically: A Tactic for Listening to Public Debates

1. For discussions of different kinds of literary silences, see Elaine Hedges and Shelley Fisher Fishkin's anthology *Listening to Silences,* particularly the essay by Kate Adams who urges academic workers to embrace silence as a means of listening to others' voices (130–32); for discussions of Adrienne Rich's categories of women's silences, see Ratcliffe's *Anglo-American Feminist Challenges* (122–26); for discussions of silence as a rhetorical art whose value is context-dependent, see Cheryl Glenn's "Silence" and *Unspoken* (6–9).

2. For Jean-François Lyotard's definitions of *differend,* see *The Differend;* for discussions of Avital Ronell's "affirmative differend," see Michelle Ballif, D. Diane Davis, and Roxanne Mountford (615–17).

3. For a history of this debate, see Alexis De Veaux's *Warrior Poet,* a 2004 biography of Audre Lorde. It narrates the public and private negotiations of Lorde and Mary Daly (via their personal conversations with one another and via the letters they wrote to one another) as well as the mediator role of Adrienne Rich. I am grateful to my colleague Judith Wilt for bringing this book to my attention.

4. Racism in the U.S. is often discussed in terms of trauma, and rightly so. I choose to employ the term *dysfunctional* in relation to a rhetoric of silence because I see this rhetoric as interfering with productive functions of communication, especially communication about and across intersections of race and gender. But make no mistake, dysfunction not only results from trauma but may also perpetuate trauma.

5. What Daly calls "African female genital mutilation" is also called "female circumcision." This practice has engendered hot debate among defenders and critics, especially after the publication of Alice Walker's *Warrior Marks.* In response to charges that Western feminists who decry this practice were imposing cultural imperialism on Africans,

> K. Anthony Appiah, professor of African-American Studies and philosophy at Harvard, [argues] that notions of cultural superiority may be at work but says that acknowledging that doesn't necessarily imply support for other cultures' traditions. " . . . I think you can agree that there is ethnocentrism there while still thinking [female] circumcision is a bad idea." (Washington)

6. Here I draw on Rich's concept of revision from "When We Dead Awaken" (35).

7. Anzaldúa also cites two other kinds of silences: (1) when a mestiza self silences and (2) when she is forced by the dominant culture to select one among her multiple identities. She argues that her project is to "overcome the tradition of silence" for women in her community (59). For a discussion of how Anzaldúa's writings inform rhetorical studies, see Foss, Foss, and Griffin (101–27).

8. hooks describes differences in the usage of the term *woman* as follows:

> White feminists did not challenge [white patriarchy's] racist-sexist tendency to use the word "woman" to refer solely to white women; they supported it. For them it served two purposes. First, it allowed [white feminists] to proclaim white men world oppressors while making it appear linguistically that no alliance existed between white women and white men based on shared racial imperialism. Second, it made possible for white women to act as if alliances did exist between themselves and non-white women in our society, and by doing so they could deflect attention away from their classism and racism. ("Race and Feminism" 140)

Barbara Christian grounds her claims about different uses of *woman* in her comparison of Toni Morrison and Virginia Woolf. Although Christian cites certain stylistic similarities, she argues that the main difference between them is that Morrison centers her texts around the concepts *black life* and *black culture* while Woolf centers hers around the concept *woman,* which really signifies *white woman.* Woolf exemplifies many white feminists' use of the term *woman.*

Common sense tells us that all feminists necessarily focus on the category *woman* as the organizing principle for a political movement; more recently, common sense tells us that feminists analyze *woman* in terms of gender as it intersects with other cultural categories, such as age, race, class, etc., in hopes of creating a better world for women and those around them. But in the arena of feminist theory, common sense is quickly complicated, and we often find ourselves debating the question: What do we really mean by the term *woman*? For example, some post-structuralist feminists define *woman* as a gendered discursive position, a lexicon of competing discourses; some psychoanalytic feminists define *woman* as a field of desires within the symbolic whose unconscious is structured like a language; some materialist feminists define *woman* as a material body in which is embodied the psychoanalytic, the textual, and the cultural.

9. For random newspaper articles that exemplify how discussions of guilt haunt our public discourses about gender and race, see Jacqueline Mitchard; letters to the editor in "Too Late for Slavery Reparations"; and especially Leonard Pitts Jr.

10. For reasons why some theorists deem the term *critique* not functional for our times, see archived entries in the February and March 2003 *Pretext* listserv (Vitanza, "Discussions").

4: Eavesdropping: A Tactic for Listening to Scholarly Discourses

1. John Poulakos provides one answer to this question by invoking a Nietzschean critical historiography:

> The critical conception of the past operates from the assumption that much of what the past has produced is dysfunctional and useless because it was not, indeed, it could not have been, produced with our present predicament in mind. Therefore, if we are to place history in the service of life [a Nietzschean imperative], we must rid ourselves of the burdens of the past and strive to create from them materials that are useful, that augment our capacity to live joyfully. (90)

Poulakos's source for this critical historiography is Nietzsche's "On the Uses and Disadvantages of History for Life," which posits three kinds of history: monumental (72), antiquarian (73–74), and critical (75–76).

2. Whiteness studies is, in part, an offshoot of critical race studies, both of which champion an antiracist agenda. For a history of critical race studies, see Kimberlé Williams Crenshaw's "First Decade"; for landmark research associated with the contemporary whiteness studies movement, see Theodore W. Allen, *The Invention of the White Race*; Kate Davy, "Outing Whiteness"; Richard Delgado and Jean Stefancic, *Critical White Studies*; Richard Dyer, *White*; Michelle Fine, et al., *Off White*; Shelley Fisher Fishkin, "Interrogating 'Whiteness' Complicating 'Blackness'"; Ruth Frankenberg, *White Women/Race Matters*; Mike Hill, *Whiteness*; bell hooks, "Representing Whiteness: Seeing the Wings of Desire" and "Representing Whiteness in the Black Imagination"; Noel Ignatiev, *How the Irish Became White*; George Lipsitz, "The Possessive Investment in Whiteness"; Peggy McIntosh, "White

Privilege"; Toni Morrison, *Playing in the Dark*; Thomas Nakayama and Robert Krizek, "Whiteness: A Strategic Rhetoric"; Vivian Gussin Paley, *White Teacher*; Adrienne Rich "Notes" and "Distance"; and Nelson M. Rodriguez and Leila E. Villaverde, *Dismantling White Privilege*. My thanks to Joyce Middleton for suggesting Wahneema Lubiano, *The House That Race Built*.

3. Drawing from the scholarship of Dyer (11), Middleton argues that the usage of the term *non-whites* is more appropriate than *people of color* because *non-white* exposes the "white" standard against which non-whites are measured and because *people of color* obfuscates the fact that *white* is also a color ("Kris" 439).

4. For other challenges to the origins mode of historiography, note Susan Jarratt's invocation of a feminist sophistic historiography (*Rereading* 10–12) and Victor Vitanza's invocation of a Nietzschean (sophistic) sub/versive one ("'Notes'" 100–101, 106–14).

5. Rich's description of the poetic moment also explains why the convergence of body, trope, and culture is often interpreted as a moment of origin: This convergence is "the crossing of trajectories of two (or more) elements that might not otherwise have known simultaneity. When this happens, a piece of the universe is revealed *as if* for the first time" ("Woman and Bird" 8; emphasis added). Her *as if* exposes that what we name "moments of origin" are actually "moments of usage," which (given our deep desire for origins) are often received *as if* they were origins.

6. One important white practice is law. As Cheryl Harris (1996) argues, within the legal system, whiteness emerges as property: "Whiteness—the right to white identity as embraced by the law—is property if by property we mean all of a person's legal rights" (105).

7. Non-whites have also been aware that whiteness represents privilege. John A. Powell claims that the use of the term "'white privilege' is a redundancy [because] Whiteness has always signified worthiness, inclusion, and acceptance" (qtd. in Roediger 100).

8. In *Massacre of the Dreamers*, Ana Castillo concretizes this safe space in terms of writing. Quoting Ivan Argüelles, she claims that white writing is "[e]vocative, finely crafted, witty, urbane, sophisticated, occasionally troubling, but always *safe* . . . politically correct, but sanitized with only faint air-brushed innuendos of anger" (168; emphasis added).

9. Another example of how whiteness informs blackness is played with in J. A. Rogers' "Debating the Senator" (1917), in which an African American Pullman porter informs a white segregationist senator from Oklahoma that:

> "The word, slave, has a white origin."
> "A white origin!"
> "Yes, sir, it comes from 'Slav,' a very white-skinned people who were reduced to slavery by the Germans." (98)

10. Lillian Smith demonstrates the "semantic" level of discursive socialization when she describes how adult, white Southerners of a certain class denigrate their childhood love for the African American women who cared for them by naming

these women "nurse" and then tearing up at spirituals for the rest of their lives instead of continuing a caring relationship with these women (130). Smith demonstrates the "somatic" level of discursive socialization when she describes how early- and mid-twentieth-century Southerners use language (she implies but never states the *n*-word) to dehumanize African Americans and justify whites' physical torture of them, in which case this socialization is being played out on both "black" and "white" bodies, obviously with very different results (161).

11. I use Lawrence Buell's term *authorial agency* to signify positions of production, that is, speaking and writing, and I use his term *readerly agency* to signify positions of reception, that is, reading and listening. While I recognize that production and reception intertwine, I also think the power differentials of these positions, as they play out in U.S. culture, are worth exploring separately.

12. Nedra Reynolds reminds us that the community in which Aristotle was writing precluded the participation of women and slaves within communal decision making ("*Ethos*" 329). Consequently, even if it were possible, simply lifting the theory and dropping it into our lives will not work. The theory must be remade for our own historical moments.

13. Margaret Rose Gladney explains the silencing of Smith in 1949:

> Although *Strange Fruit* [an interracial love story set in the South after World War I] brought Smith international acclaim and greatly expanded her sphere of influence as a social critic, *Killers of the Dream* . . . affronted too many Southerners—including powerful moderates—to be financially or critically successful. After an initial 30,000 copies, sales dropped dramatically, and when reviewers and critics refused to accord it critical notice, Smith was effectively silenced as a writer. . . . This subject matter and Smith's innovative style were met with hostility, or deliberate silence, by the literary establishment, the New Critics, and the general public of Cold War American. (iv)

14. In 1994, not only was *Killers* reviewed but Smith was hailed by critics as "original and insightful" (Hobson 1), as "bold and honest" (14), as

> one of the most important white civil rights figures of her time, virtually alone among white Southern "liberals" in condemning gradualism in all of its forms and in calling for an immediate end to institutionalized segregation in the interest of all Southerners, white as well as black. (Watson 470)

Also see C. Carr and Scott Romine.

5: Listening Pedagogically: A Tactic for Listening to Classroom Resistance

1. For discussions of how resistance is and is not addressed in composition studies, see Carl Herndl, the essays in C. Mark Hurlbert and Michael Blitz's collection, and Karen Kopelson (118–21).

2. Ruth Frankenberg discusses how racism may manifest itself via two paradigms, that is, via a focus on biological difference and via a focus on human commonality (color-blindness); both paradigms ignore race as a cultural structure and

suggest that "any failure to achieve is therefore the fault of people of color themselves" (*White* 14).

3. Ira Shor makes the same point in terms of class socialization. After providing a bulleted list of descriptors for working-class students, he claims, "Even though these general identities fill the classroom, I would say that there is no stereotypical working-class student. Their typical traits and social conditions are identifiable, but this general reality does not exhaust their individual differences" (7).

4. In *White Teacher,* Vivian Gussin Paley emphasizes the importance of acknowledging differences when teaching her elementary school students: "Our safety lies in schools and societies in which faces with many shapes and colors can feel an equal sense of belonging. Our children must grow up knowing and liking those who look and speak in different ways, or they will live as strangers in a hostile land" (131–32). She uses *our* to mean all children, not simply as a code word for white children.

5. For a discussion of how *double consciousness* has informed identities of "black folk" in general, see the first chapter of W. E. B. Du Bois's *Souls of Black Folk,* which defines *double consciousness:*

> It is a peculiar sensation, this double-consciousness, this sense of always looking at one's self through the eyes of others, of measuring one's soul by the tape of a world that looks on in amused contempt or pity. One ever feels his twoness,—an American, a Negro; two souls, two thoughts, two unreconciled strivings; two warring ideals in one dark body, whose dogged strength alone keeps it from being torn asunder. (5)

For reflections on how factoring in gender transforms double consciousness into triple consciousness, see the essays by critical race scholar Patricia Williams in *Open House.*

6. In their introduction to *Race in the College Classroom,* Bonnie TuSmith and Maureen Reddy argue that teachers should "recognize the centrality of race in all disciplines, including those that seem unrelated to racial issues" and that the "struggle with race in the classroom on a daily basis . . . constitutes a crisis in higher education" (1).

7. For an updated version of Maxine Greene's ideas, see Greene's foreword to Barbara Curry's *Women in Power.*

8. Shor names these two kinds of resistance as negative and positive—negative being "a defensive posture of 'getting by' in a non-negotiable setting" and positive being that students "begin framing purposes which reshape the process to meet their emerging intellectual interests" (149).

9. For a discussion of the epistemic grounds of white defensiveness, see Susan Sánchez-Casal (60–63).

10. Two teaching moments haunted by students' refusal to see race in play are described by Maureen Reddy; these moments could be effectively cited by other teachers in class discussions (59–61).

11. Whether or not lived experience is a necessity for teaching a topic is a contentious and context-specific issue. Nancy Sorkin Rabinowitz discusses how her lack of lived experience as a lesbian created tensions in her queer theory course;

she uses these tensions to reflect on how she would teach it differently the next time (186–93). Margaret Hunter argues that lived experience, in terms of a static identity politics, is not necessary for teaching: "[A] pedagogy of liberation should not be limited to people embedded in particular identities. However in order to teach from the standpoint of women of color, one must rely on scholarship and knowledge created, at least primarily by women of color" (253). On the other hand, Sarah Sloane made a compelling, nonnegotiable case during a particularly vigorous dinner discussion at the 4C's that, given current U.S. cultural politics, a straight woman should not teach a lesbian literature course.

12. Karyn McKinney examines the issues that commonly arise when she teaches whiteness to predominantly white students: denial of racism (130–31), a focus on liabilities of whiteness (131–34), epiphanies of whiteness (134–36), and seeing racism (136–37).

13. Although whiteness studies emerged as an antiracist project within critical race studies, it also has roots in studies of white trash culture (*white trash* being a label reclaimed by academics who study the culture of lower-class white people, particularly intersections of race and class). For an example of the latter, see several essays in Mike Hill's collection *Whiteness: A Critical Reader* and in Matt Wray and Annalee Newitz's collection *White Trash: Race and Class in America.*

14. For a more in-depth discussion of my definition of feminist pedagogy, see chapter 5 of *Anglo-American Feminist Challenges.*

15. For a discussions of how feminists have theoretically engaged this issue, see Chris Cuomo and Kim Q. Hall's introduction to *Whiteness: Feminist Philosophical Reflections,* where they argue, "In contributing to [whiteness scholarship], what we are after here is neither a melting pot nor an apolitical pastiche of interesting identities but a feminist, postcolonial, multicultural engagement with lived racial reality" (4). For discussions of how feminists have pedagogically engaged this issue, see Peggy McIntosh's "White Privilege: Unpacking the Invisible Knapsack," which contains a list of white privileges that generates interesting class discussion. Also see Mary Louise Pratt, "Arts of the Contact Zone"; Nelson M. Rodriguez, "Projects of Whiteness in a Critical Pedagogy"; and Joy Ritchie, "Confronting the Essential Problem."

16. For a theoretical explanation of how cultural categories function, see Judith Newton and Deborah Rosenfelt's introduction.

17. For a general overview of pedagogies of resistance, see Christina Hughes. For a particular discussion of white students' resistance to Latino studies, see Susan Sánchez-Casal, "Unleashing the Demons of History." For a particular discussion of U.S. students' resistance to critiques of the U.S.'s (un)witting participation in global abuse of women, see Michiko Hase, "Student Resistance and Nationalism in the Classroom." For a discussion of why listening helps counter such resistance, see Paulo Freire (101–12).

18. One caveat: If a beginning teacher (especially a young woman) is self-conscious about her body being the topic of conversation, she should select another topic. One that I sometimes use focuses on the time when my then eight-year-old

daughter was obsessed with *Grease* (the John Travolta–Olivia Newton-John movie). I discuss with students how the oily material substance is troped as *grease,* which, in turn, signifies as car oil, hair oil, body language, clothes, and a cool way of being in the world. Furthermore, these tropes generate other significations: When I watch Travolta and Newton-John, *cool* signifies a humorous nostalgia that proffers cultural rebels in ways that mask actual gender, race, and class inequalities and oppressions; however, when I imagine my daughter acting *cool* "down in the sand," in the Newton-John role, changing herself to be considered *cool* by her friends and her boyfriend, then *cool* signifies very differently for me . . . as something akin to horror. And *horror* signifies . . . and so it goes.

19. "*Acting white*" refers to the idea that non-white students pressure one another not to do well in school—that is, not to "act white." To find evidence that the term is still in play, we need look no further than local newspapers. The Milwaukee *Journal Sentinel* periodically features stories referring to the use of "*acting white*" by students in Milwaukee Public Schools (MPS).

A November 2002 story features a teacher claiming that acting white is no longer an issue for high school students:

> At Madison East High School . . . teacher Sharon McPike said she had watched such stereotypes weaken and erode over the past few years. Five years ago, she said, she might . . . overhear a minority student accusing another one of "acting white" for working hard in school and getting good grades. But she never hears that anymore. (S. Carr, "Coalition").

This report is based on a survey of forty thousand "relatively high-income" students in grades seven through eleven from Madison, Wisconsin, Evanston, Illinois, and Cambridge, Massachusetts; critics of the survey wonder if students living in poverty would show the same results (Carr).

More recently, in profiles done in 2003, successful African American students in Milwaukee claim that although the pressure to "act white" still exists in MPS, resistance is possible. Eugene Kane describes a Washington High School valedictorian, Corey Benson: "He acknowledged that some black students seemed to resist education out of fear of being accused of 'acting white.' But clearly, Benson is the kind of black student who never put much stock in that kind of silliness" ("Acing"). Tanette Johnson-Elie profiles $180,000 scholarship winner, Sable King: "Black kids too often are told that being smart is acting white and that it's better to be a rapper or entertainer than it is to have a college degree" ("Can't Fault"). Also see Felicia Thomas-Lynn.

20. Pamela Caughie's *Passing and Pedagogy* is a useful text for helping teachers contemplate pedagogy that asks teachers and students to move beyond static identity politics and even beyond postmodern impersonation (86–96); she advocates an ethical pedagogy wherein students' and teachers' "willingness to claim 'I have passed,' then becomes neither a shameful confession of inauthenticity nor a celebration of a boundary crossed but an imperative to act" (259).

21. For discussions on how to think about gender, whiteness, and pedagogy, see

Amy Goodburn, Amie MacDonald and Sánchez-Casal, Rodriguez and Villaverde, and TuSmith and Reddy.

22. This negotiation of classroom boundaries during tense discussions that spur resistance is described by Patti Duncan in "Decentering Whiteness":

> Race and racism are difficult, sometimes painful topics in the classroom, for both students and faculty. In my own classes, I have found it useful to establish ground rules early in the term, during which I ask students to discuss their own needs for creating a relatively safe space. Many students are able to articulate at this time the practices that make them uncomfortable and unsafe, and we work as a group to balance sensitivity and awareness of our differences with academic, intellectual freedom in the classroom. At the same time, I recognize that the classroom has rarely been safe for students of color, and I work to create a context for discussing race and racism through readings, films, discussion and classroom exercises. I have also found it necessary to teach and model appropriate, sensitive ways of interrupting racist remarks and other oppressive comments in class. (48)

Karyn McKinney argues, however, that we should not try to eradicate all tension because some may be productive for generating critical thinking (139); likewise, hooks argues that some tension may challenge students to question their "career choices" and their "habits of being" (*Teaching* 206). While I agree, I just want to add one caveat: Resistance-prone tension must not be romanticized; it must be carefully considered because just as its productive effects are real, so, too, are its unproductive ones.

Works Cited

Abel, Elizabeth. "Black Writing, White Reading: Race and the Politics of Feminist Interpretation." *Critical Inquiry* 19 (1993): 470–98.

Adams, Kate. "Northamerican Silences: History, Identity, and Witness in the Poetry of Gloria Anzaldúa, Cherríe Moraga, and Leslie Marmon Silko." Hedges and Fishkin 130–45.

Allen, Paula Gunn. *The Sacred Hoop.* Boston: Beacon, 1996.

Allen, Theodore W. *The Invention of the White Race.* New York: Verso, 1994.

Anzaldúa, Gloria. *Borderlands/La Frontera: The New Mestiza.* San Francisco: Spinsters, 1987.

Aristotle. *Nichomachean Ethics.* Trans. Roger Crisp. New York: Cambridge UP, 2000.

———. *The Politics of Aristotle.* Ed. and Trans. Ernest Barker. New York: Oxford UP, 1980.

———. *On Rhetoric: A Theory of Civic Discourse.* Trans. George Kennedy. New York: Oxford UP, 1991.

Baldwin, James. "White Man's Guilt." Roediger 320–25.

Ball, Arnetha, and Ted Lardner. "Dispositions Toward Language: Teacher Constructs of Knowledge and the Ann Arbor Black English Case." *CCC* 48 (1997): 469–85.

Ballif, Michelle. "What Is It That the Audience Wants? Or, Notes Toward a Listening with a Transgendered Ear for (Mis)Understanding." *JAC* 19 (1999): 51–70.

Ballif, Michelle, D. Diane Davis, and Roxanne Mountford. "Negotiating the Differend: A Feminist Trilogue." *JAC* 20 (2000): 583–625.

Barnes, Kim. "A Leslie Marmon Silko Interview." *"Yellow Woman": Leslie Marmon Silko.* Ed. Melody Graulich. New Brunswick, NJ: Rutgers UP, 1993. 47–65.

Barthes, Roland. "The Death of the Author." *The Rustle of Language.* Trans. Richard Howard. Berkeley: U of California P, 1989. 49–55.

———. *Mythologies.* Trans. Annette Lavers. 1957. New York: Hill, 1972.

Bartholomae, David, and Anthony Petrosky. *Ways of Reading: An Anthology for Writers.* 3rd ed. Boston: Bedford, 1993.

Bay, Mia. "The Color of Heaven." Roediger 67–69.

Bell, Derrick A., Jr. "Property Rights in Whiteness: Their Legal Legacy, Their Economic Costs." Delgado and Stefancic, *Critical Race* 71–79.

Berlin, James. "Revisionary Histories of Rhetoric: Politics, Power, and Plurality." Vitanza, *Writing* 112–27.

———. *Rhetorics, Poetics, and Cultures: Refiguring College English Studies.* Urbana, IL: NCTE, 1996.

Bhabha, Homi. "On the Irremovable Strangeness of Being Different." *PMLA* 113 (1998): 34–39.

Bitzer, Lloyd. "The Rhetorical Situation." *Philosophy & Rhetoric* 1 (1968): 1–14.

Bizzell, Patricia. "'Contact Zones' and English Studies." *Cross-Talk in Comp Theory.* Ed. Victor Villanueva Jr. Urbana, IL: NCTE, 1997. 735–42.

Bleicher, Josef. *Contemporary Hermeneutics: Hermeneutics as Method, Philosophy, and Critique.* Boston: Routledge, 1980.

Bonham, Vence, Jr. "Viewpoint: Race and Genomics: A Challenge to Medical Educators." Apr. 2003. Association of American Medical Colleges. 4 Dec. 2004 <http://www.aamc.org/newsroom/reporter/april03/viewpoint.htm>.

Booth, Wayne. *Rhetoric of Fiction.* 2nd ed. Chicago: U of Chicago P, 1983.

Bruns, Gerald. *Hermeneutics Ancient and Modern.* New Haven: Yale UP, 1992.

Buell, Lawrence. Introduction. "In Pursuit of Ethics." *PMLA* 114 (1999): 7–19.

Burke, Kenneth. *A Grammar of Motives.* 1945. Berkeley: U of California P, 1969.

———. *Language as Symbolic Action: Essays on Life, Literature, and Method.* Berkeley: U of California P, 1966.

———. *The Philosophy of Literary Form: Studies in Symbolic Action.* 1941. Berkeley: U of California P, 1973.

———. *A Rhetoric of Motives.* 1950. Berkeley: U of California P, 1969.

Butler, Judith. *Bodies That Matter: On the Discursive Limits of "Sex."* New York: Routledge, 1993.

Cahill, Susan, ed. *Writing Women's Lives: An Anthology of Autobiographical Narratives by Twentieth-Century Women Writers.* New York: Harper, 1994.

Campbell, Karlyn Kohrs. *Man Cannot Speak for Her.* Vol. 1. New York: Greenwood, 1989.

Carbado, Devon W. "Men, Feminism, and Male Heterosexual Privilege." Delgado and Stefancic, *Critical Race Theory* 525–31.

Carr, C. "Dreams Deferred: The Long Exile of Lillian Smith." *Village Voice* 39 (1994): 21–22.

Carr, Edward Hallett. *What Is History?* New York: Vintage, 1961.

Carr, Sarah. "Coalition Says Study Rebuts Education Myths." *Journal Sentinel* [Milwaukee] 20 Nov. 2002. 6 Sept. 2003 <http://www.jsonline.com/news/metro/nov02/97244.asp>.

Castillo, Ana. *Massacre of the Dreamers: Essays on Xicanisma.* New York: Penguin, 1995.

Caughie, Pamela. *Passing and Pedagogy: The Dynamics of Responsibility.* Urbana: U of Illinois P, 1999.

Childers, Mary, and bell hooks. "A Conversation about Race and Class." *Conflicts in Feminism.* Ed. Marianne Hirsch and Evelyn Fox Keller. New York: Routledge, 1990. 60–81.

Christian, Barbara. "Layered Rhythms: Virginia Woolf and Toni Morrison." *Virginia Woolf: Emerging Perspectives. Selected Papers from the Third Annual Conference on Virginia Woolf.* Ed. Mark Hussey and Vara Neverow. New York: Pace UP, 1994.

"Cincinnati Cools: Curfew Extended as Violent Protests Subside." *Good Morning America.* ABC. 13 Apr. 2001. 1 Sept. 2003 <http://abcnews.go.com/sections/us/dailynews/shooting_protest_2_010413.html>.

Clough, Patricia Ticineto. "Autotelecommunication and Autoethnography: A Reading of Carolyn Ellis's *Final Negotiations.*" *Sociological Quarterly* 38 (1997): 97–110.

Conley, Dalton. *Honky.* New York: Vintage, 2001.

Corbett, Edward P. J. *Classical Rhetoric for the Modern Student.* 2nd ed. New York: Oxford, 1971.

Crenshaw, Kimberlé Williams. "The First Decade: Critical Reflections, or 'A Foot in the Closing Door.'" *Crossroads, Directions, and a New Critical Race Theory.* Ed. Francisco Valdez et al. Philadelphia: Temple UP, 2002. 9–31.

———. "Mapping the Margins: Intersectionality, Identity Politics, and Violence Against Women of Color." Crenshaw et al. 357–83.

Crenshaw, Kimberlé Williams, Neil Gotanda, Gary Peller, and Kendall Thomas, eds. *Critical Race Theory: The Key Writings That Formed the Movement.* New York: New, 1995.

Culler, Jonathan. *Literary Theory: A Very Short Introduction.* New York: Oxford, 1997.

Cuomo, Chris, and Kim Q. Hall. Introduction. "Reflections on Whiteness." *Whiteness: Feminist Philosophical Reflections.* Ed. Cuomo and Hall. Lanham, MD: Rowman, 1999. 1–14.

Daly, Mary. *Gyn/Ecology: The Metaethics of Radical Feminism.* 1978. 2nd ed. Boston: Beacon, 1990.

Daly, Mary, and Jane Caputi. *Websters' First New Intergalactic Wickedary of the English Language.* Boston: Beacon, 1987.

Darwin, Charles. "Chapter 7: On the Races of Man." *The Descent of Man.* 8 Feb. 2004 <http://www.book-worm.org/darwin-charles/the-descent-of-man/chapter-07.html>.

Davis, Diane. *Breaking Up [at] Totality: A Rhetoric of Laughter for Politics and Pedagogy.* Carbondale: Southern Illinois UP, 1999.

———. "Just Listening: A Hearing for the Unhearable." Conference on College Composition and Communication. Hyatt Regency Hotel, Phoenix. 14 Mar. 1997.

Davy, Kate. "Outing Whiteness: A Feminist/Lesbian Project." Hill 204–25.

de Certeau, Michel. *The Practice of Everyday Life.* Trans. Steven F. Rendall. 1984. Berkeley: U California P, 2002.

Deck, Alice A. "Autoethnography: Zora Neale Hurston, Noni Jabavu, and Cross-Disciplinary Discourse." *Black American Literature Forum* 24 (1990): 237–56.

de Crèvecoeur, St. John. "What Is an American?" 1782. *American Literature, American Culture.* Ed. Gordon Hunter. New York: Oxford, 1999.

"Defense Mechanisms." UTMed Online manual. 1 Sept. 1999. 1 Apr. 2003 <http://utmed.com/wmanuel/psyc/defense.html>.

Delgado, Richard. "Storytelling for Oppositionists and Others: A Plea for Narrative." Delgado and Stefancic, *Critical Race Theory* 60–70.

Delgado, Richard, and Jean Stefancic, eds. *Critical Race Theory: The Cutting Edge.* 2nd ed. Philadelphia: Temple UP, 2000.

———. *Critical White Studies: Looking Behind the Mirror.* Philadelphia: Temple UP, 1997.

Derrida, Jacques. *The Ear of the Other: Otobiography, Transference, Translation: Texts and Discussions with Jacques Derrida.* 1982. Ed. Christie V. McDonald. Trans. Peggy Kamuf. Lincoln: U of Nebraska P, 1985.

———. "Otobiographies." Derrida 3–38.

———. "Violence and Metaphysics: An Essay on the Thought of Emmanuel Levinas." *Writing and Difference.* Trans. Alan Bass. Chicago: U of Chicago P, 1978. 79–153.

———. "White Mythology: Metaphor in the Text of Philosophy." Trans. F. C. T. Moore. *New Literary History* 6 (1974): 5–74.

Desser, Daphne. "Reading and Writing the Family: Ethos, Identification, and Identity in My Great-Grandfather's Letters." *Rhetoric Review* 20 (2001): 314–28.

De Veaux, Alexis. *Warrior Poet: A Biography of Audre Lorde.* New York: Norton, 2004.

Dinah Was. By Oliver Goldstock. Dir. David Petrarca. Perf. E. Fay Butler. Milwaukee Repertory Theater. 13 Jan. 2001.

Doro, Paul. "Burden in My Hand." Unpublished student essay. Marquette University, 2000.

Du Bois, W. E. B. "Dialogue with a White Friend." Roediger 29–37.

———. *The Souls of Black Folk.* 1953. New York: Modern, 2003.

Duncan, Patti. "Decentering Whiteness: Resisting Racism in the Women's Studies Classroom." TuSmith and Reddy 40–50.

Dyer, Richard. *White.* New York: Routledge, 1997.

Dyson, Michael Eric. *Race Rules: Navigating the Color Line.* New York: Vintage, 1996.

Elias, Karen, and Judith Jones. "Two Voices from the Front Lines: A Conversation about Race in the Classroom." TuSmith and Reddy 7–18.

Ellison, Ralph. "What America Would Be Like Without Blacks." Roediger 160–67.

Erdrich, Louise. *Love Medicine.* 1984. New York: HarperPerennial, 1993.

Fanon, Frantz. *Black Skin, White Masks.* Trans. Charles Lam Markmann. New York: Grove, 1967.

Fine, Michelle, et al., eds. *Off White: Readings on Race, Power, and Society.* New York: Routledge, 1997.

Fishkin, Shelley Fisher. "Interrogating 'Whiteness,' Complicating 'Blackness': Remapping American Culture." *American Quarterly* 47 (1995): 428–66.

Fiumara, Gemma Corradi. *The Other Side of Language: A Philosophy of Listening.* New York: Routledge, 1990.

Foss, Sonja, Karen Foss, and Cindy Griffin. *Feminist Rhetorical Theories.* Thousand Oaks, CA: Corwin, 1999.

Fox, Helen. *When Race Breaks Out: Conversations about Race and Racism in College Classrooms.* New York: Lang, 2001.

Frankenberg, Ruth. "'When We Are Capable of Stopping, We Begin to See': Being White, Seeing Whiteness." Thompson and Tyagi 3–18.

———. *White Women/Race Matters: The Social Construction of Whiteness.* Minneapolis: U of Minnesota P, 1993.

Freire, Paulo. *Pedagogy of Freedom: Ethics, Democracy, and Civic Courage.* Trans. Patrick Clark. Lanham, MD: Rowan, 2000.

Freud, Sigmund. *The Standard Edition of the Complete Psychological Works of Sigmund Freud.* Trans. and Ed. James Strachey. 24 vols. London: Hogarth, 1953–1974.

Fuss, Diana. *Essentially Speaking: Feminism, Nature and Difference.* New York: Routledge, 1989.

———. *Identification Papers.* New York: Routledge, 1995.

Gadamer, Hans-Georg. *Truth and Method.* Trans. Garrett Barden and John Cummings. New York: Seabury, 1975.

Gerard, Philip. *Creative Nonfiction: Researching and Crafting Stories of Real Life.* 2nd ed. Long Grove, IL: Waveland, 2004.

Gilbert, Sandra. "Ethnicity-Ethnicities-Literature-Literatures." *PMLA* 113 (1998): 19–27.

Gil-Gomez, Ellen. "The Practice of Piece-Making: Subject Positions in the Classroom." Jarratt and Worsham 198–205.

Gilligan, Carol. *In a Different Voice: Psychological Theory and Women's Development.* 1982. Cambridge: Harvard UP, 1993.

Gilyard, Keith. "African American Contributions to Composition Studies." *CCC* 50 (1999): 626–44.

———, ed. *Race, Rhetoric, and Composition.* Portsmouth, NH: Boynton/Cook, 1999.

Giovanni, Nikki. "Annual Conventions of Everyday Subjects." *Racism 101.* New York: Morrow, 1994. 83–89.

Gladney, Margaret Rose. Introduction. Smith i–vi.

Glenn, Cheryl. *Rhetoric Retold: Regendering the Tradition from Antiquity Through the Renaissance.* Carbondale: Southern Illinois UP, 1997.

———. "Silence: A Rhetorical Art for Resisting Discipline(s)." *JAC* 22 (2002): 261–91.

———. *Unspoken: A Rhetoric of Silence.* Carbondale: Southern Illinois UP, 2004.

Goodburn, Amy. "Racing (Erasing) White Privilege in Teacher/Research Writing about Race." Gilyard, *Race* 67–86.

Graves, Joseph. "Between a Rock and a Hard Place: Teaching the Biology of Human Variation and the Social Construction of Race." TuSmith and Reddy 299–314.

———. *The Emperor's New Clothes: Biological Theories of Race at the New Millennium.* New Brunswick, NJ: Rutgers UP, 2001.

Gray, J. Glenn. Introduction. Heidegger, *What* xvii–xxvii.

Green, Judith, and Blanche Radford Curry. "Recognizing Each Other Amidst Diversity: Beyond Essentialism in Collaborative Multi-Cultural Feminist Theory." *Sage* 8 (summer 1991): 39–49.

Greene, Maxine. Foreword. *Women in Power: Pathways to Leadership in Education.* By Barbara K. Curry. New York: Teachers College P, 2000.

Gregory, Marshall. "Comment and Response." *College English* 60 (1998): 89–93.

Grosz, Elizabeth. *Jacques Lacan: A Feminist Introduction.* New York: Routledge, 1990.

Gusfield, Joseph R. "The Bridge over Separated Lands: Kenneth Burke's Significance for the Study of Social Action." Simons and Melia 28–54.

Haas, Christina, and Linda Flower. "Rhetorical Reading Strategies and the Construction of Meaning." *CCC* 39 (May 1988): 167–84.

Harris, Cheryl. "Whiteness as Property." Roediger 103–18.

Harris, Joseph. *A Teaching Subject: Composition since 1966.* Upper Saddle River, NJ: Prentice, 1997.

Hase, Michiko. "Student Resistance and Nationalism in the Classroom." *Gender, Teaching, and Research in Higher Education: Challenges for the Twenty-first Century.* Ed. Gillian Howie and Ashley Tauchert. Burlington, VT: Ashgate, 2002. 87–107.

Hedges, Elaine, and Shelley Fisher Fishkin, eds. *Listening to Silences: New Essays in Feminist Criticism.* New York: Oxford UP, 1994.

Hegel, G. W. F. *The Philosophy of Fine Arts.* Trans. F. P. B. Osmaston. London: Bell, 1920.

Heidegger, Martin. "Phenomenology and Fundamental Ontology: The Disclosure of Meaning." Mueller-Vollmer 214–40.

———. *What Is Called Thinking?* 1954. Trans. Fred D. Wick and J. Glenn Gray. New York: Harper, 1968.

Herndl, Carl. "Tactics and the Quotidian: Resistance and Professional Discourse." *JAC* 16 (1996). 11 Nov. 2004 <http://jac.gsu.edu/jac/16.3/Articles/7.htm>.

Hill, Mike. Introduction. "Vipers in Shangri-La." Hill 1–18.

———, ed. *Whiteness: A Critical Reader.* New York: New York UP, 1997.

Hobson, Fred. "The Sins of the Fathers: Lillian Smith and Katharine Du Pre Lumpkin." *Southern Review* 34 (1998): 14 pp. Memorial Lib., Marquette U. 19 Apr. 1999 <http://proquest.umi.com/pqdweb?TS=...=1&Did=000000036261966& Mtd=1&Fmt=3>.

Homans, Margaret. "'Women of Color' Writers and Feminist Theory." *New Literary History* 25 (1994): 73–94.

hooks, bell. "Counterhegemonic Art: *Do the Right Thing*." hooks, *Yearning* 173–84.

———. "Homeplace: A Site of Resistance." hooks, *Yearning* 41–50.

———. "The Politics of Radical Black Subjectivity." hooks, *Yearning* 15–22.

———. "Race and Feminism: The Issue of Accountability." *Ain't I a Woman: Black Women and Feminism.* Boston: South, 1981. 119–58.

———. "Representing Whiteness in the Black Imagination." *Cultural Studies.* Ed. Lawrence Grossberg, Cary Nelson, and Paula Treichler. New York: Routledge, 1992. 338–46.

———. "Representing Whiteness: Seeing Wings of Desire." hooks, *Yearning* 165–72.

———. "Talking Back." *Talking Back.* Boston: South, 1989. 5–9.

———. *Teaching to Transgress: Education as the Practice of Freedom.* New York: Routledge, 1994.

————. *Yearning: Race, Gender, and Cultural Politics.* Boston: South, 1990.

Houston, Jeanne Wakatsuki, and James D. Houston. *Farewell to Manzanar.* New York: Bantam, 1973.

Hughes, Christina. "Pedagogies of, and for, Resistance." *Gender, Teaching, and Research in Higher Education: Challenges for the Twenty-first Century.* Ed. Gillian Howie and Ashley Tauchert. Burlington, VT: Ashgate, 2002. 59–85.

Hunter, Margaret. "Decentering the White and Male Standpoints in Race and Ethnicity Courses." MacDonald and Sánchez-Casal 251–79.

Hurlbert, C. Mark, and Michael Blitz, eds. *Composition and Resistance.* Portsmouth, NH: Boynton/Cook, 1991.

Ignatiev, Noel. *How the Irish Became White.* New York: Routledge, 1995.

"Image Archive on the American Eugenics Movement." Dolan DNA Learning Center. 8 Feb. 2004. <http://www.eugenicsarchive.org/>.

Jarratt, Susan. "Feminist Pedagogy." *A Guide to Composition Pedagogies.* Ed. Gary Tate et al. New York: Oxford UP, 2001. 113–31.

————. *Rereading the Sophists: Classical Rhetoric Refigured.* Carbondale: Southern Illinois UP, 1991.

Jarratt, Susan, and Lynn Worsham, eds. *Feminism and Composition Studies: In Other Words.* New York: MLA, 1998.

Jay, Greg. "Whiteness Studies: Deconstructing (the) Race." Nov. 2004. 5 Dec. 2004 <http://www.uwm.edu/~gjay/Whiteness/>.

Jay, Martin. "The Rise of Hermeneutics and the Crisis of Ocularcentrism." *The Rhetoric of Interpretation and the Interpretation of Rhetoric.* Ed. Paul Hernandi. Durham, NC: Duke UP, 1989. 55–74.

Johnson-Elie, Tanette. "Can't Fault the Parents Who Want to Shout Their Daughter's Achievements from Rooftops." *Journal Sentinel* [Milwaukee] 20 Aug. 2003. 6 Sept. 2003 <http://www.jsonline.com/bym/Biz2biz/aug03/163337.asp>.

Kane, Eugene. "Acing the Tough Lessons." *Journal Sentinel* [Milwaukee] 8 May 2003. 5 Dec. 2004 <http://www.jsonline.com/news/metro/may03/139264.asp>.

Keating, AnnLouise. "Interrogating 'Whiteness,' (De)Constructing Race." *College English* 57 (1995): 901–18.

King, Martin Luther, Jr. "Letter from Birmingham Jail." 1963. *The Norton Reader.* 8th ed. New York: Norton, 1992. 886–900.

Kingsolver, Barbara. *Pigs in Heaven.* New York: HarperCollins, 1993.

————. *The Poisonwood Bible.* New York: HarperCollins, 1998.

Kirsch, Gesa, and Joy Ritchie. "Beyond the Personal: Theorizing a Politics of Location in Composition Research." *CCC* 46 (1995): 7–29.

Kopelson, Karen. "Rhetoric on the Edge of Cunning; Or, the Performance of Neutrality (Re)Considered as a Composition Pedagogy for Student Resistance." *CCC* 55 (2003): 115–46.

Kristeva, Julia. "Stabat Mater." *The Kristeva Reader.* Ed. Toril Moi. New York: Columbia UP, 1986. 160–86.

Lee, Jayne Chong-Soon. "Navigating the Topology of Race." Crenshaw et al. 441–48.

LeFevre, Karen. *Invention as Social Act.* Carbondale: Southern Illinois UP, 1987.

Leitch, Vincent. *Cultural Criticism, Literary Theory, Poststructuralism.* New York: Columbia UP, 1992.

Lentricchia, Frank. *Criticism and Social Change.* Chicago: U of Chicago P, 1983.

Lerner, Gerda. *Why History Matters.* New York: Oxford UP, 1997.

Levin, David. *The Listening Self: Personal Growth, Social Change, and the Closure of Metaphysics.* New York: Routledge, 1989.

Linn, Ray. *A Teacher's Introduction to Postmodernism.* Urbana, IL: NCTE, 1996.

Lipsitz, George. "The Possessive Investment in Whiteness: Racialized Social Democracy and the White Problem in American Studies." *American Quarterly* 47 (1995): 369–87.

———. "Toxic Racism." *American Quarterly* 47 (1995): 416–27.

Logan, Shirley Wilson. "Changing Missions, Shifting Positions, and Breaking Silences." *CCC* 55 (2003): 330–42.

———. "'When and Where I Enter': Race, Gender, and Composition Studies." Jarratt and Worsham 45–57.

Lorde, Audre. "Age, Race, Class, and Sex: Women Redefining Difference." Lorde, *Sister Outsider* 114–23.

———. "From a Burst of Light." Cahill 283–96.

———. "An Open Letter to Mary Daly." Lorde, *Sister Outsider* 66–71.

———. "Poetry Is Not a Luxury." Lorde, *Sister Outsider* 36–39.

———. *Sister Outsider: Essays and Speeches.* Trumansburg, New York: Crossing, 1984.

Lu, Min-Zhan. "Composition and Postcolonial Studies." *JAC* 19 (1999): 335–57.

Lubiano, Wahneema, ed. *The House That Race Built: Black Americans, U.S. Terrain.* New York: Pantheon, 1997.

Lunsford, Andrea. Introduction. Lunsford 3–8.

———, ed. *Reclaiming Rhetorica: Women in the Rhetorical Tradition.* Pittsburgh: U of Pittsburgh P, 1995.

Lyotard, Jean-François. *The Differend: Phrases in Dispute.* Trans. Georges Van Den Abbeele. Minneapolis: U of Minnesota P, 1988.

———. *The Postmodern Condition: A Report on Knowledge.* Trans. Geoff Bennington and Brian Massumi. Minneapolis: U of Minnesota P, 1984.

MacDonald, Amie, and Susan Sánchez-Casal, eds. *Twenty-first Century Feminist Classrooms: Pedagogies of Identity and Difference.* New York: Palgrave, 2002.

Maher, Frances, and Mary Kay Thompson Tetreault. "The Making and Unmaking of Whiteness, Gender, and Class in College Classrooms." Rodriguez and Villaverde 158–75.

Mailloux, Steven. *Rhetorical Power.* Ithaca, NY: Cornell UP, 1989.

Malcolm X. *The Autobiography of Malcolm X (as Told to Alex Haley).* 1965. New York: Ballantine, 1992.

Maraniss, David. "Not Black or White, but Packer Green." *Journal Sentinel* [Milwaukee] 17 Sept. 1999: A1+. *When Pride Still Mattered: Life of Vince Lombardi.* New York: Simon, 1999.

McDonald, Christie V. Preface. Derrida, *Ear* vii–x.

McIntosh, Peggy. "White Privilege: Unpacking the Invisible Knapsack." 1988. 5 Sept. 2003 <http://www.utoronto.ca/acc/events/peggy1.htm>.

McKay, Claude. "The Lynching." Roediger 335.

McKinney, Karyn. "Whiteness on a White Canvass: Teaching Race in a Predominantly White University." TuSmith and Reddy 126–39.

Middleton, Joyce Irene. "Delivery and the Art of Listening: Toni Morrison's Nobel Lecture as an Epideictic Argument." Conference on College Composition and Communication. Hilton Hotel, Atlanta. 25 Mar. 1999.

———. "Kris, I Hear You." *JAC* 20 (2000): 433–43.

Miller, J. Hillis. "Composition and Decomposition: Deconstruction and the Teaching of Writing." *Composition and Literature: Bridging the Gap.* Ed. Winifred Horner. Chicago: U of Chicago P, 1983. 38–56.

Mitchard, Jacqueline. "Ahem! It's Not a White Man's World Anymore." *Journal Sentinel* [Milwaukee] 5 May 2002. 1 Sept. 2003 <http://www.jsonline.com/lifestyle/advice/may02/41116.asp?showheadlines=all>.

Moi, Toril. *Sexual/Textual Politics.* New York: Routledge, 1985.

Moraga, Cherríe. "The Breakdown of the Bicultural Mind." Thompson and Tyagi 231–39.

Moraga, Cherríe, and Gloria Anzaldúa, eds. *This Bridge Called My Back: Writings by Radical Women of Color.* 2nd ed. New York: Kitchen, 1983.

Morrison, Toni. *Beloved.* New York: Plume, 1987.

———. *Playing in the Dark: Whiteness and the Literary Imagination.* 1992. New York: Vintage, 1993.

Mountford, Roxanne "Reply to *Adversus Haereses.*" *JAC* 19 (1999): 6 pars. 18 Oct. 1999 <http://www.cas.usf.edu/JAC/193/mountford2.html>.

Mueller-Vollmer, Kurt, ed. *The Hermeneutics Reader: Texts of the German Tradition from the Enlightenment to the Present.* New York: Continuum, 1985.

Murphy, James. Foreword. Lunsford ix–xiv.

———. "Rhetorical History as a Guide to the Salvation of American Reading and Writing: A Plea for Curricular Courage." *The Rhetorical Tradition and Modern Writing.* Ed. James J. Murphy. New York: MLA, 1982. 3–12.

Nakayama, Thomas, and Robert Krizek. "Whiteness: a Strategic Rhetoric." *QJS* 81 (1995): 291–309.

New English Bible, The. New York: Oxford UP, 1976.

New Shorter Oxford English Dictionary, The. Vol. 1: A–M. Ed. Lesley Brown. Oxford: Clarendon, 1993.

Newton, Judith, and Deborah Rosenfelt. Introduction. "Toward a Materialist-Feminist Criticism." *Feminist Criticism and Social Change: Sex, Class, and Race in Literature and Culture.* Ed. Newton and Rosenfelt. New York: Methuen, 1985. xv–xxxix.

Nietzsche, Frederick. "On the Uses and Disadvantages of History for Life." *Untimely Meditations.* Trans. R. J. Hollingdale. Cambridge: Cambridge UP, 1983. 57–123.

Norris, Christopher. *Deconstruction: Theory and Practice.* New York: Methuen, 1982.

Oravec, Christine. "Kenneth Burke's Concept of Association and the Complexity of Identity." Simons and Melia 174–95.

Paley, Vivian Gussin. *White Teacher.* 2nd ed. Cambridge: Harvard UP, 2000.

Pennock, Pamela. "The Scopes Trial: The Textbook." University of Michigan–Dearborn. 27 Jan. 2004 <http://www-personal.umd.umich.edu/~ppennock/doc-scopesText.htm>.

Phelan, James. "Vanity Fair: Listening as a Rhetorician—and a Feminist." *Out of Bounds: Male Writers and Gender.* Ed. Laura Claridge and Elizabeth Langland. Amherst: U of Massachusetts P, 1990. 132–47.

Phelan, James, and Peter Rabinowitz, eds. *Understanding Narrative.* Columbus: Ohio State UP, 1994.

Piercy, Marge. "The book of Ruth and Naomi." *No More Masks: An Anthology of Twentieth-Century American Women Poets.* Ed. Florence Howe. New York: Harper, 1993. 277–78.

Pitts, Leonard, Jr. "An Apology over Slavery Misses Point." *Detroit Free Press* 23 July 2003. 1 Sept. 2003 <http://www.freep.com/voices/columnists/pitts23_20030723.htm>.

Plato. *Phaedrus.* Trans. Harold North Fowler. Vol. 1. Cambridge, MA: Harvard UP, 1977.

Poulakos, John. "Nietzsche and Histories of Rhetoric." Vitanza, *Writing* 81–97.

Powell, Malea. "Blood and Scholarship: One Mixed-Blood's Story." Gilyard, *Race* 1–16.

Pradl, Gordon. *Literature for Democracy: Reading as a Social Act.* Portsmouth, NH: Boynton/Cook, 1996.

Pratt, Mary Louise. "Arts of the Contact Zone." *Profession 91.* New York: MLA, 1991. 33–40.

Preston, Richard. *First Light: The Search for the Edge of the Universe.* New York: Atlantic Monthly, 1987.

Rabinowitz, Nancy Sorkin. "Queer Theory and Feminist Pedagogy." MacDonald and Sánchez-Casal 175–202.

Rabinowitz, Peter. "Fictional Music: Toward a Theory of Listening." *Theories of Reading, Looking, and Listening.* Ed. Harry R. Garvin. East Brunswick, NJ: Associated UP, 1981: 193–206.

Race Traitor: A Journal of the New Abolitionism. 8 Feb. 2004 <http://racetraitor.org/>.

Random House Dictionary of the English Language. 2nd ed. New York: Random, 1987.

Ratcliffe, Krista. *Anglo-American Feminist Challenges to the Rhetorical Traditions: Virginia Woolf, Mary Daly, Adrienne Rich.* Carbondale: Southern Illinois UP, 1996.

———. "Eavesdropping as Rhetorical Tactic: History, Whiteness, and Rhetoric." *JAC* 20 (2000): 87–119.

———. "Eavesdropping on Others." *JAC* 20 (2000): 908–18.

———. "Listening to Cassandra: A Materialist-Feminist Exposé of the Necessary

Relations Between Rhetoric and Hermeneutics." *Studies in the Literary Imagination* 28 (fall 1995): 63–77.

———. "Rhetorical Listening: A Trope for Interpretive Invention and a Code of Cross-Cultural Conduct." *CCC* 51 (Dec. 1999): 33–62.

———. "A Rhetoric of Classroom Denial: Resisting Resistance to Alcohol Questions while Teaching Louise Erdrich's Love Medicine." *The Languages of Addiction.* Ed. Jane Lilienfeld and Jeffrey Oxford. New York: St. Martin's, 1999. 105–21.

Rayner, Alice. "The Audience: Subjectivity, Community, and the Ethics of Listening." *Journal of Dramatic Theory and Criticism* 7 (1993): 3–24.

Reddy, Maureen. "Smashing the Rules of Racial Standing." TuSmith and Reddy 51–61.

Reynolds, Nedra. "*Ethos* as Location: New Sites for Understanding Discursive Authority." *Rhetoric Review* 11 (1993): 325–38.

———. "Interrupting Our Way to Agency: Feminist Cultural Studies and Composition." Jarratt and Worsham 58–73.

Rich, Adrienne. *Blood, Bread, and Poetry: Selected Prose 1979–1985.* New York: Norton, 1986.

———. "Contradictions." Rich, *Your* 81–111.

———. "The Distance Between Language and Violence." Rich, *What* 181–89.

———. "North American Time." Rich, *Your* 33–36.

———. "Notes Toward a Politics of Location." Rich, *Blood* 210–31.

———. "Split at the Root: An Essay on Jewish Identity." Rich, *Blood* 100–123.

———. *What Is Found There: Notebooks on Poetry and Politics.* New York: Norton, 1993.

———. "When We Dead Awaken: Writing as Revision." *On Lies, Secrets and Silences.* New York: Norton, 1979. 33–49.

———. "Woman and Bird." Rich, *What* 3–8.

———. *Your Native Land, Your Life: Poems.* New York: Norton, 1986.

Ritchie, Joy. "Confronting the Essential Problem: Reconnecting Feminist Theory and Pedagogy." *JAC* 10 (1990): 249–71.

Robbins, Kamenka. " . . . Some of My Best Friends are Black. . . . " Unpublished student essay. Marquette University, 2000.

Rodriguez, Nelson M. "Projects of Whiteness in a Critical Pedagogy." Rodriguez and Villaverde 1–24.

Rodriguez, Nelson M., and Leila E. Villaverde, eds. *Dismantling White Privilege: Pedagogy, Politics, and Whiteness.* New York: Lang, 2000.

Roediger, David, ed. *Black on White: Black Writers on What It Means to Be White.* New York: Schocken, 1998.

Rogers, J. A. "Debating the Senator." Roediger 85–98.

Romine, Scott. "Framing Southern Rhetoric: Lillian Smith's Narrative Persona in *Killers of the Dream.*" *South Atlantic Review* 59 (1994): 95–111.

Roof, Judith, and Robyn Wiegman, eds. *Who Can Speak?: Authority and Critical Identity.* Urbana: U of Illinois P, 1995.

Royster, Jacqueline Jones. "Borderlands and Common Spaces: Care and Maintenance in Our Neutral Zones." Conference: From Boundaries to Borderlands. Oregon State University, Corvallis, OR. 28 Aug. 1997.

———. "When the First Voice You Hear Is Not Your Own." *CCC* 47 (1994): 29–40.

Sales, Carol. "Color Me Confused." Unpublished student essay. Marquette University, 2000.

Salvaggio, Ruth. *The Sounds of Feminist Theory.* Albany: State U of New York P, 1999.

Sánchez-Casal, Susan. "Unleashing the Demons of History: White Resistance in the U.S. Latino Studies Classroom." MacDonald and Sánchez-Casal 59–86.

Scheunemann, Sara. "Matthew 13: 1–17: 'He Who Has Ears, Let Him Hear.'" Unpublished student essay. Marquette University, 1996.

Schuman, Amy. "Feminist Ethnography and the Rhetoric of Accommodation." Conference: From Boundaries to Borderlands. Oregon State University, Corvallis, OR. 30 Aug. 1997.

Shor, Ira. *When Students Have Power: Negotiating Authority in Critical Pedagogy.* Chicago: U of Chicago P, 1996.

Showalter, Elaine. *Speaking of Gender.* New York: Routledge, 1989.

Simons, Herbert, and Trevor Melia, eds. *The Legacy of Kenneth Burke.* Madison: U of Wisconsin P, 1989.

Smith, Lillian. *Killers of the Dream.* 1949. New York: Norton, 1994.

Spivak, Gayatri. "Subaltern Studies: Deconstructing Historiography." *In Other Worlds: Essays in Cultural Politics.* New York: Methuen, 1987. 197–221.

Talbot, Margaret. "Getting Credit for Being White." *New York Times Magazine* 30 Nov. 1997: 116–19.

Tan, Amy. *The Joy Luck Club.* New York: Ivy, 1989.

Tannen, Deborah. "'I'll Explain It to You': Lecturing and Listening." *You Just Don't Understand: Women and Men in Conversation.* New York: Ballantine, 1990. 123–48.

Thomas-Lynn, Felicia. "Motivating Minority Students: Group Encourages Academic Excellence in Face of Peer Pressure That Tells Kids Achieving Is Not Cool." *Journal Sentinel* [Milwaukee] 25 Dec. 2000. 20 Apr. 2001 <http://www.jsonline.com/news/Metro/jan00/scholar04010300.asp>.

Thompson, Becky. "Time Traveling and Border Crossing: Reflections on White Identity." Thompson and Tyagi 93–109.

Thompson, Becky, and Sangeeta Tyagi, eds. *Names We Call Home: Autobiography on Racial Identity.* New York: Routledge, 1996.

"Too Late for Slavery Reparations." Letter. *Journal Sentinel* [Milwaukee] 10 Mar. 2001: 10A.

Trinh, T. Minh-ha. "Not You/Like You: Postcolonial Women and the Interlocking Questions of Identity and Difference." *Longman Anthology of Women's Literature.* Ed. Mary K. Deshazer. New York: Longman, 2001. 929–33.

TuSmith, Bonnie, and Maureen Reddy, eds. *Race in the College Classroom: Pedagogy and Politics.* New Brunswick, NJ: Rutgers UP, 2002.

Tutu, Desmond. Acceptance speech. Pere Marquette Discovery Award. Marquette University, Milwaukee, WI. 12 Feb. 2003.

Villanueva, Victor, Jr. *Bootstraps: From an American Academic of Color.* Urbana, IL: NCTE, 1993.

———. "Reading Rhetoric Outside and In: Theory, Pedagogy, and Politics in *Race, Rhetoric, and Composition.*" *JAC* 20 (2000): 195–203.

Vitanza, Victor, ed. "Discussions of Empire." Feb. and Mar. 2003 pretext@listserve. uta.edu>.

———. *Negation, Subjectivity, and the History of Rhetoric.* Albany: State U of New York P, 1997.

———. "'Notes' Towards Historiographies of Rhetorics; or, Rhetorics of the Histories of Rhetorics: Traditional, Revisionary, and Sub/Versive." *Pre/Text* 8 (1987): 63–125.

———. *Writing Histories of Rhetoric.* Carbondale: Southern Illinois UP, 1994.

Walker, Alice. "The Dummy in the Window: Joel Chandler Harris and the Invention of Uncle Remus." Roediger 233–39.

Walker, Alice, and Pratibha Parmer. *Warrior Marks: Female Genital Mutilation and the Sexual Blinding of Women.* New York: Harcourt, 1993.

Washington, Harriet. "The Rite of Female Circumcision." *Emerge* 30 Sept. 1996: 30.

Watson, Jay. "Uncovering the Body, Discovering Ideology: Segregation and Sexual Anxiety in Lillian Smith's *Killers of the Dream.*" *American Quarterly* 49 (1997): 20 pp. Memorial Lib., Marquette U. 11 May 1999 <http://muse.jhu.edu/cgi-bin/access.cgi?uri=/journals/american/quarterly/v049/49.3watson.html&session =42844328>.

Weber, Rachel. "Dehumanization Suffered Yesterday and Today." Unpublished student essay. Marquette University, 1997.

Webster's New World Dictionary. 2nd ed. Cleveland: Collins, 1979.

Webster's Third New International Dictionary of the English Language. Springfield, MA: Merriam-Webster, 1986.

Weil, Danny. *Towards a Critical Multicultural Literacy.* New York: Lang, 1998.

Weiler, Ben. "Racism." Unpublished student essay. Marquette University, 2000.

Welch, Kathleen. "Interpreting the Silent 'Aryan Model' of Histories of Classical Rhetoric." Vitanza, *Writing* 38–48.

West, Cornel. "On Georg Lukács." *Keeping Faith: Philosophy and Race in America.* New York: Routledge, 1993. 143–64.

Wildman, Stephanie M., and Adrienne D. Davis. "Language and Silence: Making Systems of Privilege Visible." Delgado and Stefancic, *Critical Race Theory* 657–63.

Williams, David Cratis. "Under the Sign of (An)Nihilation." Simons and Melia 196–223.

Williams, Joe. "'White Benefit' Was Driving Force of Busing." *Journal Sentinel* [Milwaukee] 19 Oct. 1999: A1+.

Williams, Patricia. *The Alchemy of Race and Rights.* Cambridge: Harvard UP, 1991.

———. *Open House: Of Family, Friends, Food, Piano Lessons, and the Search for a Room of My Own*. New York: Farrar, 2004.

Wilson, William J. "What Shall We Do with the White People?" Roediger 58–66.

Wisconsin Department of Public Instruction. *Classroom Activities in Listening and Speaking*. Madison: Wisconsin Dept. of Public Instruction, 1991.

Worsham, Lynn, "After Words: A Choice of Words Remains." Jarratt and Worsham 329–56.

Wray, Matt, and Annalee Newitz, eds. *White Trash: Race and Class in America*. New York: Routledge, 1997.

Wright, Mark. "Burkean and Freudian Theories of Identification." *Communication Quarterly* 42 (1994): 301–10.

Yancey, Kathleen. *Voices on Voice: Perspectives, Definitions, Inquiry*. Urbana, IL: NCTE, 1994.

Index

Abel, Elizabeth, 100
academic research, listening to, 37–38
accountability, 6, 31, 98–99; logic of, 6, 8, 26, 31–32, 43
acting white, 112–13, 151, 202n19
Adams, Kate, 195n1
agency, 52, 65, 70, 74–75, 110, 194n11; authorial, 120, 124–26, 131, 199n11; cultural, 120, 129–31; discursive, 120, 121–24, 131; readerly, 120, 126–29, 131, 199n11
African genital mutilation, 80, 196n5
Alchemy of Race and Rights, The (p. Williams), 189n13
Allen, Paula Gunn, 136
Allen, Theodore, 154, 197n2
American Association of Medical Colleges, 13
American gynecology, 80
Anglo-American Feminist Challenges to the Rhetorical Tradition (Ratcliffe), 3, 4, 5, 101
Anzaldúa, Gloria, 79, 85, 93, 193n2, 196n7
appropriation, 168
Aristotle, 5, 20, 50, 61, 124, 125, 126, 131, 171, 199n12
Autobiography of Malcolm X, The (Malcolm X and Haley), 150
autoethnography, listening to, 35–36

Baldwin, James, 70–71, 117, 143, 175, 179, 180
Ballif, Michelle, 18, 20, 27, 77, 126, 190n4, 195n2
Barthes, Roland, 56
Bartholomae, David, 144
Bay, Mia, 116–17
Bell, Derrick A., Jr., 188n9
Beloved (Morrison), 8, 41, 44, 45, 96, 109, 122–23
Berlin, James, 52, 102, 107, 193n5
Bewitched, 104, 105
Bhabi, Homi, 189n12

Bitzer, Lloyd, 103
black (as a word), 122–23, 150, 156, 188n11, 196n8, 198n9
Bleicher, Joseph, 191n12
Blitz, Michael, 199n1
Bodies That Matter (Butler), 62
"book of Ruth and Naomi, The" (Piercy), ix, 25, 46
Booth, Wayne, 103
Bootstraps (Villanueva), 129
Borderlands/La Frontera (Anzaldúa), 85
Bridge Called My Back, This (Moraga and Anzaldúa), 79, 85
Bruns, Gerald, 191n12
Buell, Lawrence, 120, 125, 199n11
Burke, Kenneth, 1, 47, 49, 50, 52, 65, 66, 68–69, 72, 171, 183, 191n13, 194nn9, 10, 195n16; and identification and persuasion, 1, 28, 48, 74; and identification and rhetorical listening, 19, 53–60. *See also* consubstantiality; identity; substance; terministic screen
Butler, Judith, 7, 10, 49, 52, 62, 63, 66, 193nn2, 6

Campbell, Karlyn Kohrs, 85
Carbado, Devon, 187n4
Castillo, Ana, 85, 100, 118, 121, 126, 127–28, 198n8
Caughie, Pamela, 147, 151, 190n5, 191n10, 202n20
Childers, Maria, 5
Chinese foot-binding, 80
Christian, Barbara, 87, 196n8
Civic Biology (Hunter), 12
class, 200n3
Clough, Patricia Ticineto, 192n17
code of cross-cultural conduct. *See under* rhetorical listening
color-blindness, 15, 134, 135, 153, 164; logic of, 15, 161, 169

commonalities and differences, 2, 3, 26, 32–33, 43, 59–60, 65–66, 75–76, 83, 95–96; cultural logic of, 11
common ground, 52; coercive nature of, 47, 58–59. *See also* consubstantiality
comparable worth logic, 11
Conley, Dalton, 114, 143, 176
consubstantiality, 32, 47, 53, 55, 69
Corbett, Edward P. J., 77, 107
Creative Nonfiction (Gerard), 144
Crenshaw, Kimberlé Williams, 7, 189n13, 197n2
critical race studies, 7, 189n13; logic of, 15, 149, 164, 166, 168
Critical White Studies (Delgado and Stefancic), 197n2
critique, 97–98, 99, 197n10
cross-cultural communication, 2, 3, 25
Culler, Jonathan, 193n1
cultural biases against listening, 19–23
cultural logic, 3, 26, 33, 44, 46; of gender, 10–11; of race, 14–15
Cuomo, Chris, 201n15

Daly, Mary, 2, 3, 4, 35, 78–100, 104, 146–47, 196n3; Lorde-Daly debate, 78–100, 196n3; Sado-Ritual Syndrome, 81–82, 95
Darwin, Charles, 188n7
Davis, Diane, 30–31, 62, 77, 132, 195n2
Davy, Kate, 192n18, 197n2
De Certeau, Michel, 189n15
Deck, Alice, 192n17
De Crèvecoeur, J. Hector St. John, 124
defensiveness, 89–90, 92, 99, 138, 200n9
Delgado, Richard, 7, 189n13, 191n11, 197n2
De Man, Paul, 193n1, 194n11
denial, 88–89, 92, 99, 110, 138
Derrida, Jacques, 20, 52, 68, 72, 76, 122, 190n6
Desser, Daphne, 74, 193n6
De Veaux, Alexis, 196n3
dialogue, 32, 66
differences, 3, 59–60, 65. *See also* commonalities and differences
Dinah Was (Goldstick), 155
discourse communities, 103
disidentification, 48, 53, 60, 62–63, 65–66, 69, 70, 97, 162, 167, 168, 193nn2, 6

Dismantling White Privilege (N. Rodriguez and Villaverde), 198n2
divided *logos*, 23–24. *See also* Fiumara; Heidegger
DNA variation, 13, 188n8
"Don't Fence Me In" (Porter), 40
Doro, Paul, 167–70
double consciousness, 200n5
Douglass, Frederick, 124, 154
Du Bois, W. E. B., 107, 108, 200n5
Duncan, Patti, 203n22
Dyer, Richard, 7, 113, 197n2, 198n3
dysfunctional silence. *See* rhetoric of dysfunctional silence; silence
Dyson, Michael Eric, 16, 38, 183, 187n1, 188n6, 192n18

Ear of the Other, The (Derrida), 20
eavesdropping, 16, 101, 103, 104–7, 111, 121, 132, 171; and ethical issues, 106
Ellison, Ralph, 63, 122
Emperor's New Clothes, The: Biological Theories of Race at the New Millennium (Graves), 188n8
energy-field imagery, 69–71
equal rights logic, 10
Erdrich, Louise, 116
essence, 56
essentialism, 194n11
Essentially Speaking (Fuss), 85
ethics, 30, 31, 76–77, 120–21, 149
ethnicity, 13, 15, 164, 188n12
ethos, 124–26, 131; of teaching, 137, 145–46, 193n6
eugenics movement, 14, 188n10
European witch burning, 80
excess, 24, 94, 95

Fanon, Frantz, 59, 67, 77
Farewell to Manzanar (Houston), 40, 154
Feminism and Composition Studies (Jarratt and Worsham), 120, 151
feminist pedagogy, 135
Fighting Whites, 143
Fine, Michelle, 197n2
Fishkin, Shelley Fisher, 192n18, 195n1, 197n2
Fiumara, Gemma Corradi, 13, 24–25, 105, 106

Flower, Linda, 19
Foucault, Michel, 52
Fox, Helen, 100
Frankenberg, Ruth, 7, 38, 45, 100, 113, 114, 184, 189n12, 197n2, 199n2
Freire, Paulo, 201n17
Freud, Sigmund, 49, 54, 61, 67, 68, 193n3
Fuss, Diana, 5, 48, 49, 68–69, 76, 85, 193nn2, 6; critics of, 194n12, 195n16; and identification and rhetorical listening, 60–67

Gadamer, Hans-Georg, 28
gender, 9–12, 134, 136, 142, 149, 150–56, 187n5; as trope, 9
gender bias, 20, 112
gender-blindness, 5, 134, 135, 153
gendered-and-racialized silence. *See* silence
Gender Trouble (Butler), 62
Gerard, Phillip, 144
Gilbert, Sandra, 189n12
Gil-Gomez, Ellen, 132
Gilligan, Carol, 85
Gilyard, Keith, 7, 52
Giovanni, Nikki, 21–22, 27, 143, 176, 181, 190n5
Glenn, Cheryl, 84, 102, 132, 195n1
Goodburn, Amy, 7, 203n21
Grammar of Motives, A (Burke), 55
Graves, Joseph, 188nn8, 10
Grease, 202n18
Greene, Maxine, 137, 200n7
Gregory, Marshall, 192n20
Grosz, Elizabeth, 191n14
guilt/blame, 3, 91–92, 99; logic of, 5, 6, 32, 43
Gyn/Ecology: The Metaethics of Radical Feminism (Daly), 79, 80, 82, 83, 84, 88, 91, 94, 97, 146

Haas, Christina, 19
Hall, Kim Q., 201n15
Harris, Cheryl, 198n6
Harris, Joe, 103
Hase, Michiko, 201n17
hearing, 24, 25, 26–27, 93. *See also* listening; rhetorical listening
Hedges, Elaine, 195n1
Hegel, G. W. F., 95, 190n6

Heidegger, Martin, 23–24, 27, 29, 107, 108, 109, 110, 190n6
Herndl, Carl, 199n1
Hill, Mike, 183, 192n18, 197n2, 201n13
Hispanic (as a word), 188n12
historiography: origins mode of, 107–9, 198nn4, 5; usage mode of, 107, 109–11
history, 107–11, 132; historicizing terms, 154–55
home place, 62–63, 194n14
Honky (Conley), 114, 176
hooks, bell, 5, 7, 8, 31, 39, 71, 85, 87, 90, 96, 115, 168, 170, 191n10, 192n18, 194n12, 196n8, 197n2, 203n22
House That Race Built, The (Lubiano), 198n2
Houston, Jeanne Wakatsuki, 40, 143, 154, 176, 181–82
Howell, Wilbur Samuel, 107
How the Irish Became White (Ignatiev), 112, 155, 197n2
Hughes, Christina, 201n17
Human Genome Project, 13, 188n10
Hunter, George William, 12
Hunter, Margaret, 201n11
Hurlbert, Mark, 199n1

identification, 6, 12, 48–53, 60, 97, 110, 134, 162, 164, 165, 167, 168, 189n.2, 194n7; Burke and, 1, 28, 47, 53–60; conscious, 2, 19, 25, 32, 48; faulty, 62–63; and figuration, 52; Fuss and, 60–67, 69; with gender and race, 7, 8, 9; and identity, 51, 64, 193n6; and metaphor, 52, 67–71; and metonymy, 68, 71–74; modern, 32, 48; as place, 49; politics of, 59–60, 66–67; postmodern, 32, 48; psychical and cultural, 49, 61, 66–67; reformist potential of, 48, 53; risks of, 195n15; troubled, 2, 8, 13, 19, 27, 35, 47, 48, 150
Identification Papers (Fuss), 60, 193n4
identity, 51, 53, 57, 60, 64, 193n6, 195n16
Ignatiev, Noel, 112, 155, 192nn18, 21, 197n2
Imitation of Life, 21, 190n5
In a Different Voice (Gilligan), 85
Indian widow burning, 80
interpretive invention, 189n1. *See also* rhetorical listening
invention, 189n1, 192n23

Invention of the White Race, The (T. Allen), 154, 197n2
Isocrates, 9

Jarratt, Susan, 3, 4, 23, 35, 102, 132, 135, 145, 198n4
Jay, Greg, 143, 176
Jay, Martin, 22, 190n6
Joy Luck Club, The (Tan), 118

Keating, AnnLouise, 37, 38, 112, 183, 184
Kennedy, George, 107
Killers of the Dream (Smith), 39, 103, 118, 125, 199nn13, 14
King, Martin Luther King, Jr., 117, 124, 154
Kingston, Maxine Hong, 140
Kinneavy, James, 52
Kopelson, Karen, 145, 199n1
Kristeva, Julia, 27, 187n2
Krizek, Robert, 198n2

Lacan, Jacques, 61, 191n14
language, 9
Language as Symbolic Action (Burke), 54
Lee, Jayne Chong-Soon, 7, 15–16, 189n14
Lefevre, Karen, 192n23
legein, 23–24
Leitch, Vincent, 51, 193n1
Lentricchia, Frank, 193n1, 194n7
Lerner, Gerda, 188n6
Levinas, Emmanuel, 20, 151, 190n6, 192n16
Linn, Ray, 193n5
Lipsitz, George, 197n2
listening, 19–20, 21, 26, 105. *See also* hearing; rhetorical listening
listening metonymically, 16, 78, 98–99, 171
listening pedagogically, 16, 133–34, 136, 171; moves of, 146–59; setting scene for, 141–46
Listening to Silences (Hedges, Fishkin), 195n1
Logan, Shirley Wilson, 5, 7, 130, 132, 135
logos, 23, 27
Lorde, Audre, 2, 78–100, 192n22. *See also* Daly: Lorde-Daly debate; mythical norm
Lorde-Daly debate. *See under* Daly, Mary
Love Medicine (Erdrich), 116
Lu, Min-Zhan, 52
Lubiano, Wahneema, 198n2

Lunsford, Andrea, 18, 27, 190n3
Lyotard, Jean-François, 52, 195n2

MacDonald, Amie, 203n21
Mailloux, Steven, 27
Malcolm X, 150
Man Cannot Speak for Her (Campbell), 85
manhood, 187n4
Maraniss, David, 120, 131
Maslow, Abraham, 8
Massacre of the Dreamers (Castillo), 85, 100, 118, 127–28, 198n8
McDonald, Christie, 20
McIntosh, Peggy, 143, 157, 176, 181–82, 197n2, 201n15
McKay, Claude, 114
McKinney, Karyn, 201n12, 203n22
metaphor, 194n11. *See also* identification
metonymy, 98. *See also* identification
Middleton, Joyce Irene, 7, 77, 113–14, 132, 198nn2, 3
modern/postmodern divide, 32, 48, 52, 53, 193n1
modern rhetorical theories, 52
Moi, Toril, 187n2
Moraga, Cherríe, 79, 123, 143, 154, 176, 181–82
Morrison, Toni, 7, 8, 27, 41, 45, 94, 100, 107, 109, 110, 118, 124, 150, 156, 192n18, 196n8, 198n2
Mountford, Roxanne, 132, 195n2
multicultural logic, 15, 164
Murphy, James, 18, 190n3
mythical norm, 136, 192n22

Nakayama, Thomas, 198n2
Newitz, Annalee, 201n13
Newton, Judith, 201n16
Nietzsche, Frederic, 76, 190n6, 197n1, 198n4
non-identification, 53, 72–76, 97, 162, 193n6
nonidentification, 193n6
nonidentity, 60, 64–65
nonproductive guilt, 5, 6, 138
non-white, 113–14, 192n21, 198n3

ocularcentrism, 22–23
Off White (Fine), 197n2
one-drop rule, 188n9

On the Origin of the Species (Darwin), 188n7
Open House (P. Williams), 200n5
"Open Letter to Mary Daly, An" (Lorde), 2, 79, 83, 84
Oravec, Christine, 54, 194nn7, 8
Other Side of Language: A Philosophy of Listening, The (Fiumara), 24–25

Paley, Vivian Gussin, 198n2, 200n4
Passing and Pedagogy (Caughie), 190n5, 202n20
patriarchy, logic of, 10, 149
pedagogy, 141
persuasion, 1; unconscious, 54
Phelan, James, 18, 27, 191n12
Philosophy of Literary Form, The (Burke), 54
Piercy, Marge, 9, 25, 27
place. *See* identification
Plato, 8, 12, 20, 62, 109, 123
Playing in the Dark: Whiteness in the Literary Imagination (Morrison), 100, 118, 150, 156, 198n2
political, the, 30, 31
postmodern rhetorical theories, 52
Poulakos, John, 102, 197n1
Practice of Everyday Life, The (De Certeau), 189n15
Pradl, Gordon, 190n8
Pratt, Mary Louise, 201n15
privilege, 32, 130, 134, 157–59; earned, 157–59; unearned, 63, 92, 98, 157–59; unearned gender, 134, 187n4; unearned racial, 16, 75, 134

Rabinowitz, Nancy Sorkin, 200n11
Rabinowitz, Peter, 191n12
race, 103, 134, 149, 164; and biology, 14, 37; and composition scholarship, 7; and culture, 13, 16; definition of, 7, 9, 12–16; and ethnicity, 15–16; as false category, 13, 37; as five-races-of-man theory, 12; history of term, 187n6; rules of, 188n6
race bias, 21
race blind, 5, 6. *See also* color-blindness
Race in the College Classroom (TuSmith and Reddy), 200n6
Race Matters (West), 35, 137
Rachel, 41–46

racism, 5, 199n2
Ratcliffe, Krista, 3, 184, 189n1, 191nn13, 15, 195n1
Rayner, Alice, 8, 26–31, 76
reading, 19–20, 23, 24
reading metaphorically, 92
Reclaiming Rhetorica (Lunsford), 190n3
recognition, 96–97, 99
Reddy, Maureen, 200nn6, 10, 202n21
reidentification, 193n6
rememory, 109–10
Rereading the Sophists (Jarratt), 23, 102, 132
resistance, 133, 137; and composition studies, 199n1; and pedagogy, 137, 138, 201n17; student/teacher, 136, 137–41; as teacher fears, 139–41; types of, 138–39, 200n8
Reynolds, Nedra, 124–25, 131, 132, 199n12
rhetorical listening, 1, 9, 16, 74, 105, 171, 189n2, 191n10; biases against, 19–23; caveats of, 33–34; as code of cross-cultural conduct, 17, 34–41, 46, 48, 78; definition of, 13, 17, 19, 25; idealism of, 27, 38; need for, 23–25; origins of, 2–8; places of, 48–53; and questioning the *logos*, 18, 36, 39, 40, 46; as trope for interpretive invention, 17, 24, 25–34, 43, 46. *See also* accountability; commonalities and differences; cultural logic; identification; understanding
rhetorical situation, 103
rhetorical stance, 103
rhetoric of dysfunctional silence, 80, 84–93; functions of, 85, 87, 88, 92, 196n4
rhetoric of listening, 80, 94–99; functions of, 94, 95, 96, 98
Rhetoric of Motives, A (Burke), 1, 55
Rhetoric Retold (Glenn), 102, 132
Rich, Adrienne, 3, 4, 7, 22, 35, 39, 69, 77, 79, 84, 88, 102, 143, 152, 154, 162, 176, 179–80, 195n1, 196n6, 198nn2, 5
Richards, I. A., 52
Ritchie, Joy, 201n15
Robbins, Kamenka, 165–66
Rodriguez, Nelson, 198n2, 201n15, 203n21
Rodriguez, Richard, 144
Roediger, David, 113, 114, 184
Roof, Judith, 192n19
Rosenblatt, Louise, 190n8

Rosenfelt, Deborah, 201n16
Royster, Jacqueline Jones, 1, 3, 7, 17, 18, 27, 52, 62, 75, 76, 77, 121, 126–27, 128, 132, 171, 187n1, 195n15
Ruth, ix, 25, 46; book of, 190n9

Sado-Ritual Syndrome, 81–82, 95
Sales, Carol, 162–65
Salvaggio, Ruth, 158
Sánchez-Casal, Susan, 200n9, 201n17, 203n21
Scheunemann, Sarah, 34
Schuman, Amy (and strategic romanticism), 27
Scopes "monkey" trial, 12
Sexual/Textual Politics (Moi), 187n2
Shakespeare, William, 140
Shor, Ira, 141, 145, 200nn3, 8
Showalter, Elaine, 85, 187n5, 189n12
sight, 22–23
silence, 195n1, 196n7; dysfunctional, 80; gendered and racialized, 79. See also rhetoric of dysfunctional silence
Silko, Leslie Marmon, 121–22
Sloane, Sarah, 201n11
Smith, Lillian, 39, 91, 103, 114, 118–20, 123, 125, 128–29, 130–31, 143, 175, 177–78, 179, 180, 198n10, 199nn13, 14
Sommers, Nancy, 5
Sorenstam, Annika, 152
Souls of Black Folk (Du Bois), 200n5
speaking, 19–20, 24
Speaking of Gender (Showalter), 85
Spivak, Gayatri (and strategic essentialism), 27
standing under, 28–30, 191n13
standpoint, 3, 28
Stanton, Elizabeth Cady, 154
Stefancic, Jean, 7, 189n13, 197n2
stories of self and others, listening to, 38–41
strategic idealism, 27, 38, 159
strategy, 189n15
student learning outcomes, 142, 143
substance, 32, 52, 53, 55–57, 73, 98, 194nn10, 11; Burke's first- and second-nature, 57, 69, 194n11, 195n16

tactic, 189n15
Tan, Amy, 118

Tannen, Deborah, 20–21, 39
teacher goals, 142, 143
Teacher's Introduction to Postmodernism, A (Linn), 193n5
terministic screen (Burke), 70
Thompson, Becky, 7, 184
Toulmin, Stephen, 52
Towards a Critical Multicultural Literacy (Weil), 135
Trinh, T. Minh-ha, 48, 73–74, 77, 93
triple consciousness, 200n3
trope, 9, 46, 124, 147–49; definition of, 111–12; embodiment of, 53, 111, 156–57
TuSmith, Bonnie, 200n6, 203n21
Tutu, Desmond, 74

understanding, 26, 27–31, 43, 191n12. See also standing under
Unspoken: A Rhetoric of Silence (Glenn), 84, 195n1

Vickers, Brian, 107
Villanueva, Victor, 7, 129–30
Villaverde, Leila, 198n2, 203n21
Vitanza, Victor, 18, 27, 107, 197n10, 198n4

Walker, Alice, 4, 5, 116, 196n5
Warrior Marks: Female Genital Mutilation and the Sexual Blinding of Women (Walker), 196n5
Warrior Poet: A Biography of Audre Lorde (De Veaux), 196n3
Washington, Dinah, 155–56
Watson, Jay, 192n17
Weil, Danny, 135
Weiler, Ben, 159–62
Welch, Kathleen, 7, 121
Wells, Ida B., 115
West, Cornel, 35, 58, 137, 146
What Is Called Thinking (Heidegger), 23, 108
When Race Breaks Out (Fox), 100
When Students Have Power (Shor), 141
white (as a word), 14, 113–14, 150, 154–55, 158, 192n21, 196n3
White (Dyer), 197n2
whiteness, 3, 5, 6, 45, 102, 132, 136, 142, 149, 150–56, 192n18; as consumption, 115–16;

as denial of language play, 121–23; as denial of race issues, 117, 129; dysfunctions of, 104, 121, 131; as hypocrisy, 116–17; as ignorance, 118; as invisible performance, 113; and pedagogy, 199–203nn1–22; as privilege, 37, 113, 157–58, 166, 198n7; as property, 115, 188n9, 198n6; as (desire for) stasis, 113, 114, 131; as terror, 114–15, 119; as trope, 9, 12, 37, 104, 111–20, 143, 144–45, 159; as visible performance, 112–13. *See also* privilege

Whiteness: A Critical Reader (Hill), 197n2, 201n13

Whiteness: Feminist Philosophical Reflections (Cuomo and Hall), 201n15

whiteness studies, 7, 102–3, 183–84, 197n2, 201n13

white privilege. *See* whiteness

white supremacy, logic of, 14–15, 149, 164, 165, 168

White Teacher (Paley), 197n2, 200n4

White Trash: Race and Class in America (Wray and Newitz), 201n13

white-trash studies, 201n13

White Women Race Matters (Frankenberg), 100, 189n12, 197n2

white writing, 198n8

Who Can Speak? (Roof and Wiegman), 192n19

Wiegman, Robyn, 192n19

Williams, David, 68, 72, 194n11

Williams, Patricia, 189n13, 200n5

Woman Warrior (Kingston), 140

Woods, Tiger, 151, 152

Woolf, Virginia, 3, 4, 28–29, 35, 196n8

Worsham, Lynn, 7, 100, 104, 120, 132, 151, 152

Wray, Mark, 201n13

Wright, Mark, 193n3

writing, 19–20, 24

KRISTA RATCLIFFE is an associate professor of English at Marquette University in Milwaukee, where she directs the first-year English program and teaches undergraduate and graduate courses in rhetoric and composition theory, writing, autobiography, and women's literature. She has served as president of NCTE's College Forum and as president of the Coalition of Women Scholars in the History of Rhetoric. Her research focuses on intersections of rhetorical theory, feminist theory, and composition pedagogy. Her publications include *Anglo-American Feminist Challenges to the Rhetorical Tradition: Virginia Woolf, Mary Daly, Adrienne Rich* (1996) and *Who's Having This Baby* with Helen Sterk, Carla Hay, Alice Kehoe, and Leona VandeVusse (2002). Her articles and reviews have appeared in edited collections as well as in *CCC, JAC, Rhetoric Review,* and *College English.*

Studies in Rhetorics and Feminisms

Studies in Rhetorics and Feminisms seeks to address the interdisciplinarity that rhetorics and feminisms represent. Rhetorical and feminist scholars want to connect rhetorical inquiry with contemporary academic and social concerns, exploring rhetoric's relevance to current issues of opportunity and diversity. This interdisciplinarity has already begun to transform the rhetorical tradition as we have known it (upper-class, agonistic, public, and male) into regendered, inclusionary rhetorics (democratic, dialogic, collaborative, cultural, and private). Our intellectual advancements depend on such ongoing transformation.

Rhetoric, whether ancient, contemporary, or futuristic, always inscribes the relation of language and power at a particular moment, indicating who may speak, who may listen, and what can be said. The only way we can displace the traditional rhetoric of masculine-only, public performance is to replace it with rhetorics that are recognized as being better suited to our present needs. We must understand more fully the rhetorics of the non-Western tradition, of women, of a variety of cultural and ethnic groups. Therefore, Studies in Rhetorics and Feminisms espouses a theoretical position of openness and expansion, a place for rhetorics to grow and thrive in a symbiotic relationship with all that feminisms have to offer, particularly when these two fields intersect with philosophical, sociological, religious, psychological, pedagogical, and literary issues.

The series seeks scholarly works that both examine and extend rhetoric, works that span the sexes, disciplines, cultures, ethnicities, and sociocultural practices as they intersect with the rhetorical tradition. After all, the recent resurgence of rhetorical studies has not so much been a discovery of new rhetorics; it has been more a recognition of existing rhetorical activities and practices, of our newfound ability and willingness to listen to previously untold stories.

The series editors seek both high-quality traditional and cutting-edge scholarly work that extends the significant relationship between rhetoric and feminism within various genres, cultural contexts, historical periods, methodologies, theoretical positions, and methods of delivery (e.g., film and hypertext to elocution and preaching).

Queries and submissions:
Professor Cheryl Glenn, Editor
  E-mail: cjg6@psu.edu
Professor Shirley Wilson Logan, Editor
  E-mail: Shirley_W_Logan@umail.umd.edu

Studies in Rhetorics and Feminisms
Department of English
142 South Burrowes Bldg.
Penn State University
University Park, PA 16802-6200